STEEL
AND
TARTAN

'It was pure Hell let loose – shrapnel bursting above our heads, shells dropping alongside of you and German machine guns and snipers picking off the men by scores. It was a pitiable sight to see some of the boys coming down the road without kilts, jackets, haversacks and drenched to the skin. Anyone who came out of it alive should be thankful. You will see it for yourself in the papers. I can't explain it, and what's more, I'm not going to try.' (Festubert, 18 May 1915)

STEEL AND TARTAN

THE 4TH CAMERON HIGHLANDERS IN THE GREAT WAR

PATRICK WATT

The History Press

'Cuimhnich air na daoin'e o'e d'thainig thu'
('Remember the men from whom you have come')

Highland proverb

For my grandfather, Peter Bruce, who got me interested in the subject, and to the memory of all the officers, non-commissioned officers and men of the 4th Cameron Highlanders.

First published 2012
This new paperback edition first published 2024

The History Press
97 St George's Place, Cheltenham,
Gloucestershire, GL50 3QB
www.thehistorypress.co.uk

British Library Cataloguing in Publication Data.
A catalogue record for this book is available from the British Library.

ISBN 978 1 80399 589 2

Typesetting and origination by The History Press
Printed and bound by TJ Books Limited, Padstow, Cornwall

FSC www.fsc.org MIX Paper from responsible sources FSC® C013056

Trees for Life

Contents

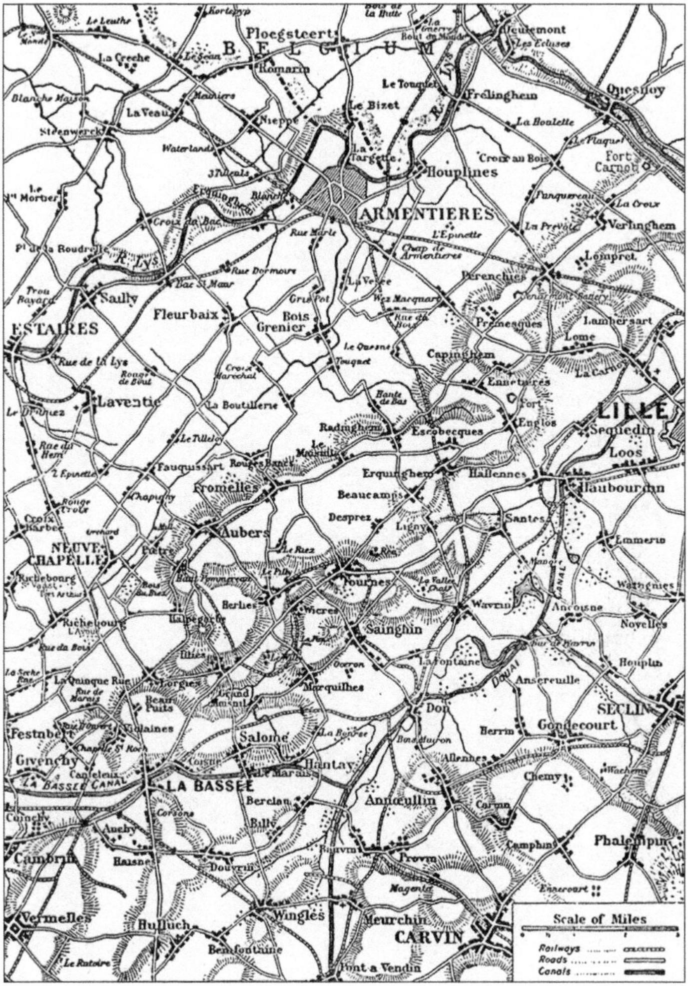

The battlefields of the Nord Pas de Calais, 1915.

Acknowledgements

I would like to thank the following individuals and institutions who helped me in my research for this book: Karen Mee of the Special Collections Department of Leeds University for her assistance with the papers of the Liddle Collection; Sue Skelton of the Reference Department of Inverness Library for her wonderful help with the contemporary newspaper reports; Sabrina Rowlatt of the Imperial War Museum, Harry Brown of Bridgnorth, Shropshire for his permission to publish extracts from the papers of J.B. Mackenzie; Michael Roemmele of Perth for providing me with a photograph of his father; Stuart Farrell of Nairn for his fantastic assistance in providing me with images of the battalion Roll Book amongst other things; Dr Andrew Bamji of Queen Mary's Hospital in Sidcup for providing details of my great-grandfather's treatment there; and the extremely knowledgable and generous moderators of and contributors to the 1914–1918 online forum without whom research into all aspects of the First World War would be a hundred times more difficult to conduct.

I would also like to thank the Imperial War Museum who are the curators of the papers of 2nd Lieutenant M.S. Goodban, Lieutenant-Colonel Charles Bowdery, J.B. Mackenzie and S. Bradbury. Every effort has been made to trace copyright holders and the author and the Imperial War Museum would be grateful for any information which might help to trace those whose identities or addresses are not currently known. Likewise, the Special Collections Department of Leeds University who hold the papers of Hector Macdonald; the National Archives of Scotland who hold the wills of soldiers who died during the war; the National Archives in London who retain the battalion war diary, service and pension records, and medal index cards of First World War soldiers; and the staff of the National Library of Scotland.

In addition, I would like to thank everyone at The History Press for all their efforts in producing this work.

Finally, I would like to thank my friends and family, in particular Blythe Robertson, who acted as my proof reader and my mother Trish for enduring endless hours of rather one-sided conversations on the 4th Cameron Highlanders. Lastly, I would like to thank my wife, Hande Zapsu Watt, without whom I would never have had the inclination or patience to put all my research down on paper, and who now knows as much as anyone on the subject.

Introduction

In February 1916 the future of the 4th Battalion, the Queen's Own Cameron Highlanders was hanging in the balance. The War Minister Lord Kitchener and the Imperial Chief of Staff Sir William Robertson had visited the Adjutant General in St Omer on 9 February. Amongst other business, they had informed him that all under strength battalions at the front, without the prospect of adequate reinforcement, would cease to be fighting units and would be amalgamated with other battalions of the same regiment.

On 16 February, Lieutenant-Colonel Murdoch Beaton, commanding officer of the 4th Cameron Highlanders, was summoned to St Omer. Beaton was told, along with the commanders of other such distinguished battalions as the 4th and 5th Battalions, Black Watch, that their units were to be disbanded. As there were no other Territorial Force battalions of the Cameron Highlanders in France, the men of the 4th Battalion were to be sent as drafts of reinforcements to the 1st Cameron Highlanders, the only Cameron battalion more senior to them in France.

Beaton fought as hard for his battalion as he had done throughout the battles of 1915. The 4th Camerons had been in France for five days short of a full calendar year and had won the respect and admiration of all they had met, going 'over the top' five times, at Neuve Chapelle, Aubers Ridge, Festubert, Givenchy and Loos. In a passionate speech in the House of Commons, Annan Bryce, Member of Parliament for the Inverness Burghs, spoke of the ingratitude expressed by the breaking up of 'a battalion that has won deathless renown on the fields of Flanders'.[1]

It was all to no avail, as one month later the 4th Cameron Highlanders sent 550 men to a holding unit called Number 1 Entrenching Battalion, with the task of building trenches in the vicinity of Poperinghe in Belgium. From there, they supplied drafts of men when required to the 1st Cameron Highlanders who were fighting with such gallantry on the Somme. As a concession from the Adjutant General, Lieutenant-Colonel Beaton was able to ensure that a nucleus of the battalion, three officers and 100 men, remained in Étaples. In August 1916, a formal request was lodged with the Adjutant General to reconstitute the battalion. It was turned down, but a further assurance was given that after the war the 4th Cameron Highlanders could be rebuilt in Inverness by its surviving members.

That February 1916, the 4th Cameron Highlanders moved south from Artois to the town of Corbie on the banks of the river Ancre, a tributary of the Somme. Whilst there, two photographs were taken, one of the officers, and one of the non-commissioned officers of the battalion. In the officers' photograph, only five men remained from a similarly posed photograph taken exactly a year before, when the battalion left their training ground in Bedford for France. It was a similar story for the men.

In total, 1402 men had served with the battalion in France in 1915 and a further 180 had arrived as reinforcements in 1916, including many who had served more than one period in the trenches, and returned after being wounded. The battalion sustained 607 casualties, 257 of which had been killed in action or died of their wounds or disease, their bodies buried by their comrades in cemeteries in France or else left where they fell, their names etched on one of the memorials to the missing. The 4th Cameron Highlanders had sustained a casualty rate of 43 per cent in 1915, including 18 per cent of their number who had paid the ultimate sacrifice for their country.

Of the 930 men who left their training camp at Bedford in February 1915 only 220 remained with the battalion a year later. The officers fared equally badly. In total, 79 officers had served with the 4th Cameron Highlanders but by March 1916, 12 were dead and 25 were evacuated wounded. Of the original 30 4th Camerons officers who left Bedford, only five remained, with Lieutenant-Colonel Beaton himself being the only officer to have come through all five battles fought by the battalion. Of the 4th Camerons' first year in France, they had spent 110 days in the front line and reserve trenches. The 4th Cameron Highlanders were one of the first battalions of the Territorial Force to see action in France and sadly, were one of the first to be disbanded. The part-time soldiers of Inverness-shire and Nairnshire had gone from being farm workers, servants, postmen and carpenters to seasoned veterans, and had earned the admiration of all for their bravery, attitude and determination.

This book is the culmination of five years research into the 4th Cameron Highlanders. My great-grandfather, Peter Bruce, joined the 4th Camerons on 31 March 1909. He worked full time for the shoemaker firm of Alexander Napier based in Nairn High Street, and carried on this trade into his military career. He served as the battalion shoemaker-Sergeant throughout 1915 and went to Étaples with the battalion nucleus in March 1916 before finally being transferred to the 6th Battalion, the Cameron Highlanders in June 1917. He was promoted to Warrant Officer Class II and was wounded in action on 29 July 1918 at Buzancy near Soissons. A shell had exploded in his trench, killing one man and injuring four others including Sergeant-Major Bruce, who was hit in the face by shrapnel. He was evacuated to King George V Hospital in Dublin before being transferred to Queen Mary's Hospital in Sidcup, Kent, for surgery in February 1919. At Queen Mary's, an army surgeon, Sir Harold Gillies, had founded a specialised clinic to treat victims of facial injuries caused by service in the First World War. In total some 5000 men were treated by this pioneering doctor and his team. My great-grandfather was operated on by Major Geoffrey Seccombe-Hett, a specialist in repairing damage to the nose, and made an excellent recovery. He was discharged from the army in September 1919 and returned home to Nairn and his wife and young daughter.

In trying to piece together what happened to my great-grandfather, I hit upon that brick wall for researchers of First World War soldiers: the destruction of service and pension records in a fire caused by German bombing in 1940. With no leads to go on I tried to gather as many clues as possible about his life from the details of the lives of those men who served with him in the 4th Cameron

Highlanders. I found a variety of official papers, newspaper articles, diaries, photographs and publications detailing the actions of the men of the 4th Camerons from their creation out of the old Volunteer Force Battalion in 1908, up to their disbanding in March 1916 and beyond.

The title of this book is taken from the Reverend Dugald MacEachern's work *The Sword of the North: Highland Memories of the Great War*. The Reverend MacEachern described how, during the night of 17 May 1915, the 4th Cameron Highlanders took the Southern Breastwork trench at Festubert against all odds, the enemy fleeing 'before the onset of steel and tartan'.[2] That phrase seemed to sum it up perfectly.

The 4th Cameron Highlanders had come a long way from the glens of Lochaber, the beaches of the Inner Hebrides, the farms of the Moray Firth coast and the county towns of Inverness and Nairn. They had seen such horrors and experienced such danger that even after years of reading their testimonies I struggle to comprehend what must have gone through their minds as they defended the Moated Grange at Neuve Chapelle, stormed the Southern Breastwork at Festubert or repelled countless bomb attacks at Loos. That my great-grandfather was there made it all the more real.

This is the story of the 4th Battalion, Queen's Own Cameron Highlanders.

1

Fourteen New Divisions

Alexander Fraser – a future commanding officer of the 4th Camerons – was born in the Highland village of Beauly on 6 May 1865. His father, also Alexander, was an agent for the Commercial Bank of Scotland and his mother, Elizabeth Spray, was the daughter of the vicar of the Parish of Kinneagh in Ireland. Young Alexander led a privileged life, being educated at Inverness Royal Academy and Inverness College before progressing on to study law at Edinburgh University, graduating in 1890.

In the spring of 1883, shortly after his eighteenth birthday, Alexander Fraser joined the 1st (Inverness Highland) Volunteer Battalion of the Queen's Own Cameron Highlanders. He joined as a private soldier and served with them in that capacity until leaving for university in 1887. On his arrival in Edinburgh, Fraser again sought out the military, joining a volunteer battalion of the Royal Scots, the Edinburgh Volunteer Regiment, with whom he served until November 1889.

After completing his degree, Alexander Fraser returned to the family home at 67 Church Street in Inverness and took up employment as a solicitor in 1890, and as a notary public two years later. The year 1890 also saw Fraser obtain a commission in the Inverness Volunteer Battalion as a 2nd Lieutenant. Clearly, he must have excelled in his new role as he was promoted full Lieutenant in 1892, Captain in 1898 and Major in 1905. Fraser took every opportunity to advance himself in his military pastime, undertaking qualifications in musketry, organisation and equipment, tactics and military topography.

In the meantime, Alexander Fraser met and married Isabella Menzies, the daughter of Colonel Duncan Menzies, the former commander of the 1st Sutherland Highland Rifle Volunteers. They moved after their marriage to the house Westwood on Drummond Road, a 20-room mansion in the south of Inverness. Alexander and Ella had nine children: Duncan Menzies in 1894, Elizabeth Sibell in 1896, Mary Millicent in 1898, Muriel Janet in 1900, Alexandra Dorothy in 1903, Eleanor Beatrice in 1905, Alexander Redmond in 1908, Margaret Iris in 1910 and Frances Alice in 1912.

Alexander Fraser's private life couldn't have been better and his professional life soon followed suit. Along with business partner David Ross, he founded the legal firm of Fraser & Ross where he became factor for the Highland estates of Culloden and Ferintosh. He became a prominent member of the local Freemasons, rising to become the Right Worshipful Master of St John's Lodge in Inverness. He also took a keen interest in all things to do with the town, taking appointments with several organisations, including the Territorial Force Association for the county, as secretary of the northern branch of the Royal

Arborical Society, as Clerk to the Deacons Court of the United Free High Church and as President of the Sanitary Association of Scotland.

In 1908 the Minister for War, Richard Haldane, decided to reform the organisation of the volunteer and militia units of the British Army. In their place would be a newly created set of 14 divisions of the Territorial Force. The 1st (Inverness Highland) Volunteer Battalion became the 4th Battalion, Queen's Own Cameron Highlanders. The renamed battalion was to take its place in the newly created Seaforth and Cameron Brigade of the Highland Division.

On 12 February 1909 the commanding officer of the 4th Cameron Highlanders, Lieutenant-Colonel James Leslie Fraser, died after a long battle with illness. In his place, Alexander Fraser was promoted Lieutenant-Colonel commanding the battalion. One of his first tasks as commanding officer was to lead the Colour Party of the battalion to Windsor Castle where King Edward VII presented new Colours to each of the newly created Territorial Force battalions. Accompanying Fraser were Lieutenants Ronald MacDonald and Murdoch Beaton, and Colour Sergeants William Ross, Duncan Cameron and J. Angus.

The 4th Cameron Highlanders, as part of their obligation as members of the Territorial Force, had to attend up to 15 days annual training at a camp every summer. They were joined at these camps by the other members of their brigade, and in turn, by the remainder of the Highland Division. The camps took place at locations all over the Highland Divisional recruiting area, with training camps at Burghead in 1909, Aviemore in 1910, Tain in 1911, Burghead again in 1912, Dornoch in 1913 and Kingussie in 1914. At these camps, the men would practise marching, musketry, bombing, machine gunning and a variety of other skills.

In accordance with the Haldane Reforms, on 31 March 1908 all existing members of the Inverness-shire Volunteer Battalion resigned their positions and re-enlisted on 1 April. The men were then allocated a unique service number which would see them through to the renumbering of the Territorial Force in 1917. The new numbers were allocated in ascending order, starting from number 1 for the first man who re-enlisted on 1 April, up to approximately 1700 for those who enlisted on the eve of war in August 1914. Therefore, of the men who went to France in 1915, Company Quartermaster Sergeant Kenneth MacKenzie – who transferred from the Highland Volunteers on 1 April 1908 – was given the service number 3, and Private Angus MacDonald – who enlisted directly into the 4th Cameron Highlanders at Fort William on 9 May 1914 – was given the service number 1693. Some of the 1700 men who enlisted between 1908 and 1914 were, of course, no longer serving with the 4th Cameron Highlanders, having transferred to other regular or territorial units or resigned from military service.

The *1908 Regulations for the Territorial Force*[3] set out the organisation of a territorial force battalion such as the 4th Cameron Highlanders. Their total complement at full strength stood at 29 officers and 980 men organised into 8 companies named A–H based at locations throughout the recruitment area. The men of the 4th Camerons found themselves spread over one of the largest recruitment areas for any battalion of the British Army with A and C Companies based at Inverness, B Company at Nairn, D Company at Broadford, E Company at Fort William,

F Company at Kingussie, G Company at Beauly and H Company at Portree.

As commanding officer, Lieutenant-Colonel Alexander Fraser found himself based at the battalion's drill hall in Inverness along with the rest of the unit's training and administrative personnel. In recognition for his 25 years service in the Volunteer Battalion and then the Territorial Force, Colonel Fraser was awarded the Long Service Medal, the Volunteer Decoration and the Coronation Medal of King George V, awarded in 1911. On 23 August 1913, 48-year-old Lieutenant-Colonel Alexander Fraser decided to resign his commission and concentrate on spending time with his young family and working on his numerous business affairs. Fraser did not retire completely from military life, however, as he joined the Reserve of Officers, meaning he was prepared to be called upon to serve his country in time of war. He would not be long parted from his battalion.

The new commanding officer of the 4th Cameron Highlanders was Lieutenant-Colonel Ewan Campbell. Colonel Campbell was born in Kingussie on 18 November 1856, the son of John Campbell, an innkeeper in the village, and his wife Margaret Aitchison. Campbell had strong connections to the 4th Cameron Highlanders, with both his brother John and eldest son, also called John, serving as officers.

The battalion he inherited had been well trained and disciplined by Lieutenant-Colonel Fraser and Ewan Campbell carried on his work admirably. The 'Saturday night soldiers' of the Territorial Force may have been looked down upon by the officers and men of the regular army but they were undoubtedly a source of pride in the towns and villages of Inverness-shire and Nairnshire. This pride followed the battalion for the next 18 months as it grew from an untried home defence battalion into an experienced and hardened military unit, the equal of any in the British Army.

2

Preparing for War, August 1914–February 1915

On 3 August 1914 the German Army swept through Belgium, Luxembourg and northern France with the aim of encircling Paris before moving their conquering armies across Germany to fight Russia on their eastern borders. This attack on neutral Belgium prompted the British government to declare war on Germany and prepare to despatch the British Expeditionary Force for service in France. As soon as war was declared, the government sent word to the units of the Territorial Force to mobilise for war.

Lieutenant-Colonel Ewan Campbell ordered that the eight companies of the 4th Camerons, who were spread all over the Highlands and Islands, muster in Inverness. On 5 August the five companies from Inverness, Nairn, Beauly and Kingussie went by train to Fortrose before marching to Cromarty, where their wartime posting was to man the coastal defences. The Portree, Broadford and Fort William companies joined up with the rest of the battalion on 7 August, having waited for the call to arms at their drill halls.

A list of the officers of the battalion in the early days of training was published in the *Historical Records of the Queen's Own Cameron Highlanders*:[4]

Lieutenant-Colonel Ewen Campbell	Commanding Officer
Major Hector Fraser	Second in Command
Captain Garden B. Duff	Adjutant
Major John Lockie	Quartermaster
Captain Robert A. Lindsay (RAMC)	Medical Officer
Lieutenant John D. Macpherson	Transport Officer
2nd Lieutenant William MacKay	Signalling Officer
2nd Lieutenant Harold B. Law	Machine Gun Officer
Captain Murdoch Beaton	A Company (Inverness)
Lieutenant David F. MacKenzie	A Company
Lieutenant Ian MacKay	A Company
Lieutenant A.J. MacKintosh	B Company (Nairn)
Lieutenant Peter M. Cram	B Company
Lieutenant James H. Leigh	B Company
2nd Lieutenant William J. Shaw	B Company
Captain James MacPherson	C Company (Inverness)
Lieutenant Frederick W. Fraser	C Company
Lieutenant Charles Campbell	D Company (Broadford)
Captain Thomas Allison	E Company (Fort William)

Lieutenant Nigel B. MacKenzie	E Company
Major John Campbell	F Company (Kingussie)
Lieutenant John Campbell	F Company
Captain Roderick MacLean	G Company (Beauly)
Captain William MacKintosh	G Company
2nd Lieutenant Murdo MacKenzie	G Company
Captain Ronald MacDonald	H Company (Portree)
2nd Lieutenant Angus Ross	H Company
2nd Lieutenant Archibald M. Fletcher	H Company

Two thirds of the officers were Gaelic speaking, which was roughly the same proportion as the men, possibly the highest percentage in any battalion in the British Army. The majority of the officers were firmly middle class with a large number being made up of members of the legal and teaching professions. In the end, several of the battalion's officers who mobilised in August 1914 would not serve in France; Captain William MacKintosh of Glenurquhart was left in Inverness as the officer commanding the Cameron Territorial Force Depot and Captain James H. Leigh was employed training recruits at the base. Others such as Captain Roderick MacLean and Lieutenants Peter Cram, A.J. Mackintosh and Murdo Mackenzie were ordered, in September 1914, to recruit and organise a second line unit, the 2/4th Cameron Highlanders[5] to take on the home defence duties of the 1/4th if they were sent to France.

At Cromarty the 4th Cameron Highlanders spent most of their time digging trenches during the day and camping in the open fields during the night, only once or twice having to be turned out of their tents to defend their camp. Every instance was a false alarm. The first casualty of war occurred that week when an unnamed soldier sustained an unfortunate injury when he sat in a pan of boiling fat!

On 11 August, the battalion returned to Inverness to join up with the 4th, 5th and 6th Battalions of the Seaforth Highlanders with whom they were brigaded in the Seaforth and Cameron Brigade of the Highland Division. The Regimental Journal, *The 79th News*, reported that 6000 troops were concentrated in Inverness at this time, taking over all the available accommodation. The following day, Lieutenant-Colonel Campbell paraded the battalion in Bell's Park and after a stirring speech asked for volunteers for service abroad. Over 80 per cent of the men volunteered to fight in France. When the deductions in manpower for those who did not volunteer for overseas service, those who were too young and those who were deemed medically unfit were taken into consideration, the 4th Cameron Highlanders stood at a strength of 600–700 men. It became clear that more recruits would be needed to send the battalion abroad at anything close to its full fighting complement of over 1000 men. This recruiting would have to be done away from their Highland home as, on 15 August, the Highland Division was ordered to their new training area at Bedford. The *Bedfordshire Times and Independent* reported the arrival of the Highland Division on 21 August 1914:

> The Highland Territorials arrived in Bedford on Saturday and received a very hearty welcome from the townsfolk. At an early hour the southern side of the town presented an animated scene. The soldiers who had had a long and trying journey appreciated to the full the cups of hot cocoa generously provided by the

people in the Southend District and wherever they were billeted.[6]

The 4th Cameron Highlanders and their colleagues in the Seaforth and Cameron Brigade were allocated billets in the district between Kimbolton Road and Bromham Road, some men settling in the grammar and high schools. Bedford High School was converted into the 4th Camerons' headquarters and can be seen in a photograph of the officers before their departure to France.

The *Inverness Courier* of 13 October described how the townsfolk of Bedford embraced their Highland visitors, accommodating them in their houses and serving them hot coffee and cocoa as soon as they stepped off the train. The paper also told of the diversions available to the men; the local pubs closed their doors at 8.00pm, but the men were also entertained by concerts, boating on the river and walking the promenades, while the officers were made honorary members of the local libraries and clubs. Some of the men even went to the trouble of learning French!

In the opening two weeks of the war over 100 men volunteered for service with the 4th Cameron Highlanders at either their central depot in Inverness or the Company depots in their local towns. However, still more were needed, so brothers Lieutenant Ian MacKay and 2nd Lieutenant William MacKay were sent to the headquarters of the London Scottish Regiment in the capital which was being inundated with volunteers of Scottish origin who wished to join Highland regiments. Approximately 250 new soldiers were recruited this way between 4 and 11 September 1914. These London Scots would be subject to particularly heavy losses when the battalion finally made it to France, with one in every five being killed within a year.

The new recruits had to sign Army Form E.624 stating their agreement to serve at any place outside the United Kingdom in times of emergency. In recognition of this agreement, the soldiers were entitled to wear an Imperial Service Badge on the right breast of their tunic.

One of the men who volunteered in September 1914 was Max Alexander Roemmele. He had been born in Kirkintilloch, Dunbartonshire, in 1892 to German immigrant parents Carl Hugo Roemmele, an iron merchant from Stuttgart, and his wife Amelia Bost. In order to join the 4th Camerons, Roemmele travelled from Glasgow to Inverness and enlisted at the depot as Private Number 2223. On his return to Glasgow, proudly sporting his new uniform, his neighbours promptly reported him to the police as a German spy. Luckily, nothing came of it and Private Roemmele travelled to Bedford with the rest of the 4th Cameron Highlanders. While there, he applied for a commission in the battalion, which was accepted on 25 February 1915 and he served as an officer withdistinction throughout the 1915 campaign.

In Bedford, the 4th Camerons embarked on a vigorous routine of training to prepare them for action at the front. One unidentified soldier, writing home to his friend in the Highlands, told of his daily routine in a letter reproduced in a local newspaper:

> We are getting a lot of recruits just now coming down every day from Inverness; others have arrived from London, over 80 coming in one day. So great is the rush of recruits that there are not enough tunics to rig them out so they have to wear their own clothes. All the same

> they look quite a smart lot. We are kept hard at it every day. Up at 6am, physical culture until 8am, out again from 9.15am until 1pm, dinner then out from 2.15pm until 4pm. After that we are free for the night. We go to the baths 3 times a week and as the heat here is terrific you can be sure we enjoy a refreshing plunge. We had a ten-mile march the other night for recruiting purposes and I hear there is to be another shortly. Everybody is in the best of spirits and take the most arduous of duties good humourdly. We rebel sometimes all the same over the grub. We kicked up a dust the other morning over breakfast. We had cause too as you may guess, when I say that the Adjutant came up and gave us another breakfast. We have been asked if we are ready for active service and over 80% of the battalion has volunteered for the front. We expect to be sent when we have completed 3 months training. I have no idea whether we will ever see France for no one has any idea where we may be sent.[7]

Another member of the 4th Camerons, in a letter published in the *Inverness Courier,* gave a further account of the training in Bedford, describing how they spent their time: 'Skirmishing overs fields, hedges, ditches, dykes and fences after an imaginary enemy whom we usually put to complete rout in the end by a bayonet charge.'[8]

It was whilst at Bedford on 4 September that a most unfortunate event befell the battalion when Lieutenant-Colonel Ewen Campbell fell from his horse and had to be hospitalised. It was initially thought that Campbell was making significant, if slow, progress and would be able to rejoin the battalion, but it was not to be, and on 10 November it was decided that he would need to be replaced as commanding officer. The only person deemed capable of leading the battalion was the former commander, Alexander Fraser. Since the outbreak of war, Lieutenant-Colonel Fraser had been in command of the 2/4th Cameron Highlanders in Inverness and was the natural choice to succeed Colonel Campbell, given his knowledge of the officers and men.

The Battalion continued its programme of training in Bedford. On Friday 9 October it suffered one of its first serious casualties when in one of C Company's billets at 6 Albert Terrace, Union Street, Private Arthur Charker was stabbed with a bayonet by Private John Fraser during a fight. Six men of the 4th Camerons were in the billets and three – Charker, Fraser and John MacVinish – were drunk. MacVinish had wanted a fight but, as reported by Sergeant Kenneth MacKenzie at the inquest, had been quietened by the time MacKenzie left. However, ten minutes later, Sergeant MacKenzie returned as the disturbance had started up again and found Fraser and another man named Macdonald fighting. They were separated by some of C Company's sergeants but Fraser grabbed a bayonet and Sergeant MacKenzie left to gather up men to place Private Fraser under arrest. It seems that Charker and Macdonald tried to take the weapon from Fraser and in the ensuing scuffle Charker somehow fell on the blade. All the witnesses at the inquest reported that Fraser and Charker were friends and that the incident had been out of character for both men. Fraser was charged with wounding and intent to cause grievous bodily harm but when he appeared in court on the following Monday morning it was announced that Private Charker had died, so the charge was changed to wilful murder. The case was heard on 16 October and Fraser pleaded guilty to a reduced charge of manslaughter. He was sentenced to 15 months hard labour.

During their time at Bedford the battalion underwent a structural reorganisation, changing from eight companies to four, A–D. The old A and D Companies merged to form A Company, B and C merged to become B Company, E and F became C Company and G and H became D Company. As some of the officers had been sent back to Inverness to raise the second line battalion, several of the men were commissioned from the ranks to take their places. The *Historical Records of the Queen's Own Cameron Highlanders* showed the new posts for the battalion's officers.[9]

Lieutenant-Colonel Alexander Fraser	Commanding Officer
Major Hector Fraser	Second in Command
Captain Garden B. Duff	Adjutant
Major John Lockie	Quartermaster
Captain Robert Lindsay	Medical Officer
Lieutenant John D. MacPherson	Transport Officer
Lieutenant Harold B. Law	Machine Gun Officer
A Company	
Captain Murdoch Beaton	in command
Captain David F. MacKenzie	
Lieutenant Ian MacKay	Assistant Adjutant
Lieutenant William MacKay	Signalling Officer
2nd Lieutenant Francis E. Laughton	
2nd Lieutenant John D.M. Black	
B Company	
Captain James MacPherson	in command
Captain Frederick W. Fraser	

Lieutenant Charles Campbell
Lieutenant William J. Shaw
2nd Lieutenant John F. MacLaren
2nd Lieutenant Frederick J. Kelly

C Company

Captain Thomas Allison	in command
Captain John Campbell	
2nd Lieutenant Andrew Sutherland	
2nd Lieutenant William Calder	
2nd Lieutenant Ian T. Nelson	

D Company

Major John Campbell	in command
Captain Nigel B. MacKenzie	
Lieutenant Angus Ross	
Lieutenant Archibald M. Fletcher	
2nd Lieutenant Joshua Thompson	
2nd Lieutenant Cameron R. Carruthers	

At the end of October 1914 King George V inspected the Highland Brigade at Bedford. The King was met at the station by General Sir Bruce Hamilton, commanding the Highland Division, and General Bannatyne-Allason, commanding the Seaforth and Cameron Brigade. The troops of the Seaforth and Cameron Brigade, the Gordon Brigade and the Engineer and Artillery units mustered for review on the golf links just outside Bedford and the Argyll Brigade, the Army Service Corps and the Royal Army Medical Corps drew up in the pastures beside the course. The Division marched past the King with pipes playing, taking 80 minutes to complete the review.

From the middle of October onwards many of the officers and men of the 4th Camerons chose to make out wills in order to ensure their effects were disposed of as they wished in the event of their death. As always, Lieutenant-Colonel Alexander Fraser led by example. In his will dated 23 October 1914, Fraser left all his worldly possessions to his wife, Ella Menzies Fraser. The document was witnessed by Captain Thomas Allison and Orderly Room Sergeant James MacDonald.[10] Some of the men wrote their wills right up to the time they were sent into battle, with Corporal Duncan Fraser of Beauly writing his on 19 February on board the troopship taking him to France. Lance Corporal John Hossack of Cawdor stipulated that he wanted to have his pocket revolver and diary sent to his father back home in Scotland.[11]

Although the main focus of the battalion's time at Bedford was training, there was still time for the men to enjoy themselves. For the New Year of celebrations 1915, Hogmanay suppers were provided, the festivities costing £1000. Most of the funding had been raised in Scotland, and dignitaries such as the Lord Provost of Aberdeen and the editor of the *Aberdeen Journal* visited Bedford to see in the New Year with the troops. Dinners were given, reels danced, pipes played and Auld Lang Syne was sung in the market square at midnight, much to the delight of the onlooking locals.

Back in Scotland the 2/4th Battalion was not idle, recruiting and training men who would, in time, be sent to the front. One training initiative was the screening of a short recruiting film made by Gaumont of the 4th Cameron Highlanders in Bedford. Entitled *The Highlanders at Bedford* it was shown at the Central Hall in

Inverness in the last week of November. Captain Ian Baillie of Lochloy near Nairn was present, and after each showing gave a stirring speech which prompted many of the watching men in the packed theatre to volunteer for service with the 4th Camerons. Adverts prompting men to do their duty and join their local battalion were printed every week in the *Inverness Courier, Highland News, Northern Chronicle* and many other local newspapers. Men flocked to the recruiting stations.

The 2/4th Cameron Highlanders were to be attached to 191 Brigade of the 64th (2nd Highland) Division. As a reserve formation, they recruited men who wished to serve both on home defence and those who volunteered for foreign service duty, and would be sent to the 1/4th Camerons when required. On 4 November Lieutenants Peter Cram and Murdo Mackenzie left Inverness for Bedford with 100 men of B Company, the 2/4th Camerons. They were tasked with forming a reserve at the Highland Division base, from where they could despatch reinforcements more quickly to France. From 6 December 1914 the battalion was under the command of Lieutenant-Colonel J.G.O. Fitzmaurice, and soon after the 2/4th Camerons recruited many officers and men who would later serve in France.

During the last months of 1914 the Bedford base was plagued by a measles epidemic. The 4th Camerons had been holding themselves ready to depart for the front since the end of October, but at the last minute the orders were cancelled, due to the outbreak. As many of the men hailed from the remote islands and glens of the Scottish Highlands, where measles was rare or unknown, they had little immunity to the disease. An article in the *Bedfordshire Times* in January 1915 reported that between 17 August 1914 and 9 January 1915 the Highland Division lost 27 men to measles, as well as 3 to scarlet fever, 3 to diptheria, 3 to pneumonia, 1 to uraemia and 2 to violence, including the 4th Camerons' Arthur Charker. Of the 27 men killed in the measles epidemic,[12] 14 of them were 4th Cameron men, and in total the battalion had 141 confirmed cases. Men who were deemed susceptible to measles were moved to special huts at Howbury, and then if they contracted the disease, were moved to the measles hospitals at Goldington Road and Ampthill Road.[13] The bodies of the men who died were either buried in a Commonwealth War Graves Commission plot in Bedford Cemetery or repatriated to Scotland for burial.[14]

As the epidemic had delayed the departure of the 4th Camerons to France, other troops of the Highland Division were sent in their place. The 4th Seaforth Highlanders, the 6th Gordon Highlanders and the 7th Argyll and Sutherland Highlanders departed to join other divisions across the Channel, and were replaced by their recently formed second line units at Bedford. In February 1915, after further training from platoon to division level, the 4th Cameron Highlanders were informed that they too were being detached from the Highland Division. They were chosen, along with the 4th Gordon Highlanders and the 9th Argyll and Sutherland Highlanders, to proceed to France immediately.

Before the departure the Provost of Inverness wrote to Lieutenant-Colonel Fraser on 12 February:

> My dear Colonel Fraser,
>
> Permit me, in the name of myself and the other members of the Town Council, as well as the whole of the community, to congratulate you and the battalion under

your command on being selected for foreign service. It is a signal honour for you personally that you should have been selected to lead the battalion now going on active service, after your retiral from the active command; but it is not only an honour to you personally and the gallant 4th Cameron Highlanders, but also to the Town and County of Inverness, and I am sure I voice the feelings and the wishes of the whole community when I wish you in their name Godspeed.

May every officer and man uphold the worthy traditions of our Territorial Regiment, and be distinguished by gallantry in the face of our country's enemy, and may you all return to receive the honour and thanks which you so well deserve at the hands of your home and country which you are going to defend. Your movements in the field will be followed by those at home with intense interest, and may God bless and protect you all.

I remain, yours very truly, John Birnie[15]

3

Arrival in France and First Blood, 18 February–9 March 1915

On 18 February 1915, the 4th Cameron Highlanders formed up for an inspection by Brigadier-General Bannatyne-Allason, commander of the Highland Division, and Brigadier-General Ross, commander of the Seaforth and Cameron Brigade. The same day, Lieutenant-Colonel Fraser issued orders that detailed procedures for the movement of the 4th Camerons to France the following day:

> Routine: The Battalion will proceed abroad tomorrow. Reveille 3am. Breakfast 3.30am. The first party, which consists of A Company and all the cooks, all the signallers, one strong platoon of B Company and a detail of Transport will parade in Tavistock Street at 5am under Colonel Fraser.
>
> The second party which consists of C Company, Machine Gun Section and one and a half platoons of D Company and a detail of Transport will parade in

> Tavistock Street at 7am under Major Fraser. Dr Lindsay will accompany the party. The third party consisting of B Company less one platoon and D Company less one and a half platoons and a detail of Transport, Medical Orderlies, Orderly Room Staff, CQMS's and Quarter Masters Staff will parade in Tavistock Street at 8.30am. The third party will be under Major Campbell. The Quartermaster and Adjutant will go by this train. All officers will be in their Company lines at 3.15am and report to the Orderly Room that everything is going all right by 4.30am. Officers baggage will be at the Headquarters by 4.30am.[16]

The Battalion's passing from Bedford and the Highland Division was recorded in a poem entitled 'The Departure of the 4th Cameron Highlanders' ('*Cha Til MacCruimein*' in Gaelic) by Lieutenant Ewart Alan Mackintosh of the 5th Seaforth Highlanders. Mackintosh was born in Brighton in 1893 and joined the 5th Seaforths on the outbreak of war. He was awarded the Military Cross for gallantry in the field in June 1916 and was killed in action on the second day of the Battle of Cambrai on 21 November 1917 whilst serving with the 4th Seaforth Highlanders. He is buried in Orival Wood Cemetery near Flesquieres.

The pipes in the street were playing bravely
The marching lads went by
With merry hearts and voices singing
My friends marched out to die
But I was hearing a lonely pibroch
Out of an older war
'Farewell, farewell, farewell, MacCrimmon
MacCrimmon comes no more'

And every lad in his heart was dreaming
Of honour and wealth to come
And honour and noble pride were calling
To the tune of the pipes and drum
But I was hearing a woman singing
On dark Dunvegan shore
'In battle or peace, with wealth or honour,
MacCrimmon comes no more'

And there in front of the men were marching
With feet that made no mark
The grey old ghosts of the ancient fighters
Come back again from the dark
And in front of them all MacCrimmon piping
A weary tune and sore
'On the gathering day, for ever and ever,
MacCrimmon comes no more'[17]

These opening days of the 4th Camerons' journey to the front and through the first battles of 1915 were chronicled by two A Company diarists, Private Montague Goodban and Private Charles Bowdery, and their prolific letter-writing officers, brothers Lieutenants Ian and William Mackay. These diaries and letters give a wonderful insight into the day-to-day activities of the 4th Camerons and, whilst being mainly concerned with the rudiments of an army on active service, are often tinged with moments of great humour and sadness.

Montague Sidney Goodban was born in 1891 in the London Borough of Paddington to Sidney Goodban, a china salesman, and his wife Elleanor. He was educated at St John's College in Margate in Kent and on graduating began working for his father in the family's china and glass shop at 129 High Street in Clapham. Goodban joined the 4th Cameron Highlanders at the recruiting centre in the first week of September 1914, drawn like so many of his countrymen to the ranks of a Scottish regiment.

Charles Dudley Bowdery was born in 1893 in Lambeth, London. In 1911 he lived at 52 Thirsk Road South West in Wandsworth with his mother Matilda and his sisters Gladys and Irene. As his diary shows, Bowdery was an intelligent man, which led to him taking employment as a clerk. Bowdery joined the 4th Camerons at the same time as Private Goodban and became one of the many London Scots in A Company.

The brothers Ian and William Mackay were born in 1883 and 1885 respectively, the sons of prominent solicitor William Mackay and his wife Margaret Elizabeth Mackay who lived at Craigmonie House in Inverness. They were educated at Inverness College and Edinburgh Academy before both went to Edinburgh University to study law. On his return to Inverness, Ian joined the Inverness Volunteers as a Private soldier and was commissioned as a 2nd Lieutenant on 20 December 1909 before being promoted full Lieutenant in March 1913. William joined the 4th Cameron Highlanders in 1913 and was promoted full Lieutenant in September 1914 whilst the battalion was based at Bedford. Both wrote detailed letters to their parents and sister Kathleen during their time in the trenches, describing in detail their parts played in battle, their social life in the army and their living conditions.

As the troops prepared to leave for the front, Private Bowdery's girlfriend travelled from London to Bedford to spend one last night with him. He recalled in his diary entry for 19 February, the day of embarkation, how difficult it was saying goodbye:

> Had a farewell breakfast at Smiths, Bedford at 3.30am. Paraded at Tavistock Street at 5am, entrained at 6am. Lillian saw me off from siding. Poor dear girl breaks down in tears on train leaving. My heart feels full. Saw last of Bedford at 6.40am arriving at Southampton at 12 noon after somewhat tiring journey.[18]

The 4th Cameron Highlanders embarked on the SS *Empress Queen*, the *Archimedes* and the *Duchess of Argyll* at 6.00pm along with the 4th Gordon Highlanders and the 9th Argyll and Sutherland Highlanders. Montague Goodban recorded in his diary that the crossing started out well enough but after a dinner of bully beef and biscuits had been served at 8.30pm the weather turned and it had its effect on the men, many of whom emptied their stomachs over the side of the ship, if they could make it there quick enough! They arrived at Le Havre at 1.00am on 20 February and after an early breakfast disembarked at 9.00am. The Battalion then marched 4.5 miles to rest at No.1 Camp Le Havre, where the men spent the rest of the day having their first wash since leaving Bedford; it was to be their last for a month. Men were quartered 12 to a tent, and were roused for a 10.00am church parade. The Camerons, less two platoons under Captain David F. MacKenzie who were quarantined for scarlet fever, left the Le Havre camp at 2.15am the next morning and embarked by train for Merville at 7.20pm, having waited at the station all day. The journey to Merville took an unbearable 23 hours, as described by Private Bowdery: '34 men packed like sardines into a horse truck. Straw spread on floor. Spent a most uncomfortable time. Slept little. Never mind, still quite happy. Smoking and eating passes the time.'[19] Private Goodban noted:

> There is no thinking of going on holiday this time; we are packed in like sardines. The train is composed of horse boxes and we are packed 34 in each box and no light. What a game! We sort ourselves out and try to settle down but sleep is out of the question, such cries of 'get off my ear' and 'whose ****** leg's that in my dining room?!' etc keep rending the air. However we pass the night singing and smoking and eating the 3 B's.[20]

According to Bowdery, the train passed through Rouen, Beauvais, Amiens, Boulogne, Calais, St Omer and Hazebrouck before arriving at Merville at 6.30pm on Monday 22 February. From there they marched to La Gorgue, a distance of four miles, where they were billeted in a school with heaps of straw as their bed. At this time La Gorgue was approximately six miles behind the firing line, but had been occupied by the German Army at the start of the war, and bore the scars of the previous winter's fighting. The 4th Cameron Highlanders were immediately posted to 24 Brigade in the British 8th Division where they were brigaded with the 1st Worcester Regiment, the 2nd East Lancashire Regiment, the 1st Sherwood Foresters, the 2nd Northamptonshire Regiment and the 5th Black Watch. Whilst in La Gorgue the two platoons detached the previous day rejoined the battalion.

The Cameron men spent the next few days searching La Gorgue for cafes, or as Private Goodban writes, 'Estaminets'. Lieutenant Ian MacKay – in a letter to his parents of 23 February – described that time: 'All the men are very fit and in high spirits and some of their efforts at French are very amusing. Most of them say 'Oui, oui' to everything and the Skyemen usually stare and say nothing.'[21]

Whilst billeted in La Gorgue, Private Bowdery saw one of the wonders of modern warfare – a dogfight in the air:

> During the afternoon I witness a fight in mid-air between English and German aeroplanes. These fellows run great risks and from below one can watch the effects of shrapnel fire directed against them. None of them were hit but at any rate the Germans were driven off.[22]

On 25 February, a party of eight officers and eight sergeants were sent to spend the night with the Worcestershire Regiment in the front line trenches to gain an idea of how they operated. Lieutenant Ian Mackay was one of the officers selected, and he later described how, in the advance to the trenches, bullets were flying all around them. The trenches the Camerons viewed were 70–100 yards from the Germans, who kept firing all night. Mackay reported that the trenches were very muddy and it was bitterly cold at night but the Worcesters' Captain shared his dug out with him and they managed to light a fire, cooking their own dinner. Even though he proclaimed the trenches to be a safe place, MacKay had a close encounter when a bullet passed straight through his glengarry (bonnet). He was undeterred by the incident. A sergeant from Inverness, eager to test the marksmanship of the Germans, raised his own on a stick, which instantly drew fire and left him with two holes in the headgear.

Whilst in these trenches Lieutenant Mackay got word that the 4th Camerons were moving closer to the firing line and he returned to join them in their new billets in Black Watch Lane, which they reached at 7.40pm on 26 February, eight days after their arrival in France. The officers were billeted in a cottage and the A Company officers formed their own mess there. Captain Murdoch Beaton, Captain David F. Mackenzie, Lieutenants Francis E. Laughton, John Black, Charles Campbell and the Mackay brothers all messed together.

On 28 February, the 4th Cameron Highlanders took their place in the front line trenches for the first time. In the sector running north from the village of Neuve Chapelle the trenches were known as A to F Lines. A and B Companies took over from two companies of the Middlesex Regiment and took their positions in part of the C Lines trenches just north of the Estaires to La Bassee Road. C and D Companies were in reserve billets in Cameron Lane, just behind the battalion Headquarters which were in a farmhouse in Rue Bacquerot, about 1000 yards behind the firing line.[23] Lieutenant-Colonel Alexander Fraser had the honour of being in command of the whole sector.

The conditions in the trenches were particularly trying. There were no communication trenches linking the fire trench to the reserve positions and no duckboards providing flooring in the front line trenches. This lack of flooring – when combined with the snowfalls which peppered northern France in the first week of March 1915 – meant that the trenches became a quagmire. Ration parties were forced to move in the open at night under persistent rifle fire from the enemy positions.[24]

Private Bowdery described his first day in the trenches:

> Well Sunday today, and who would have thought that I would see a Sunday as near the firing line as I am now. Nothing much doing in the early part of the day. Aha! We hear about 12 orders now that we are to go into the trenches this evening, my word the excitement

> in A Company. Now for fatigues, yes I thought, my name yes Bowdery, just give a hand with these blankets. Right-oh Sergeant off I trot, come back, more fatigue – rations this time. Eventually we are ready then comes 'fall in' and off we go for our first baptism of fire. We march to trenches through mud over our ankles. Eventually we get within the bullet area and my word don't they whistle. Everyone keeps as low as possible and probably wonder if any are coming his way. We reach the trenches at last and we are told that we are safe enough if we keep low, which one might be sure we do with the result that our backs ache within about 5 minutes. At 10 o'clock pm I am put on Sentry, that is to look out over the top of the trench for Germans. One might guess that hearing the bullets whistling about I feel somewhat dubious about putting my head over, but I eventually get over that feeling and do my duty. Nothing happens.[25]

The Inverness, Broadford and Nairn men of A and B Companies spent that first day in the C Lines trenches and were relieved after two days by the Strathspey, Fort William and Portree men of C and D Companies. Each platoon had a front of about 100 yards to call their own.

The first casualties sustained by the 4th Cameron Highlanders were taken on 1 March. When the Machine Gun Section was retiring to their billets half a mile behind the trenches a shell came through the roof of the billet and exploded, killing Sergeant Ronald R. MacDonald and wounding Privates John Kowin, Albin Rous, William Feiling, Reginald Murray, Daniel Stanger and Robert Dingwall. A correspondent, writing to the *Inverness Courier,* described the explosion:

> I jumped up on the wall and was in the act of jumping over when a shell burst through the roof and blew me off the wall, half-blinding and deafening me and I was nearly choked with fumes. When I realised my whereabouts I was sitting under a horse. I got up and rushed for the fresh air. I then heard shrieks and groans from within and shouts for stretchers. I bolted to the doctor and got three stretchers, and in them we carried three of the worst cases and three walked to the doctor.[26]

By 6 March all four companies of the 4th Camerons were in the front line trenches of C Lines. On 8 March a German shell exploded in the trenches of C Company, killing Private Colin Fraser and Bugler William Campbell and wounding six of their comrades, one of whom, Private Ralph Edwards, died on 9 March. Company Sergeant Major William A. MacIntyre became the most senior member of the 4th Camerons to become a casualty. He was shot in the leg on 8 March and died on the 23rd of his wounds.

These early days in the trenches were full of new experiences for the men of the 4th Cameron Highlanders. Corporal Roderick Ross described the situation in a letter to his sister in Inverness:

> On Monday night I took a team into the firing line, and on the way up had to pass a bullet-swept road. It made one feel rather nervous to hear a biz-z-zip above your head and not knowing but that the next would get you. The trenches themselves are safe as houses once we get in. The dangerous part is getting in and out. The mud is terrible. I wish you could have seen me when I came out last night. I walked into a shellhole, sinking almost to

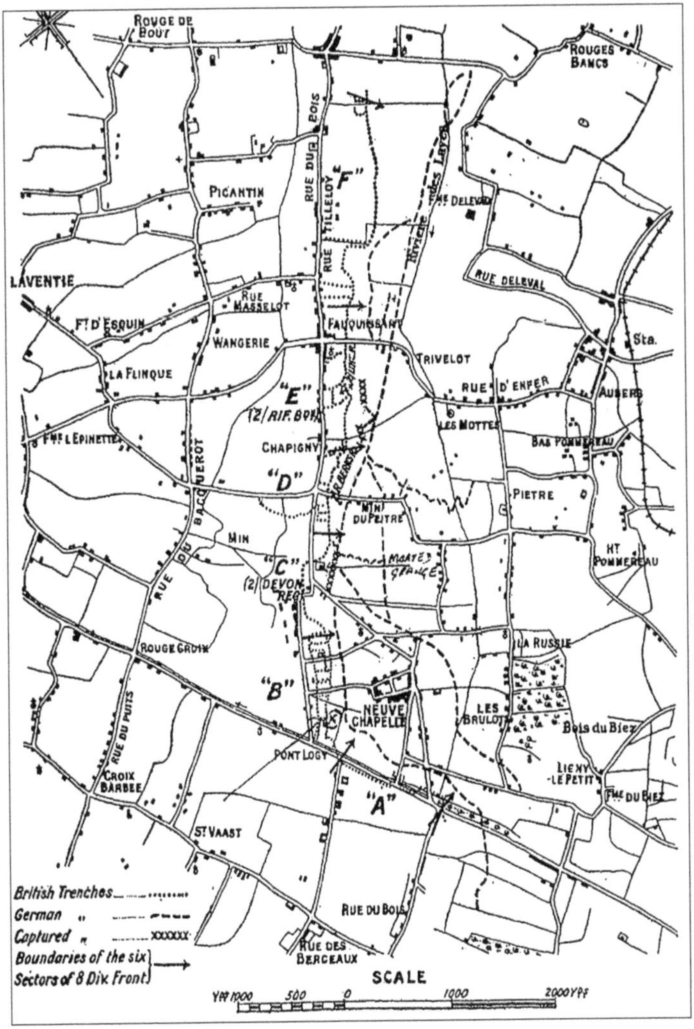

A to F Lines trenches, Neuve Chapelle Sector, March 1915.
(8th Division History)

> the waist in liquid clay. About half a dozen star shells blazed up near us as we were crossing the exposed part of the field but we were so mad and out of temper that we kept straight on even though we were showing up quite distinctly. We are so close that we can hear the Germans talking and singing. They have a very nasty habit of shooting just when we are at meals and when a lump of clay falls into your tea, which is none too plentiful as water is scarce, it's none too pleasant. I had a few shots at their loopholes, and did some damage to their cookhouse chimney.[27]

The Battalion, with their colleagues in the 8th Division, were about to take part in the first major attack of 1915. The village of Neuve Chapelle had to be taken.

4

The Battle of Neuve Chapelle, 9–15 March 1915

In March 1915 Neuve Chapelle was a small village in the Nord Pas-de-Calais region of France, nine miles south-west of Armentières. The area had been the scene of sporadic fighting in the final months of 1914, which culminated in the Germans taking possession and incorporating the village into the defences of the strategically important position of Aubers Ridge, a mile to the east of the village. The overall battle plan was to capture the salient in which the village was situated and, if the British Army was successful, to assault Aubers Ridge itself.

There were several key features of the battlefield. On the extreme north of the British position, at the point where C Lines met D Lines, was a farm called Moated Grange. It had been largely destroyed on 27 November 1914 by British artillery, in an attempt to eliminate a German sniper position. By March 1915 the buildings were technically in no man's land between the British and German lines. To the south of the farm, the Sunken Road ran past an orchard and then on to meet a road coming from the village of Mauquissart and a group of houses called Nameless Cottages. Just south of the Sunken Road was Signpost Lane. This was another road running almost parallel to the Sunken Road just outside of Neuve Chapelle. Further still to the south, in the centre of the British line, was the village itself and at the extreme south of the position was Port Arthur, which was to be assaulted by the Lahore and Meerut Divisions of the Indian Corps.

The popular image of First World War trenches was inspired by those of the later years of the conflict: complex trench systems carved into the earth, extending from the North Sea to the Swiss border. The Neuve Chapelle sector in March 1915 did not have these cavernous subterranean homes and the British soldiers relied on something much more basic, the breastwork. Speaking in 1977, Private Hector Macdonald from Daviot, near Inverness, described them:

> You could stand in the trench and look over the breastwork towards the German frontline but of course ... the weather was wet and you were nearly up to your knees in mud in this trench. Everything was mud. Both sides of the trench all mud. The trench would be about five foot deep and then you could look over it towards the German front.[28]

The Battle of Neuve Chapelle was the first large scale offensive carried out by the BEF in 1915. The disposition of the British troops at the start of the battle was as follows. From the Port Arthur position to the start of the B Lines trenches was the area manned by the Indian Corps, comprised of the Lahore and Meerut Divisions. In the B and

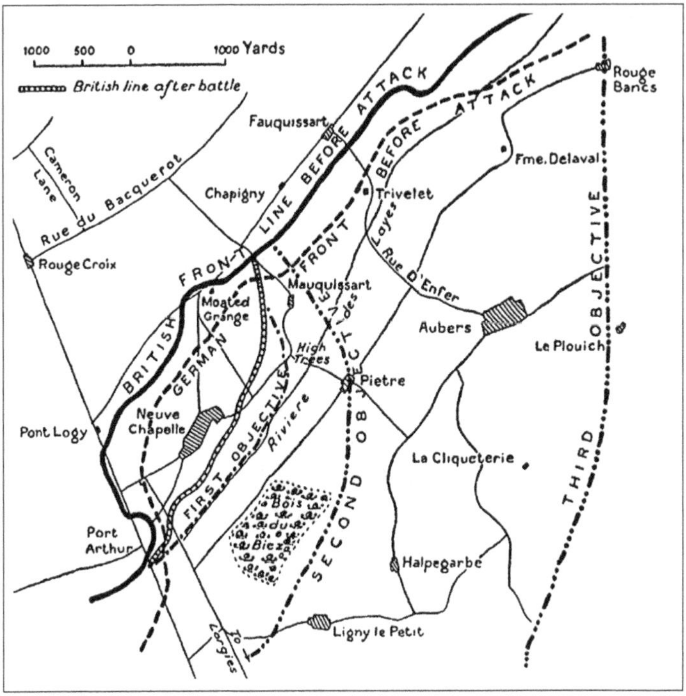

The Neuve Chapelle battlefield and objectives, March 1915. (*7th Division History*)

C Lines trenches were 23 and 25 Brigades of the British 8th Division who were to lead the assault on the village. Farther to the north were 20, 21 and 22 Brigades of the 7th Division. 24 Brigade of the 8th Division were to be the Divisional reserve, but at the opening of the battle several of their battalions were in holding positions in the front line. This included the 4th Cameron Highlanders whose A Company was on the extreme left of the battlefield in the right hand portion of the D Lines trenches. To their right was B Company in the left portion of C Lines and the trenches curving round behind the Moated Grange. Next came D Company, still in C Lines, and lastly C Company, who garrisoned the right hand section of C Lines up to the junction of C and B Lines, to the north of Signpost Lane.

The aim of the 8th Division attack was for 23 and 25 Brigades to push on and capture the first line objectives. 24 Brigade had supplied the 5th Black Watch and the 2nd Northampton Regiment to garrison B Lines in addition to the 4th Camerons in C and D Lines. 21 Brigade of the 7th Division was to assemble along the Rue de Tilleloy, behind B Lines, and occupy the trenches vacated by the assaulting brigades of the 8th Division, with 20 Brigade taking over their reserve trenches. 22 Brigade was to remain in reserve trenches in E and F Lines to the north of the main attack. Facing the British troops were the German 13th and 14th Divisions, the 6th Bavarian Reserve Division and the 11th Jaeger Regiment.

The battle commenced at 7.30am on 10 March with a massive artillery bombardment. Around 350 artillery pieces had been collected for use in the offensive and they set about their aim of pulverising the Germans' front line trenches and destroying the protective works of barbed wire. There followed a barrage which was the largest yet seen in the war and prompted one officer in the 4th Seaforth Highlanders to remark: 'the din was terrific, the whole air and the solid earth itself became one quivering jelly.'[29] Another account stated that: 'a wall of dust and smoke, from 50 to 100 feet high had shot up from the German trenches, as the shells fell thick and fast on the enemy's barbed wire and front line.'[30]

The bombardment was largely successful, with one exception – the trenches in front of 23 Brigade from Signpost Lane to the Sunken Road, held by two companies of the 11th Jaeger Regiment. This was to prove costly for the attack.

Twenty-four-year old Kingussie man Sergeant Donald P. Fraser of the 4th Camerons C Company described the barrage:

> The men were wonderfully cool and confident the night before the battle, and quite ready at any moment to drive off an attack. At 7am the guns opened like thunder, shot and shell screaming overhead, and men, earth and debris flying high in the air from the German trenches. We kept up a rapid fire on anyone who tried to retire.[31]

The artillery bombardment lasted for 35 minutes before lifting to its secondary targets in the German second defensive line. At 8.05am, the infantry attacked. The 2nd Middlesex Regiment and 2nd Scots Rifles, in the first wave of 23 Brigade's attack on the right of the 4th Camerons, ran into trouble immediately. Their 400-yard front to the immediate north of Signpost Lane had been largely untouched by the artillery barrage and the German defenders inflicted such losses on them that they were unable to advance very far and were pinned down by machine-gun and shell fire. The second wave of the 23 Brigade assault, the 2nd West Yorkshire Regiment and the 2nd Devon Regiment, were ordered to support the attack of the Scots Rifles as they were less bogged down than the Middlesex to their left. They were then to turn north and attack in the flank of the enemy positions holding up the Middlesex.

Corporal Alistair MacDougall[32] of the 4th Camerons, writing to his father in the Highlands, described the initial advance of the British Army:

> After breakfast the advance began, the Scottish Rifles leading. For all the world you would think that they were going to a football match; smiling, smoking and joking, their manner did not suggest war. They were followed by battalion after battalion, and as they were under fire you could see every now and again a fellow stumble and fall, but the advance continued. When our men arrived at the German trenches they had nothing to do but walk in.[33]

At approximately 10.00am a fresh artillery bombardment of the lines in front of the Middlesex commenced. Major-General Francis Davies, commanding the 8th Division, ordered most of 24 Brigade to take up new positions to continue the attack. The 1st Worcesters and the remainder of the 2nd West Yorkshires were to support the Middlesex men and occupy the trenches vacated by the 11th Jaegers. The 2nd Northamptonshires, the 1st Sherwood Foresters and the 2nd East Lancashires, all of 24 Brigade, took up their new positions in the area of the old British front line, from where 23 and 25 Brigade had launched their assault. The East Lancashires took up positions where Signpost Lane met the Armentières Road, filling the gap of several hundred yards between the attacking brigades. Major-General Davies realised the difficulties of 23 Brigade's position and accordingly authorised General Pinney, the commander, to call on the services of 24 Brigade as and when needed.

At 11.30am, Sir Henry Rawlinson, commander of IV Corps, ordered the 2nd West Yorkshires and the battle-weary remains of the Middlesex Regiment to rush the Orchard position on the north of the Sunken Road. After a brief artillery bombardment, they did so, and at 12.30pm the Orchard was taken and the Yorkshires moved north towards the Moated Grange and the 4th Camerons' position.

Situated to the north of the Middlesex attack, the 4th Cameron Highlanders themselves were not directly involved in the first stage of the battle, but neither were they idle. Private Montague Goodban of A Company, situated in the D Lines trenches, reported how the artillery barrage took its toll on the German defenders:

> During the 3 hours from 4am to 7am we had orders to pour rapid fire on to the 'Allemands' who were retreating from their trench to seek safer quarters. With the constant rapid fire my rifle steamed like a boiling kettle and became so hot that I could scarcely hold it. During this time I think we managed to bag a good few of the enemy between us. Their parapet was so badly damaged by our high explosives that they stuffed the gaps up in it with their dead.[34]

The Camerons were still the target of German attention, with shells continuously hitting the trenches around their position, causing casualties. Captain James MacPherson of B Company became the first 4th Camerons officer to be killed by enemy fire; he died alongside seven of his men. A further 23 men were wounded, one of them, Sergeant Alexander Johnston of Nairn, dying the next day. An unnamed Private writing in a letter published in the *Inverness Courier* told of the German shellfire:

> The air was simply thick with shrapnel. One shell knocked down a bit of our parapet, passed through a

> group of men without hitting anyone and buried itself in the wall of the dugout. Fortunately it did not burst.[35]

Lieutenant William Mackay was in command of a farmhouse to the north of the Moated Grange which had been strengthened, loopholed and garrisoned by his platoon of A Company.

> It was quite amusing, quite near the German lines so we could not leave the building during the day time and had to keep all lights well shaded at night. Through chinks in the roof we could observe with field glasses the Germans and see them running about in their trenches. The farmer had gone, his wheat lay unthreshed in the barn, his cows lay dead in the fields but his two dogs remained and became very friendly with us![36]

By 1.00pm the battalions of 23 Brigade were in possession of their second line objectives and had cleared the Germans from the trenches on the left of their advance to the Moated Grange. At once the troops of 23 Brigade began to put this area of newly captured ground into a state of defence to prepare for a counterattack. Their colleagues in 25 Brigade dug in on a line from the easterly houses of Neuve Chapelle to the road junction at Signpost Lane where its flank met that of 23 Brigade.

Around 2.15pm 21 Brigade was ordered forward from its reserve positions on the Rue de Tilleloy. The 2nd Yorkshire Regiment and the 2nd Royal Scots Fusiliers advanced through the 23 Brigade positions 100 yards east of the Moated Grange, and gained about 300 yards from the enemy. On their left, the 2nd Wiltshire Regiment took up a position just in front of, and joined up with, the

4th Cameron Highlanders in the C Lines trenches. These fresh troops were to attack towards Moulin du Pietre as soon as 24 Brigade were in position on their right flank. But it was not to be so straightforward.

At 1.30pm, 24 Brigade had received fresh orders to be ready for the attack. The Sherwood Foresters and the Northamptons deployed along the Armentières Road each side of Signpost Lane. Due to numerous breakdowns in communication they finally advanced at 5.30pm and received a light peppering of fire from the German positions at Nameless Cottages and the Layes Brook Redoubt. Taking casualties, the battalions halted and dug in, awaiting support. The new British line ran from a point near the German defences north of the Moated Grange to the junction of the Signpost Lane–Layes Bridge Road where it met Nameless Cottage Lane.

By 7.00pm, 21 and 24 Brigades had lost touch with each other and both had dug in for the night to prepare to renew the assault in the morning. That evening, in the Camerons' sector, parts of B and D Companies occupied the Moated Grange and trenches taken from the enemy. A wounded officer of B Company, recuperating in Inverness at the end of March, recounted the tale of occupying the farm:[37]

> They were ordered to occupy a moated grange, a large farm building that had been wrecked by the German shells. The moat round the building was reached by the Camerons in safety. Operations were immediately done to fortify the place and while the Camerons were busily engaged digging themselves in, a hail of German bullets assailed them. A number of the men dropped wounded, but the German counterattack was repelled promptly, and the Camerons were able to dig themselves into the

> position they had taken up, and to hold them against the enemy. During this operation there were several casualties among officers and men and these were promptly attended to. The whole operation was a fine piece of work.[38]

11 March did not start well for the British troops. The weather was particularly misty and the 15-minute artillery barrage which preceded the morning's action was ineffectual. Shells by now were in short supply. Under the cover of night and and a thick mist the Germans had been able to dig new defensive positions in relative comfort, these areas being missed by the British gunners, who never even knew they existed. The troops of 21 Brigade – in dugouts in the area between the Orchard on the Sunken Road and the village of Mauquissart – could make no progress in their attack against these new positions. Reinforcements from 20 Brigade advanced at 7.00am from the Moated Grange to try and get in touch with 21 Brigade but were hit by rifle, machine-gun and artillery fire. This bombardment was to last for three hours. 21 Brigade suffered many casualties, especially amongst the 2nd Gordon Highlanders, who dug in southeast of the Moated Grange and to the north of the orchard.

Corporal MacDougall, of the Cameron's Fort William Company, described how the German artillery bombardment affected the 4th Camerons:

> It was at that time that I had the misfortune to be hit. The Germans had brought up fresh artillery and men. In our part of the trench, Captain Allison, Lieutenant Calder, Sergeant K.K. Cameron, Sergeant Donald Cameron, Corporal R. Cooper, Corporal Donald

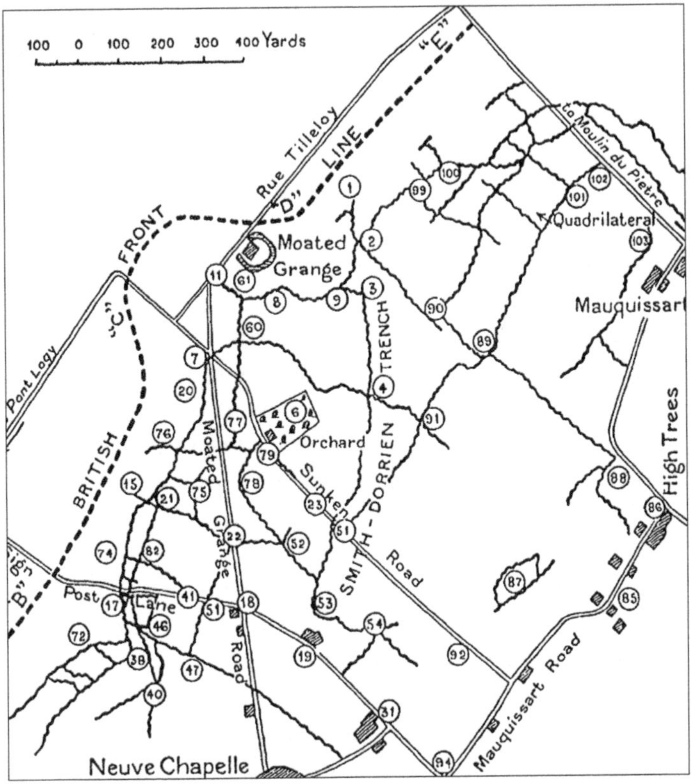

The northern sector of the Neuve Chapelle battlefield.
(*7th Division History*)

Grant and myself. Shells were dropping too near to be comfortable and one landed just behind the trench and almost buried us all. I had to be dug out and the Captain also had to be helped out. We shifted over to where 9 Platoon were and had not been there very long when a shell burst about 6 yards away and fairly peppered Lieutenant Calder and myself.[39]

The Germans did not have it all their own way. In the Camerons sector around the Moated Grange the German trenches had taken a severe pounding from the British artillery. Private Charles Bowdery of A Company described how the enemy reacted:

> We have the satisfaction of seeing the Germans put up their white flags all along their line and we shout across to them to surrender and come over, which they do, poor wretches. They leave all the rifles and equipment behind and run across with their hands up. We capture about 300 in our section, most of them wounded owing to the terrific fire they have been subjected to. Poor devils they seem dazed and only too pleased to be taken prisoner.[40]

Lieutenant Ian Mackay, serving in A Company with his brother William, also watched the surrender, before taking posession of the vacated German trench:

> Some of our troops collected them and they came across to our lines so we had a good look at them. It was a guard of our men that marched them off. They seemed to be delighted to be taken prisoner and be out of the fight as they waved their hands to us and shook hands with our men and slapped them on the back and some gave up their helmets in exchange for biscuits etc.[41]

Lieutenant William Mackay, writing to his mother in Inverness on 14 March, described the part the Camerons played in the surrender and in particular the role of one of the toughest men in the battalion, Corporal James Macbean of Achnabeachan,[42] who would later achieve legendary status as the finest fighting man in the battalion:

> Of course the flank attack and artillery fire really caused them to surrender but we did our share too and picked them off whenever they showed up – Achnabeachan in particular doing great execution, remaining at a loophole all day like a leech! Whilst the bombardment was going on amidst the fearful noise one of my platoon, a Skyeman looked over the parapet and seeing sandbags etc being hurled from the German trenches by the explosions exclaimed in awestruck tones 'Good Graaashus, God have mercy on them' to which I replied 'I hope he will have more than you Norman, for I am sure if you get at them you won't have much!' The man in question being very small made the joke complete.[43]

At 12.19pm, General Rawlinson ordered that the buildings at Moulin du Pietre and at the Mauquissart-Pietre crossroads should be assaulted. Regrettably, the only troops to hear of this were two companies of the 1st Worcester Regiment. Their attempt to capture the position, and a later attack by the Sherwood Foresters and 2nd Northamptonshires, met with failure and severe loss of life. The 24 Brigade front now stretched from the Northamptons in the extreme north, in touch with 7th Division on their left, directly east of Nameless Cottages. The Worcester Regiment was on their immediate right with the Sherwood Foresters facing the German position at the eastern end of Sunken Lane. The West Yorkshire Regiment of 23 Brigade held their right flank, in a position straddling the Layes Bridge Road. These battalions remained there for the rest of the day and made preparations to renew the attack the following morning.

In the 4th Cameron Highlanders War Diary, Adjutant Captain Garden B. Duff recorded that in the evening of 11 March two platoons of C Company occupied trenches in support of the Middlesex Regiment where they remained for the night.[44] The trench system occupied by the 4th Camerons was now much more spread out than at the start of the battle two days earlier. A Company still held the left flank in D Lines but B Company now held the right of C Lines, the Moated Grange and the captured German trenches to the east. They were ably supported by D Company who had moved forward from their position in the salient to a position to the southeast of the Moated Grange, and C Company on the extreme right of the Camerons' front was now in support of the Middlesex Regiment.

As night fell on 11 March 1915, the German 6th Reserve Bavarian Division moved into position to assault the ground gained by the British and Indian assault and recapture the village of Neuve Chapelle. Their aim was to force the Allied troops to retreat along the whole of the captured territory, from Port Arthur in the south to the Moated Grange in the north. The 13th Infantry Regiment, two companies of the 15th Infantry Regiment and one battalion of the 179th Saxons would attack the area of the Moated Grange.[45]

On that misty Friday morning, following an artillery bombardment, the German troops were able to advance as close as 50 yards from the British lines before being spotted. 21 Brigade managed to hang on to their position south of the Quadrilateral, near the Moated Grange, despite the 2nd Wiltshire Regiment being temporarily overwhelmed by the enemy bombers, and their A and C Companies were driven back to the Camerons' trench. The Green Howards to the immediate right of the Wiltshires, directly facing the Quadrilateral, repulsed the Germans but only when the enemy was in their front line trenches. Further round the line the Germans broke through the ranks of the 2nd Royal Scots Fusiliers, but were swiftly dealt with by reinforcements from the 2nd Bedfords. The Bedford War Diary records the battalion's losses as 15 men killed, 66 wounded and 5 missing and at least 3 officers wounded.[46] The Northamptonshires and Worcesters further to the right of the British line repulsed an attack by the 21st Bavarians and the 133rd Saxons but the Sherwood Foresters, holding the line between the Sunken Road and Layes Bridge Road, we not so fortunate. Their section of the line was the first to be attacked and most of the defenders were killed. At the same time, the Germans attacked the Foresters in the trench along Nameless Cottage Lane and forced them to retreat.[47]

The Bavarians and Saxons then found themselves in a salient and were charged by elements of the 1st Worcesters and the West Yorkshires who drove them back and secured the Nameless Cottages position. The Sherwood Foresters also rallied and regained the trenches that had been lost earlier.

The 4th Cameron Highlanders were also in the thick of it that morning. The previous evening, the officer commanding the D Lines trenches had issued an order to Lieutenant-Colonel Alexander Fraser:

> To enable the 7th Division to support an attack with key close artillery fire the whole of D Lines will be very quietly cleared of troops by 6.30am tomorrow morning. Half will close onto C Lines and half onto E Lines. Two

18-pounder batteries will be firing from Rue Bacquerot towards Moulin du Pietre from 7am. Troops so cleared to close back again after artillery bombardment which will commence at 7am and last half an hour. If morning very misty bombardment may be postponed a little. The Yeomanry will go into E Lines, the Cyclists and Camerons into C Lines. The move will be made as quietly as possible.[48]

Lieutenant Ian Mackay summarised the actions of Highlanders that morning:

About 4.30am we got the word to quit our trench as our guns were going to heavily bombard the German trench in front, part of which had not been captured by our men the previous day. We accordingly started before dawn to go over to the next trench on our right which was held by our B Company. To get to it we had to go through a ditch up to our middles in water and thick with mud. Just as we were getting across and most of us flopping about in the water the Germans attacked. They opened a heavy fire on us and also the Wiltshire Regiment, who were holding the part of the German trench captured the previous day. They drove the Wiltshires out with bombs and they retreated back to our trench to the very point we were making for. Consequently there was a fearful block in the entrance to the trench and we could not get on.

Those of us who were across the trench got into the next trench, those behind had to lie low in the watery ditch and those at the end of the line who were not across the ditch (among whom were Willie and DF)[49] went back to our old trench and manned it. I was at the head of the line as my command is Number 1 Platoon and I was following Beaton, our Captain. We got across alright but when we got into the next trench we found it blocked with the Wiltshires who had been bombed out of the trench in front and that there was absolutely no room for us. We had therefore to file down a narrow trench behind and there we were stuck for about half an hour over the ankles in mud and water. We had to stoop very low to get cover and bullets were flying thick. I looked across with my field glasses and made out Willie and McErlich[50] in it. Gradually the block eased and we were able to make our way back to the firing trench.

While we were in the narrow trench behind we expected every minute to be charged by the Germans but when we got back to the firing trench we found that the Wiltshires had rallied and charged the Germans and recaptured the bit of trench they had been bombed out of in the morning. We accordingly took our place in the firing line and had a lovely time. Our fellows enjoyed it awfully and you could see the Germans being bowled over like rabbits. After a bit we made our way back to our old trenches. The heavy guns again bombarded the German trenches while we kept up a constant fire and after a bit, a large number (300) of Germans again surrendered, again coming through our lines. The Brigadier sent us a note congratulating us on our co-operation in these captures. These captures were very exciting, like winning a good football match.[51]

The letters of Lieutenants Ian and William Mackay and the diaries of Privates Montague Goodban and Charles

Bowdery are full of references to the exciting and even enjoyable life on the front line. However, some moments provided a sobering reflection on the horrors of war. Writing to his mother on 14 March from billets in Cameron Lane, Ian Mackay described one such event:

> That morning we had one of the little tragedies of war. When we crossed the ditch in the early morning we had with us a young officer of the Welsh Fusiliers who had come along the line to reconnoitre. When the Wiltshires were beaten back he took a prominent part in rallying them and behaved very bravely and when we recrossed to our old trench he came back with us. We lit a fire in the open and sat round it and had some breakfast and discussed the events of the morning. After a while he got up to go back to his own lines but he had only gone a few yards when he looked over the breastwork and fell dead, shot through the head. I believe he is to be recommended for the DSO for the part he played in the morning's proceedings.[52]

The officer in question was 25-year-old 2nd Lieutenant Horace Parkes from Bournemouth. He had joined the 1/28th London Regiment, the Artists Rifles, and was given a temporary commission into the Royal Welch Regiment in December 1914. On the day of the battle he was in the C Lines trenches in his capacity as liaison officer with the 21st Brigade. For his efforts in trying to rally the 2nd Wiltshire Regiment he was mentioned in the despatches of General Haig. 2nd Lieutenant Parkes' body was not recovered after the battle and he is commemorated on the Le Touret Memorial to the Missing.

At this time D Company of the 4th Camerons were dug in to the southeast of the Moated Grange. Private Arnold Theobald described his experiences of this position:

> I was in a short trench for an hour or so only, a trench to the right of my own section. While there shrapnel broke overhead and a 'Jack Johnson' almost at the same time carried away the parapet, with the result that four were wounded and one killed. How I escaped I cannot explain. But some explanations are not for us to fathom, I'm sure. The above incident is simply one of hundreds.[53]

One of B Company's wounded officers, recuperating in Inverness in April, spoke of the casualties caused by shell-fire in an interview with the *Inverness Courier*:

> In some of the breastworks occupied by the 4th Camerons the floor was littered with shell fragments. In one case where there was practically no cover the men were ordered to lie close to the breastwork and hold their packs above their heads for protection.
>
> It was during this bombardment that the 4th Camerons suffered most heavily losing about 6 officers wounded and 80 to 100 men killed and wounded.[54]

At 5.45pm, 23 Brigade instructed the 2nd Devonshire Regiment and the 2nd Scots Rifles to capture the Pietre Road. 24 Brigade, still holding their earlier positions, deployed the 4th Cameron Highlanders to assist in the attack.

At about 5.00pm the battalion and the 2nd Battalion, Devon Regiment, were ordered forward to take part in a bayonet attack on the new enemy front at Pietre[55] which commenced at 7.30pm. As the battalion was very scattered, the men went forward by companies. Lieutenant-Colonel Fraser and Captain Duff, the Adjutant, led C Company forward to scout the route. They lost touch with the 2nd Devons[56] and in endeavouring to find them C Company and the Commanding Officer came in touch with the enemy's trenches unexpectedly.

The experiences of Lieutenant-Colonel Alexander Fraser were recounted in the *Inverness Courier:*

> [G]oing forward in front of the men they heard some talking but could not make out whether English or German. So they got forward to listen and came to the conclusion it was German. The Germans then sent up a flare light and the party was discovered, and the Huns opened fire very hotly. The officers in question were certainly not more than 20 yards from, and in front of, the German line but they lay flat on the ground, as flat as possible and never moved: then after a little the firing stopped and the CO, moving very cautiously a few inches a time, crawled first backwards into a hollow, then sideways and then straight back until he came to a firing trench, into which he rolled, and was then able to go in its shelter on his hands and knees for a little, after which he got up and walked away, completely untouched.[57]

Captain Duff followed Fraser and the 170 men of C Company followed him. Miraculously, there was not one casualty in the whole company. The Battalion was reorganised and once again ordered forward for a bayonet attack. The battalion war diary recorded:

> The Battalion which was now collected was ordered forward again, but owing to the dark and the intersected nature of an unknown country much time was lost and the battalion which had been in file was being assembled in an open field under heavy fire preparatory to moving to the correct position.[58]

Private Charles Bowdery described in his diary entry for 12 March how the men were exceedingly tired and in no fit state to make a bayonet charge, but were led forward in single file, across fields strewn with dead and wounded British and German soldiers. The wounded were crying for water but there was nothing the Camerons could do for them. Bowdery described it as the most gruesome thing he had ever seen in his life. His A Company colleague Private Montague Goodban could only sum it up in one word – heartbreaking.

The area over which the 4th Cameron Highlanders marched for their bayonet charge was between their position in the captured German trench in front of the Moated Grange and the 24 Brigade frontline positions facing Nameless Cottages around the sector held by the Worcester Regiment. The Camerons took up positions on a slight hill in no man's land about 100 yards from the new German positions. The Battalion had reached its launching position unobserved by the Germans and intended taking them by surprise. All of a sudden they were ordered to lie down and await further orders. The field they were in was full of rotting turnips and the constant shellfire had turned it into a quagmire. Here they stayed, expecting orders to attack at any moment, for 2–3 hours. The Germans continuously sent up flares to try and find approaching British troops, and once the Camerons were spotted the enemy opened

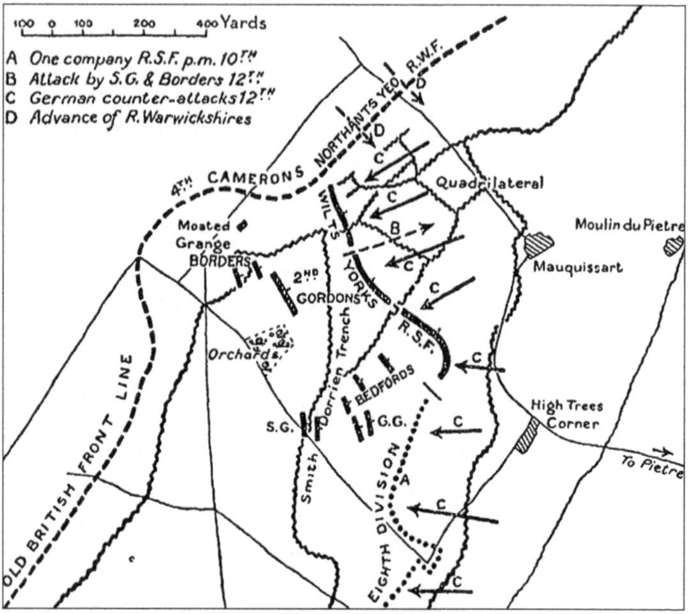

The Moated Grange sector at the Battle of Neuve Chapelle, 12 March 1915. (*7th Division History*)

up a terrific barrage of rifle, machine-gun and artillery fire. Lieutenant Ian Mackay, again writing to his parents in Inverness, noted with levity that the men were so tired from the exertions of the previous days that even under such hellish conditions they all fell asleep. He wrote that he was afraid the noise from the Highlanders' snoring would alert the Germans to their presence!

After the Germans opened fire, the 4th Camerons and the other battalions at their side were ordered to retire. Someone further up the chain of command had realised that an attack in that sector would be unwise and it was aborted. Private Bowdery described the retreat:

> Evidently someone has made a mistake and bungled orders for we are given the order to retire as best we can. We got up and shrapnel plays havoc with us, our poor chaps are hit and their cries are heartrending for we dare not stop to help them.[59]

Private Goodban echoed Bowdery's sentiments:

> For reasons I am unable to find out we get the order to get back on to the road as quickly and as best as we can, the road is about half a mile in our rear. As soon as the Huns discovered us they opened a terrific fire of machine guns, rifles and artillery and cries of chaps getting hit go up on all sides.[60]

A member of the Maxim gun section wrote home that the battalion had been ordered to charge the Germans out of a wood. The soldier reported that it was just as well the Camerons were ordered to retire as the Germans had brought up so many reinforcements that the Scots soldiers would have been annihilated.[61]

The men retired about 3.00am on 13 March. In the confusion following the retreat, many of the 4th Camerons lost their way when trying to get back to their original position beside the Moated Grange. At this time, Private Goodban's and Private Bowdery's accounts converge, as they and two other men got lost together. According to Bowdery:

> Myself and the other 3 got lost and mixed up with the Worcesters etc, eventually we strike the road towards our headquarters and after struggling along for about 3 hours dead tired we reach headquarters but cannot find anywhere to sleep so trudge off again about another

> mile to our old barn. We were fall down whacked. It is about 5.30 Saturday morning I have never spent such an awful time in all my life and hope to God that I never repeat it.[62]

Goodban continues:

> Eventually myself and 3 pals get clear but we find we have lost touch with our battalion and are mixed up with a bunch of Warwicks. We decide we had better make for Headquarters which we find after a great deal of tramping and arrive there at 5.30am on Saturday morning absolutely done up. All day Saturday chaps keep turning up who had got lost in a similar manner to ourselves.[63]

Lieutenant Ian MacKay also got lost during the retreat, having stayed behind – with Sergeant John Roake and four men – to bringing in the wounded left in no man's land during the German barrage. He described it in a letter to his parents in Inverness:

> The men ... got confused in the dark and followed the battalion home, so the Sergeant and I were left alone and we had a little adventure together. We started off across the field and went over the ground thoroughly but could not find the men we were looking for so concluded that they must have been picked up by RAMC men, who were going about in parties picking up men wounded in that day's battle. We then turned to make our way back but owing to the dark and the frequent turnings we had in our search we lost the direction and could not find the road back. Every now and again, the Germans, who seemed to be all around us, sent up fire balls and opened

> fire and we had to fall flat down. Wandered about for some time not knowing if we were going towards the British or German lines as the two were not parallel but zigzagging about but gradually by my compass I made out the right direction. We heard some voices and crawled up to them to hear what language they were speaking. We were glad to hear a good English swear word and found the party to be some RAMC men who were taking in a wounded officer who was shot through the shoulder. Shortly afterwards we fell in with some of our own men who had been delayed on the way home and we all made our way back to the trenches together.[64]

The operation had been a costly affair and the Adjutant, Captain Garden Duff, writing in the battalion war diary, summed it up most succinctly: 'Casualties about 70.'[65]

At 10.40pm on 12 March 1915, while the Camerons were lying in the field in no man's land, General Sir Douglas Haig officially ended the Battle of Neuve Chapelle. First Army Operation Order No.13 stated:

> The 4th and Indian Corps will continue to hold the advanced line reached by them today. This line to be established as a defensive line and secured against attack including wiring. The general advance will not be continued tomorrow without further orders and reliefs may be carried out within Corps accordingly.[66]

Speaking later, Sir John French, commander of the BEF, gave the fatigue of the troops and, above all, the want of ammunition as the reason for the cessation of the attack. Many units of the 7th and 8th Divisions still came under fire on 13 March and the 4th Cameron Highlanders War

Diary records that A Company sustained heavy losses during the German attack. This aside, the Camerons took little share in any action that day, and on 14 March they and the rest of 24 Brigade were placed in reserve billets at Cameron Lane before moving to the old C Lines trenches they had previously occupied. In his diary entries of 15 and 16 March, Montague Goodban described taking possession of the German trenches that day:

> These reserve trenches are situated on the ground captured from the Germans on the 10th, 11th and 12th. Rifles, equipment and dead litter the ground all round. There is an old German trench close by which I went and had a look at, it is full of dead Huns, some terribly mutilated, but I have by now got quite used to these gruesome sights. The Huns go in for comfort much more in their trenches than we do – some of their dugouts are quite cozy [sic] affairs with chairs, windows and even pictures on the walls, all of course taken from the houses behind their lines. As I write these notes shrapnel is bursting thick overhead. 6.20pm we leave here and go over to the German trenches of which I have just spoken and proceed to reverse them and make them suitable for our own occupation. We are digging until midnight when we get an hour or two's sleep and continue our operation at daybreak. We finished our job and leave here at 4pm for a rest back at La Gorgue where we arrive at 11pm.[67]

Private Bowdery, writing in his diary on the same day, his 22nd birthday, recalled how he never thought he would spend his birthday in such conditions. He remained cheerful, however, as he received letters and parcels from home. He also described the conditions of the German trenches:

> Move on to more trenches recently occupied by the Huns. I have now an opportunity of going over the German trenches and God the awful sights here inc a poor German who has had his head taken completely off and another with only half a head, others terribly mutilated. I am getting used to this now and find myself gazing on these awful sights without even a shudder. The fields round about are strewn with rifles, equipment etc both English and German, the result of our advance. While I think of it I remember that the shells and shrapnel are flying about us and a number of our chaps are falling.[68]

In La Gorgue, the 4th Cameron Highlanders rested, cleaned themselves and their equipment and refitted for their next duty in the front line. Lieutenant William Mackay, looking back on his experiences of the Battle of Neuve Chapelle, compared the German soldier to his own men:

> They are splendid snipers but in actual fighting cannot compare with the British man for man, and in fact are rather a funk of the British I think. I don't believe our fellows would have been turned out of those trenches – they are so strong and don't give a damn about anything. The more one sees of the British Tommy, the more one admires him and can understand how the British Empire has been made.[69]

His brother Ian, who served with him in A Company, reflected on the previous days:

> For a Territorial battalion just out we have had a pretty stiff time. Out of the last 10 days we have been 9 in the trenches and severely shelled which is very trying – also that abortive night attack took it out of the men very much. There is nothing so trying for Territorials or Regulars as to lie out for hours under fire, besides that we have a fair number of killed and wounded.[70]

An unidentified officer writing to a friend in Inverness described the loss of men during the battle. The letter was reproduced in the *Scotsman* of 23 March: 'I volunteered to hold an advanced redoubt until the assault was ordered, and managed to do so with a platoon of men. I lost some of the best, however, with that awful combination – snipers and shrapnel.'[71]

German snipers were a particular problem for the 4th Camerons, but they had their own share of excellent marksmen. Men used to stalking deer in the Highland glens proved adept at returning the enemy snipers' fire.

Writing in the *Scotsman* on 24 March, a 4th Cameron Highlander officer described the conditions. Iron plates with small loopholes for observation and firing were provided in the front line fire trenches, however the Germans were such good shots that one could not look through these loopholes during the day. The officer lamented the fact that the loopholes in the German trenches had iron shutters. He noted that the battalion favourite, Corporal James MacBean of Achnabeachen, Lieutenant Roderick McErlich and himself managed to locate a particular point in the German trench opposite where a sniper had been causing significant problems for the Highlanders. The three men had many shots at it, and after the battle, whilst inspecting that section of the enemy's trench, were satisfied to find many battered and silenced loopholes.

Charles Bowdery also had a salutory experience with a sniper:

> They have got a sniper posted so that his fire catches right at the side of my trench. I was bending down near the 2ft wall when without any warning I got a smash in the face by sand and mud which somewhat startled me. I got up and looked around and over the bank and found that the sandbag had been hit just below where my head had been. I thanked God it was low otherwise I should have been put out.[72]

Private Goodban recorded in his diary entry of 3 March how the German snipers used disguises:

> I drop in for Billet Guard today, 1 hour on and 3 hours off. My first attempt at this job out here. My Lieutenant has just come round to try and comfort me with the news that 3 sentries have been shot outside this billet during the last fortnight and advises me to keep a sharp look out. The sniper who did the dirty work is dressed as an old peasant woman.[73]

The snipers, trench mortars, machine guns and artillery of the German Army had taken its toll on the 4th Camerons. Casualty lists published in the *Scotsman, Inverness Courier* and *Soldiers Died in the Great War* give the names of the battalion's dead and wounded from the Battle of Neuve Chapelle. In the period from 28 February–9 March the battalion lost 7 men killed and 17 men wounded. During the battle itself, the 4th Camerons lost 28 men killed in action and died of wounds and 111 men wounded, half of whom were in A Company. The majority of the battalion's casualties took place on 12 March, presumably during the abortive attack on the German position.

The officers fared equally badly. Captain James MacPherson, commanding B Company was killed and Major John Campbell (D Company), Captain Thomas Allison (C Company), Lieutenant William J. Shaw (B Company), Lieutenant Angus Ross (D Company), 2nd Lieutenant James R. Park (B Company), 2nd Lieutenant Alexander R. Wallace (D Company) and 2nd Lieutenant William Calder (C Company) were wounded.

The casualties of the 4th Cameron Highlanders from before the Battle of Neuve Chapelle are buried at Rue de Bacquerot Number 1 Cemetery near Laventie, behind the British front line. Captain James MacPherson and four of his men lie there with them. One man, 20-year-old Private Donald MacDonald from Inverness, is buried in the Royal Irish Rifles Cemetery in Laventie. The remaining casualties' bodies were either never found or identified but their names live on, etched into the Memorial to the Missing at Le Touret.

For all their suffering at Neuve Chapelle, the Camerons were singled out for praise, both by senior officers and in the press back home. One of B Company's officers wrote:

> Instances worthy of the VC were performed by members of the 4th Camerons. When the advancing soldiers were hit in the open in front of the Cameron trenches several members of the battalion boldly left their cover and succeeded in succouring and bringing in wounded men.[74]

It had been a difficult start to their time in the trenches. From their arrival in France on 19 February until the end of the Battle of Neuve Chapelle on 16 March the 4th Camerons had spent twelve days in the front line, six days in support and eight days out of the line in reserve. Even though they had not been an attacking battalion at Neuve Chapelle, they had paid a high price; they marched on without 170 of their men.

5

The Battle of Aubers Ridge, 15 March–11 May 1915

On 16 March 1915, the 4th Cameron Highlanders were withdrawn to the village of La Gorgue in the rear of the British lines where they spent four days resting, recuperating and refitting after their first experiences of battle. Many of the battalion took the time to express their relief at being out of the firing line, even if the five-mile march to La Gorgue had taken its toll on them. In his diary entry of 16 March, Private Montague Goodban wrote: 'By jove what a march, we are all absolutely fogged out and can hardly get one foot before the other, every step is painful, however we know we are in for a rest, this fact helps us to keep going.'[75]

Private Charles Bowdery also struggled after the exertions of being in battle for the first time: 'My goodness, what a time. We have been working solidly for days and am just about dead and then this march with full pack. We hardly know how walking one foot after the other every step is really agony but we keep going as it is nearer resting.'[76]

An unnamed member of the Camerons wrote home, describing the battalion's time in La Gorgue:

> Chapter 1 has finished off quite nicely with a couple of days beautiful weather at our rest base. I had one day's fatigue during that time. It consisted of riding back in transport waggons to the battlefield and loading up with spare ammunition, equipment, and arms left there by the dead and wounded. We left at 4am in a blinding snowstorm, finished our job and got back to billets around 4pm, after being allowed to spend a few hours in a neighbouring town.[77]

While at La Gorgue, a series of promotions took place within the ranks of the 4th Cameron Highlanders to replace men who had been killed or wounded in battle. In the most senior of the changes to take place in the ranks, Harry Keates was confirmed Regimental Quartermaster Sergeant. Keates was born in Westbury in Wiltshire in 1872 and had enlisted into the 1st Cameron Highlanders on 12 February 1892 transferring from the 3rd Battalion, King's Royal Rifle Corps. He had served in Malta and Gibraltar before fighting in South Africa during the Boer War. Further service followed in Ireland, Hong Kong and Peking before he retired from the army. On 8 February 1915 he re-enlisted, this time in the 4th Cameron Highlanders, and was immediately given the rank of Acting CQMS. He was later to be promoted to Regimental Sergeant Major and served in France until 1917, when he was posted back to Scotland.

On 18 March, the newly formed Battalion Grenade Platoon, commanded by 2nd Lieutenant Francis Laughton, joined Headquarters. On the same day D Company lost Lieutenant Archibald Fletcher and B Company lost Lieutenant Frederick Kelly, both going to hospital sick.

After four days in reserve at La Gorgue the Highlanders got a well deserved bath, their first since arriving in France a month earlier. Private Bowdery described the process:

> Parade at 6.30am for bath which we have in an old soup factory, about 20 in one bath about 12 x 20 x 5, a most uncomfortable procedure but nevertheless welcome seeing that this is the first hot bath I have had since leaving dear old England. Our uniforms are disinfected and clean underwear etc are issued to us.[78]

Private Goodban also attended the battalion bathing on 20 March but he had grabbed an earlier, more opportune chance to wash off the grime of battle: 'Get up and proceed to have a gigantic clean up – the first decent wash for a fortnight, how grand and what a novelty to feel clean. I washed from head to foot under the pump in the middle of the street.'[79]

The 4th Camerons were soon required back in the trenches. On 21 March the battalion paraded at 5.30pm and marched to the Rue du Bacquerot, from where guides took them to their new front line position in the D Lines trenches at Champigny. B, C and D Companies replaced the 2nd Royal Scots Fusiliers while A Company took over an 'observing station' 300 yards behind the front line trenches. This position was an old farm which had been partially destroyed by shellfire but had been fortified by other British soldiers. Private Bowdery described the situation:

'No lights are allowed at night as we might have the place spotted and shelled, which, if that did happen, would mean a serious loss. Have to cook our own grub here and manage to have a fairly good meal now and then.'[80] An unidentified member of the battalion, writing to a friend in Inverness, described his time in these trenches: 'The Germans succeeded in putting a house on fire not 150 yards to the right of our trench yesterday. They send a shrapnel shell or two over our heads, occasionally, just to remind us that they know we are there.'[81]

The Camerons held this position for a rather uneventful two days, until on 23 March they were relieved by the 41st Dogras Regiment. Private Geoffrey Corbett was wounded during the handover. The Battalion then marched to billets at Ferme Epinette half a mile in the rear. Over the next few days the 8th Division marched north to take over trenches which had been occupied by the 7th Division since the Battle of Neuve Chapelle. They reached Neuf Berquin on the 24th and Sailly on the 25th before moving into reserve billets at the Rue des Quesnes for three days. At Sailly the first draft of officers arrived to replace those who had been killed or wounded at Neuve Chapelle: Captains Peter Cram, Ronald MacDonald and Ian Baillie and 2nd Lieutenants Alexander MacKenzie, Thomas Chalmers and James Bookless. Some of the billets during this movement north were better than others. In Neuf Berquin the troops were billeted in a barn that was fairly comfortable but the following night in Sailly the men of A Company were stuck in an old weaving factory, on a cold stone floor with only two feet of space each.[82]

On 29 March, the 4th Camerons continued their move north into the F Lines trenches in the front line south of Rouge de Bout. The trenches in this sector were in a much better condition than the battalion had been used to, as the breastworks were continuous and there was a practicable communication trench leading from the front lines to the reserve positions. In this sector the German trenches were 300–450 yards away and, after the battle two weeks earlier, neither side had much appetite for a fight. There were two officer casualties during this three-day tour: Lieutenant John Macpherson, the battalion's Transport Officer, was slightly wounded on 31 March and returned to duty within a week. Lieutenant John Black was wounded on 1 April when leaving the trench. While recuperating in hospital in Versailles, Lieutenant Black wrote to a friend in Inverness of the circumstances of his wounding:

> Our glengarry crests shine so much in the sun that for sniping purposes we put them in our pockets. On Wednesday night we were being relieved in the trenches and I hurriedly put my crest on my cap. Luckily for me I did as shortly after dark, when passing a rather exposed corner, a random bullet took the ground, or an old disused trench in front, and then struck me on the side of the head. It cut through part of the crest and was stopped by the holding pin underneath. My head was not cut but it bore and still bears to a certain extent the imprint of the pin![83]

The 4th Camerons were relieved on 1 April by the 2nd Rifle Brigade and went into reserve billets at Bac St Maur. According to the newly promoted Lance Corporal Charles Bowdery, the highlight of the tour came that same day: 'Anniversary of Bismarck's birthday – we can hear the Germans rejoicing, singing and having a good time. Endeavour to supply them with some amusement by sniping. Getting quite a good shot.'[84]

On 3 April, the 4th Camerons played the 5th Black Watch at football, winning 1–0. Whilst in Bac St Maur, the news came through that the battalion had been transferred to 21 Brigade in the 7th Division, a move which was to take place on 9 April. Through their change of division, the Camerons had new battalions as colleagues in 21 Brigade. They were the 2nd Bedford Regiment, 2nd Green Howards, 2nd Wiltshires and the 2nd Royal Scots Fusiliers, all of whom they had fought alongside in front of the Moated Grange at Neuve Chapelle.

Writing to his mother on 11 April from Estaires, Lieutenant Ian Mackay commented:

> We were sorry to leave the old brigade as we were beginning to settle down in it and getting to know the staff etc. We were at first not sure if the transfer was a compliment or the reverse. However, our new brigade was [in need of] a Territorial regiment that would be of real use to them, so we were sent. The Brigadier dined the Colonel and Duff one night and said he was exceedingly sorry to lose us.[85]

On 6 April the Camerons went into billets at Fleurbaix before marching to Estaires to join their new division. At Fleurbaix, Private Goodban made an observation on the habits of the locals:

> One of the peculiar things is that some of the French peasants are still working the land close to the trenches, notably at Fleurbaix where men were at work sowing

> corn only ½ a mile behind the firing line. Sometimes 1 or 2 get killed or wounded by a shell but they seem quite willing to risk it. And when a shell makes a big hole in the newly sown field they shake their fists towards the Germans and say 'Allemans no bon'.[86]

In April 1915 the newspapers back in Britain were full of tales of the gallantry displayed by the British soldiers at Neuve Chapelle. In the Scottish Highlands the *Inverness Courier* reproduced letters from the officers and men of the 4th Camerons. The officers writing back to Inverness were obviously very proud of their men and were eager to display their confidence in their abilities to the public: 'Officers and men are all very cheery and ready to try anything they are asked to do, and if all our forces are like the 4th Camerons in this respect there is a bad time in front for the Germans.'[87]

Life in the reserve lines was much more comfortable for the officers of the 4th Camerons than for their men. They were able to book themselves into a local convent to take hot baths and were even able to dine in a hotel behind the lines where they showed the locals their Highland customs. Ian Mackay recalled:

> Last night some of us had dinner at the hotel. Beaton, D.F. [Mackenzie], Laughton, Thomson, W. [William Mackay] and self and others. The Colonel and Duff came in too. We got the Pipe Major in later and Laughton, Thomson, W. and I danced a reel. The Pipe Major has composed a march which he has called 'The 4th Camerons at Neuve Chapelle' and he played it to us. The French people in the hotel were rather astonished at the proceedings.[88]

On 12 April, while in the reserve billets at Estaires, the Commander-in-Chief of British Forces, Sir John French, inspected the troops of 21 Brigade. A Cameron Highlander reported the parade to the *Inverness Courier*:

> We had the honour of being inspected and addressed by Sir John French this afternoon, and heard him say some very nice things about the Territorials in general and the 4th Camerons in particular. We made quite a good show in the brigade although our 'handling of arms' was not as finished in style as that of our regular comrades.[89]

All through the first months of 1915 the officers and men of the 4th Cameron Highlanders spoke with pride of being one of the first Territorial battalions sent to the front. The fact that the Camerons were part-time soldiers was not lost on the regulars either, and at all times they were happy to give pieces of advice to their less experienced countrymen. Even Sir John French commented on it:

> I never forget the difference between the Regular and Territorial Armies. We have made soldiering our life's work, and we are paid for it, but you have, though nominally enlisted for the defence of your country only, left your homes and businesses to come out here and help and I cannot sufficiently express my feelings of admiration.[90]

The day after the inspection by Sir John French, two more officers joined from the second line battalion back in Scotland. 2nd Lieutenants Henry Scott and William Dobie were posted to their companies and prepared for their first tour in the trenches.

On 14 April the Camerons took up positions in the E Lines trenches at Fauquissart, relieving the Royal Warwicks. One man, Private Duncan MacDonald of B Company, was wounded in the handover. The following day three men from A Company – Privates Thomas Gurney, A. MacQueen and William Withers – were wounded and on 16 April, Lance Corporal John MacLean of A Company was killed and Private George Grist of D Company wounded. Also on the 16th, Lieutenant William Mackay was wounded by a bullet passing through a loophole which hit him in the thumb, cheek and chest but luckily these were only flesh wounds. He was removed to an aid station and then taken to hospital in the rear. Accompanying him was his batman, Private Ian MacKinnon, who was described by Lieutenant Mackay as a 'Skyeman of the very best type, one of nature's gentlemen.'[91]

This tour in the trenches saw the 4th Camerons getting back to the more routine elements of soldiering. Private Goodban occupied a listening post: 'We have a listening post here about 20 yards in front of the parapet. I do one hour on two hours off in it during the night, blooming uncomfortable job as one has to lay flat in the mud and listen and watch.'[92]

Lance Corporal Bowdery fired pot shots at the enemy. 'Fighting calmed down but these are rather dangerous trenches. I was firing through a loop hole at a German and he fired first and hit the plate just about 2 inches away from my head. Near thing but I waited for hours and saw him drop.'[93]

The 4th Camerons were relieved by the 2nd Bedfords in the evening of 18 April and moved to billets in Laventie where they remained in the divisional reserve for ten days. Here they experienced the best billets they had had since coming to France two months previously; some of the men were billeted in a farm where they were treated to beds with proper spring mattresses. The troops trained during the day on the Grenade Company parade ground, went on route marches and practised their musketry and drill. In the evenings they were treated to picture shows and concerts designed to keep up their spirits. Whilst at Laventie, Lieutenants Angus Urquhart and Hugo Donald Ross joined up from the 2/4th Camerons in Scotland and Lieutenant Ian Mackay conducted a draft of 104 men from Rouen, the first rank and file replacements the 4th Camerons had received since leaving Britain.

On 21 April 1915, the 3/4th Battalion Cameron Highlanders were formed in Inverness. Their objective was to send reinforcements when necessary to both the 1/4th Camerons in France, and the 2/4th Camerons on home defence duty in Inverness. The 3/4th Battalion was commanded by Lieutenant-Colonel Horace Kemble of Knock on the Isle of Skye. Recruitment into the Cameron Highlanders in the summer 1915 had faltered and in order to gather new recruits Lieutenant-Colonel Kemble had to look further afield. Caledonian Societies in English towns were asked if they could help obtain recruits to the 4th Camerons, preferably men of Scottish heritage. The response was excellent and many recruits were taken on strength from towns across the north of England, predominantly from Leeds, Stockton on Tees and Sheffield. These men would go on to make up a large proportion of the drafts sent from the 3/4th Camerons to the front between August and November 1915. The 3/4th Battalion was also the first stop for 1/4th Cameron men who had

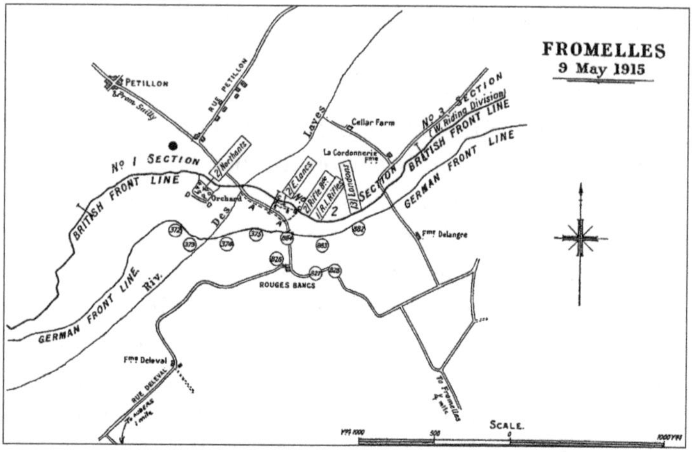

The Battle of Aubers Ridge, 9 May 1915. (*8th Division History*)

been wounded and released from hospital. Once attached to the 3/4th Camerons, the men trained with the new recruits and awaited their return to France.

Back at Laventie, on 27 April, orders were received that the 4th Camerons should be prepared to move at short notice to another sector of the Western Front. At midday on the 28th the battalion fell in and joined the rest of 21 and 22 Brigades in marching via Estaires, Neuf Berquin and Vieux Berquin to Strazeele, eleven miles north. The march was a trying one. The weather had taken a turn for the better but the hot sun caused problems for the men, although the officers were pleased – only one man fell out on the march, which was by far the best in the brigade. The men had the extra burden of additional ammunition; for some battalions it was 220 rounds per man, which added to their already heavy packs and equipment.

The move north had been precipitated by a German gas attack at Ypres on 22 April. It was possible that the

Germans would break through the British and French defensive lines to the east of Ypres and when the call for more troops was given, the First Army sent these two brigades of the 7th Division. The 4th Cameron Highlanders remained near Fletre and Strazeele until 5 May when they marched back to rejoin the Division at Estaires. During the tour the battalion occupied its time training in the beautiful sunny weather against the dangers of poison gas. At the end of April, while based at Strazeele, Lieutenant William Dobie, who had joined the battalion two weeks earlier, was seconded for service with the Army Cyclist Corps.

It was soon time to return to the trenches. On 6 May, the 4th Camerons occupied the left of E Lines and the right of the F Lines trenches from Fauquissart in the south to just opposite the village of Picantin in the northeast. The Battalion was around 200 yards away from the enemy. The men soon encountered the scourge of many an army, as described in Montague Goodban's diary entry for that day: 'Feel very crawly all over, examine my togs and find … ugh! I've clicked at last, have a good hunt and considerable slaughter. The enemy is completely routed but alas once lousy here always lousy.'[94]

The following day the Camerons were ordered to extend their line half a mile up the trenches in order to relieve the 2nd Wiltshire Regiment. Directly facing the battalion were six companies of the 17th Bavarian Reserve Regiment. In this sector the trenches were not as good as the previous ones and the soldiers had to spend time making the dugouts secure against shrapnel. All through 7 and 8 May the Germans opposite B Company subjected the Nairn men to heavy trench mortar fire, which wounded Privates John MacDonald, William MacDougall and Alexander MacLachlan. On the same day, it was reported that Private David Ross of Cawdor was accidentally killed by a bullet which was fired from his own rifle,[95] a statement which was disputed in an angry letter to the *Inverness Courier* by an unnamed 4th Camerons officer, who wanted to make it clear that Private Ross was killed by the enemy.[96]

At the end of March, following on from the success of the British Army at Neuve Chapelle in March, General Joffre, commander of the French Army, had approached Sir John French in order to gain British support for a proposed French attack on Vimy Ridge. Joffre suggested that a simultaneous British attack, again in the Neuve Chapelle sector, would greatly assist the French Tenth Army to capture the Ridge and advance on to Lens and Douai.[97]

French passed the planning for the British attack to Sir Douglas Haig who suggested a double attack on Aubers Ridge in the north and Neuve Chapelle in the south. The ridge itself was only 20 metres in height but proved to be a formidable defensive position for the German Army, with an excellent view over the British front line. The southern attack was to be carried out by the men of the 1st Division with the 2nd and 47th Divisions in support. The task of capturing Aubers Ridge in the north was given to the old comrades of the 4th Cameron Highlanders, the 8th Division. 21 Brigade, including the 4th Camerons, was detailed to be in the 7th Divisional reserve for the battle, with 20 and 22 Brigades given the task of following up the successes of the 8th Division.

At the start of the battle, the 4th Camerons held the front line trenches to the immediate south of the northern attack from Fauquissart to Picantin facing the Layes Brook and the Rue Deleval. The 2nd Royal Scots Fusiliers, 2nd Bedfords and 2nd Green Howards were based on the Rue du Bacquerot with the 2nd Wiltshires in immediate reserve to the Camerons at Petillon. Opposite their position were six companies of the 17th Bavarian Reserve Infantry Regiment. The Camerons would have the best seats in the house for the ensuing battle.

At 8.00am on 9 May 1915, the 8th Division attacked Aubers Ridge. Lance Corporal Charles Bowdery recorded in his diary:

> Big bombardment starts to our left and right. Commencement of a big advance at 3am. Immediately our guns started so the Germans replied and gathering from what our troops have told me it undoubtedly seems that the Germans knew of our plans. I believe the attack succeeded on our right but am somewhat dubious as to the left. After taking the first two lines of trenches, it seems from what I gather, serious opposition arose and our poor fellows were mown down.[98]

The attack was a disaster; the British bombardment had not damaged the well made German positions nearly as much as expected. Instead of finding few troops in destroyed positions, the advancing British battalions were cut down by heavy rifle fire from undamaged defences. Furthermore, the German artillery opened up a fearful bombardment on the British front line trenches, killing and wounding many before they could advance. In total, the Battle of Aubers Ridge resulted in over 12,000 British and Indian casualties.

The 7th Division, detailed to support the 8th if they were successful, spent the day in inactivity. The 4th Cameron Highlanders received heavy artillery shelling all during the day, which resulted in the deaths of Privates John Charles, Francis Lowe, John Williamson, Duncan MacKenzie and Frederick Smith. A further nine men were wounded; two of them, Privates Thomas Gallacher and Duncan MacLennan, died of their wounds on 11 May.[99]

In the evening of 10 May the battalion was relieved by the 6th Scottish Rifles and marched south through the night to Locon. The reason for the move was Sir John French's anxiety to continue the attack in order to divert German reserves from fighting the French at Vimy Ridge. In the fighting that followed, the 7th Division was not going to play a supporting role as it had done at Aubers Ridge. The men would be in the thick of the fighting and the 4th Cameron Highlanders would make their name at Festubert.

6

The Battle of Festubert, 11 May–19 May 1915

The area around Locon was new territory for the 7th Division. *The Seventh Division 1914–1918* by C.T. Atkinson describes this area as 'flat country, in places marshy, intersected with ditches, devoid of good artillery positions or facilities for observation, little improvement on the waterlogged meadows with which the Division was so painfully familiar.'[100]

The attack was to combine another assault southwest of Neuve Chapelle with an advance eastward from Festubert on the other flank of a salient in the German lines northwest of Ferme Cour d'Avoue.[101] The attacks were to be preceded by a hurricane bombardment which would let the artillery commanders see which areas of the German line needed more special attention to cut the barbed wire fences. To confuse the enemy, feint barrages were planned which were not followed by the main infantry attack as usual but by a further artillery bombardment designed to kill the enemy manning his trenches.[102]

On 11 May, the 4th Cameron Highlanders marched to billets at Rue de L'Epinette, where they bivouacked in an orchard. This position was a mile north of Festubert village and half a mile behind the front line trenches occupied by 20 and 22 Brigades. At L'Epinette a draft of 35 men joined the battalion. The Camerons stayed put, making trenches and dugouts under heavy shell fire for the next five days. Private Montague Goodban of A Company recorded in his diary entry for 12 May the work he was doing:

> Make dug outs in a field for protection against shell fire. Parade at 9pm and proceed towards the firing line to dig trenches (1st reserve), rotten job this under fire without any cover, but of course it is dark and we only stand the chance of stopping stray ones – return again at 3am.[103]

Lieutenant Ian Mackay, also of A Company, writing home to his parents in Inverness also described the days immediately before the battle:

> In the evening we marched two or three miles nearer the firing line and found ourselves in a pretty hot corner. We were billeted in a small farm about 1000 yards behind the firing line and were constantly under shell and rifle fire. We were told that an attack was coming off at that quarter and were warned to make good dugouts for ourselves in case of being shelled. We worked there for three days before the attack began, during which we worked hard and made some splendid dugouts in fields, sufficient to accommodate the whole battalion. All this time our guns, which were just behind us, kept up a heavy bombardment of the German lines and the noise was terrific.[104]

In a letter of 15 May a member of the battalion known only as 'a well known Invernessian' described the conditions in the billets:

> We are situated just now, and for the last three days in a scattered little hamlet some hundreds of yards from the 'Great Divide', each company in an old farmhouse with dugouts attached, to which resort is made if our 'friends' shell us uncomfortably. The house has been extensively patronised by the British Army for the last six months and after the first night I flitted to the dugout where the insect world were not quite so numerous or active. In the midst of all the shelling a family of five – grandfather, grandmother, daughter and two kiddies – have stuck where they were and though every minute such windows are as left rattle with gun explosions, they reap the reward by selling us coffee and eggs.[105]

The area of operations for the 7th Division stretched from Willow Corner in the south to the Rue du Bois in the north. Here, the British and German trenches ran parallel for some 2000 yards, 20 Brigade holding the northern sector around the Princes Road facing the Quadrilateral strongpoint, and 22 Brigade straddling the Rue des Cailloux facing a German trench known as the Northern Breastwork. At 3.15am on Sunday 16 May, the attack began. In the north, the Ferme Cour d'Avoue was the objective of 20 Brigade who despatched the 2nd Border Regiment and the 2nd Scots Guards to attack. 22 Brigade sent the 2nd Queen's Regiment and the 1st Royal Welch Fusiliers, supported by the 1st South Staffordshires and the 2nd Warwickshires up the Rue des Cailloux. Against these two brigades stood one battalion of the 57th Royal

Prussian Regiment.[106] After taking the first line of German trenches the aim of these two brigades was to advance on an orchard between the Rue du Marais and La Quinque Rue,[107] where 20 Brigade would then extend their line north to Ferme Cour d'Avoue and link up with the 2nd Division who were attacking from the Rue du Bois. 22 Brigade were to turn south and occupy the Northern Breastwork trench facing the Rue d'Ouvert.

On 16 May, 21 Brigade were the Divisional reserve. At the start of the battle the 2nd Bedfords and the 2nd Yorkshires were holding the front line trenches from the Rue de Cailloux to the Princes Road, the 2nd Royal Scots Fusiliers were in support 200 yards behind them and the 2nd Wiltshires along with the 4th Cameron Highlanders were in the reserve positions on the Rue de l'Epinette.

Private Montague Goodban, with the 4th Camerons in reserve, described the situation:

> Bombardment and general advance starts on this part of the line today. We came out of our billets and occupied the dug outs we have made previously at 1.30am. Bombardment commenced at 3am. We are in reserve and ready to be called up and quit at 5 minutes notice. At 4am wounded start to stream down the road from the trenches and continue to do so all day long, mixed in with them comes an occasional batch of German prisoners under escort. We are heavily shelled all day – shrapnel and high explosive dropping thick and fast, so many narrow escapes are experienced. Weather grand. This is at Festubert.[108]

At around midday on 16 May, Lieutenant Ian Mackay was asked by Captain Garden Duff to accompany him to reconnoitre the battlefield. They picked two men to act as a bodyguard and set off:

> We passed through the village of Festubert, which is in ruins, and along La Quinque Rue about which you will have read. Shells were flying about but we were lucky. We got up to the British trench and then across the open to the German trench which had been captured that morning. The Germans still held the trench to the right, but they apparently did not see us, or think us worth firing at. At the point we entered the German trench there was a ruined house round which there had been a stiff fight in the morning, and the sights we saw bore evidence of this. The bodies were principally of British – brave fellows who were making for the house when hit.
>
> Duff and I got the information we wanted, then made our way back to our headquarters. All that afternoon we 'stood by' in our dug outs expecting orders to go forward.[109]

By the evening of 16 May a mile of the German front line trenches had been captured and held by 20 and 22 Brigades. In the north, the attack had been particularly successful with the 2nd Queens, 2nd Warwicks, 2nd Scots Guards and 1st Royal Welch Fusiliers holding the line of the Northern Breastwork. At the junction of the Rue des Cailloux and Dukes Road the 2nd Wiltshires and the 2nd South Staffords held a further communication trench which joined the old German front line to the Northern Breastwork. From there the 7th London Regiment held the old German front trenches roughly on continuation of Dukes Road south. The successful advance by 20 and 22 Brigades had left their right flank unprotected from an attack along La Quinque Rue. By the end of the day the Division had pulled back slightly from its most advanced positions in the Northern Breastwork and Orchard. The 2nd South Staffords held a line to the south of La Quinque Rue astride the German second and third lines, connecting to the 7th Londons at point L2 (see map page 103).[110]

The 4th Cameron Highlanders waited in their newly dug positions at Rue de l'Epinette from the outset of the battle until the afternoon of 17 May. At 4.00pm, the order came through that the 2nd Bedford Regiment and the 4th Camerons were to mount an attack in conjunction with an attack of the 4th (Guards) Brigade to the north.

The Bedfords and Camerons were ordered to pass through the 7th London Regiment and advance to capture the Southern Breastwork, a communication trench which ran from the Rue d'Ouvert to the German second and third line defences at point K5 (see map). At the end of the Southern Breastwork closest to the Cameron Highlanders was a German redoubt bristling with machine guns, which had held up the advance the previous day.

Lieutenant Ian Mackay described the advance to the front line trenches:

> We paraded and moved off, not knowing where or to what we are going to do. We marched through Festubert, up La Quinque Rue again, and formed under the shelter of the British trench. The Germans were shelling the road heavily but although they were bursting all around us we had extraordinary luck, only one shell doing damage.[111]

That one shell exploded over B Company, its shrapnel fragments hitting 2nd Lieutenant James Bookless of

Inverness, Sergeant Kenneth MacLennan of Auldearn and three men. 2nd Lieutenant Bookless had joined the battalion in March as one of the replacements for the casualties incurred at Neuve Chapelle. On 2 May he had celebrated his 21st birthday in the trenches. Bookless was taken back to a Casualty Clearing Station and from there to Boulogne, where he died of his wounds on 24 May.

The 2nd Bedford Regiment formed up on the right on a line from positions L1 to L2 and the Camerons formed on the left from M3 to L1. Following an artillery bombardment of 15 minutes, the Camerons started their advance at 7.30pm with a two-Company frontage in two waves, C Company on the left and D Company on the right. A and B Companies were following in support but slightly to the left with the Bedfords in the same formation on their right.

As soon as the two battalions climbed out of the trenches the Germans opened up a terrific artillery, machine gun and rifle fire. A 4th Camerons member of the 21 Brigade bomb throwers described the early stages of the Highlanders' advance:

> We were all enjoying it till we started. The two companies lined up in the trench, that was the old German second line. At last the words came – 'First line, 4th Camerons, charge!' – and everybody goes over. In fact some never got over, for they got it just as they got to the top.[112]

Once over the parapet the Camerons were faced with 600–800 yards of open ground to cover before they reached the Southern Breastwork. The ground over which the battalion charged was strewn with deep, intersected ditches full of mud. As they were one of the first British battalions to advance over this section of the front, the ground over which they attacked was relatively untouched by artillery fire. The terrain consisted of fields of course grass covered by a vast number of bright red poppies.

Private Hector Macdonald described the tactics employed by the men in the attack: 'Each man was about 4 yards apart when we went across. Of course, we went, we actually ran about 70 yards and then laid flat for 10 or 15 seconds and then get up and go forward again.'[113]

All during the advance, German artillery on the left of C Company and machine-gun emplacements – which had not been destroyed by the bombardment – on the right of D Company, opened up a murderous barrage. In his diary, Lance Corporal Bowdery recorded the scene presented to A Company on the extreme left when they followed their comrades over the top:

> After advancing about 150 yards in the dark we come across a big ditch about 6 feet across and 6 or 7 feet deep, full of muddy water, this represents rather an awkward obstacle and we have to get across the best way we can, most of us tried to jump it, but with our heavy equipment it is impossible and the majority fall in, including myself, thus getting soaked through to the skin and our rifles choked with mud.[114]

D Company, on the right of the 4th Camerons struggled from the off. The *Inverness Courier* reported that Captain Ronald MacDonald, commanding D Company and 2nd Lieutenant Joshua Thompson were hit soon after going over the top. The paper described the conditions:

> We had gone forward only a few yards when we were up against a deep ditch full of filthy water, which none

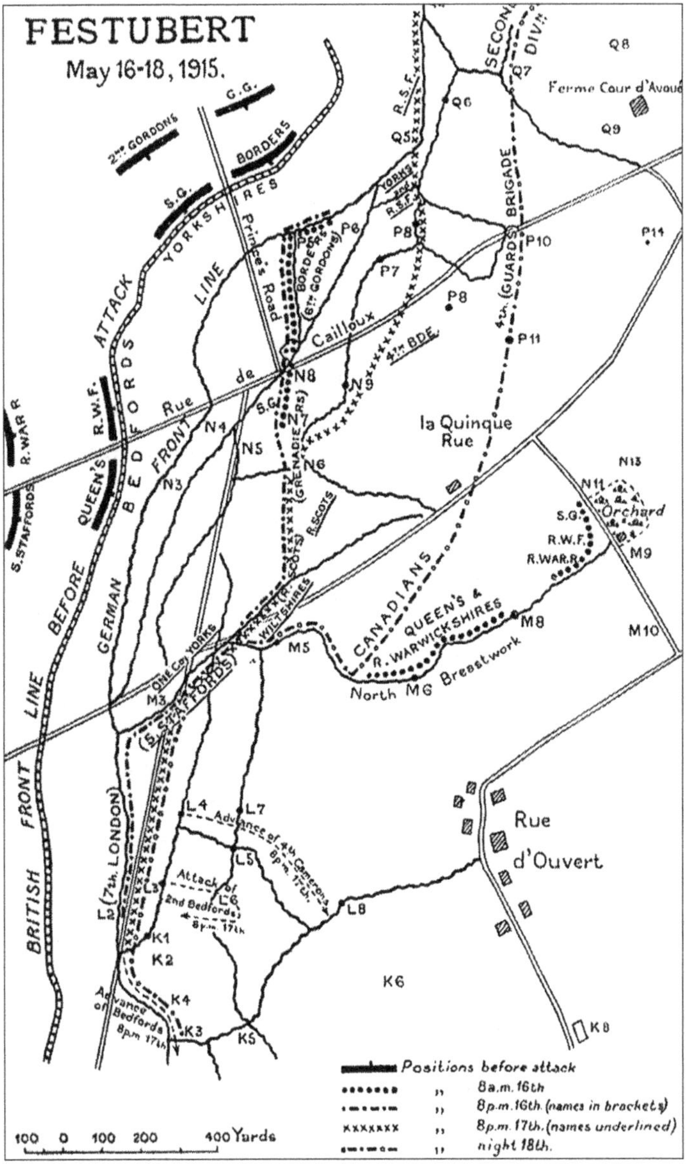

The attack of the 4th Camerons and 2nd Bedfords, Battle of Festubert, 17–18 May 1915. (*7th Division History*)

> but the strongest and most agile could jump, weighed down as we were with arms and equipment. And it was now pitch dark and rain was falling heavily. The majority of the men failing to clear the ditch disappeared up to the neck in slimy water, and it was with much difficulty that they were pulled out on the opposite bank by their stronger comrades. In the course of the advance, two such ditches and several less formidable had to be negotiated.[115]

If the conditions weren't bad enough, the German defence provided an equally stern test. On the 2nd Bedfords' front, to the right of the Camerons, no progress could be made and Lieutenant-Colonel Thorpe commanding the Bedfords called a halt to their advance, not having enough men to continue over the uncompromising terrain and into the hail of German fire.[116]

The Highlanders however, bravely continued their advance alone. Captain Thomas Allison, commanding C Company on the Camerons' left, was shot first in the ankle and after rising to encourage his men, was killed by a bullet to the head. Command of C Company passed to 32-year-old Captain John Campbell, son of the former Colonel, Ewan Campbell. D Company on the right lost the remainder of their officers, Captain Nigel MacKenzie, Lieutenant Cameron Carruthers, 2nd Lieutenant Alistair Paterson[117] and 2nd Lieutenant Thomas Chalmers. Company Sergeant Major Bill Ross of Portree took charge of the situation and ordered the now much depleted D Company forward, determined to take the Southern Breastwork.

In the confusion of the German fire and broken up country, C and D Companies lost touch with both each other and the now retreating Bedfords, but still the Highlanders pressed on, wave after wave.

The *Inverness Courier* reported:

> Each line thinned as it went, kept moving silently and doggedly towards its objective. At a hundred yards from the German trench where the ground favoured us slightly, there was a momentary pause to steady and strengthen the line in preparation for the charge. Then the caution, 'Ready', was whispered along the line, and on a given signal each man moved on at a rapid pace, which broke into the double as the German trench came into view. With loud cheers and bayonets gleaming in the enemy's flare lights the Camerons leapt into the trench.[118]

Shouting the Regimental cry '*A chlannaibh nan con*', the Camerons took the German trench. The defenders did not wait to be bayoneted where they stood but retreated over the open ground towards the Rue d'Ouvert and rushed to the rear. Lieutenant Ian Mackay, with A Company, described the taking of the trench and an apparent moment of treachery:

> The survivors of D Company under the Company Sergeant Major 'Bill' Ross, Portree, a fine big Skyeman and the 'father' of our battalion, kept on with C Company and they charged the German trench with bayonets fixed, cheering as they went. When they got near, the Germans bolted, all except four, who held up their hands, when our lads entered the trench. Old Bill Ross went up to them and called on them to surrender and one of them who previously held up his hands, shot old Ross dead. Needless to say our boys at once shot all four Germans.[119]

In a supporting role, A Company had their own trials that night. The left flank of the attack was unsupported and they were given the job of guarding that flank against a German counterattack. Lieutenants Ian Mackay and Roderick McErlich took out their two platoons in the first wave along with A Company's second in command, David F. MacKenzie.[120] Captain Murdoch Beaton, in command of A Company, took up the remaining two platoons in the second wave. Lieutenant Mackay wrote to his mother of the difficulties of the advance:

> Altogether it was very difficult to keep the platoon together. We lost touch with McErlich's platoon, and kept on ourselves thinking we were following up the company in front of us. We came to another broad ditch and I was trying to find the best place to cross, when a heavy fire was opened on us from about 20 yards off.[121]

The men of A Company were not sure if it was the Germans who had opened fire or Camerons who had mistaken A Company for the enemy. They could see the outline of a trench in front of them and could hear voices coming from it but could not make out if they were speaking English or German. They opened fire again, causing casualties in the ranks of Lieutenant Mackay's men. Mackay sent out a patrol to find out what was going on but they too were fired upon. When they returned, carrying two wounded men, they reported that it was definitely the Germans opposing them.

Lieutenant Mackay realised that A Company were in the wrong place so he withdrew his platoon 200 yards to a less dangerous position. In the course of repositioning, Lieutenant Mackay came across Captain Beaton with Number 4 Platoon in conference with Lieutenant-Colonel Alexander Fraser. Together they worked out that A Company had been given the wrong point to advance on and had drifted too far to the left. Fraser, Beaton and Mackay sent out a patrol, under Corporal James MacBean of Achnabeachan, to get in touch with C and D Companies in the Southern Breastwork trench. They succeeded and the remainder of the men proceeded after them, again MacBean guiding them. Lieutenant Mackay takes up the story:

> It was pitch dark and raining hard, and we moved in single file. We crossed several ditches and presently came up against a broad deep one. In the dark we could not see the opposite bank and several men had to swim for it. We had wounded men with us and by the time that Beaton and I had got them across we found that the party in front had disappeared in the dark. We found ourselves there with about 50 men and without a guide, not knowing in what direction to go to get to the trench now occupied by C and D Companies. We thought that a guide would come for us but none came, and after a while we started off to find the trench ourselves. We sent our patrols who had to swim ditches several times, but they failed to find the trench and it was only when it began to dawn that we gave it up and made for the British lines, the direction of which we knew from the compass. If we had continued out in that open after dawn we would have been spotted by the Germans and all wiped out.[122]

The part of A Company led by Colonel Fraser did manage to reach the Southern Breastwork trench and linked up with the remains of C and D Companies. Some men of B Company, supporting the main attack, also reached the captured German trench. By now it was around 10.00pm on 17 May and problems for the 4th Cameron Highlanders were starting to mount up. The failure of the 2nd Bedfords to capture the right hand portion of the Southern Breastwork, combined with A Company being given the wrong area to advance on, left the men in the trench with heavily armed Germans on three sides. Their only retreat was over 800 yards of uneven country interwoven with the deep ditches and canals that had broken up the main attack. The fact that many of the Camerons had to swim or wade across the ditches had caused their rifles to become clogged with mud and water and many men lost their bombs in the scramble to take the German trench. This made defending the 500 yards of captured trench a near impossibility.

An unnamed member of A Company, writing to the *Inverness Courier,* told of the work done in the trench:

> We settled into the trench and started to repair the parapets for certain shelling next morning. Patrols were thrown out to the left and right but could get in touch with nothing but Germans. The fact gradually dawned on us that the Regulars had failed to make their objective and that we were isolated. The Germans began to bomb us. We had a few bomb throwers with us but by morning only one was available. At dawn enfilade fire and bombing on our right and left made the position untenable.[123]

One of the patrols included Lance Corporal Charles Bowdery, who wrote in his diary:

> Our Adjutant sends three of us out to find B Company on our left. We start out quite confident but soon find out that it is a German redoubt. We walk up and look over and ask them who they are and get no answer. At the third time of asking they endeavour to tell us in broken English that they are Bedfords. We immediately drop down at the bottom of their parapet and lay there while they fire upon us. We manage to crawl away and all get safely back but my word it was a near touch.[124]

The Adjutant of the 4th Cameron Highlanders, Captain Garden B. Duff, was in the Southern Breastwork with Colonel Fraser during this time of uncertainty. He wrote to Fraser's wife on 20 May:

> We worked hard to put the trench in a fit state to defend, and sent back message after message asking for support. No answer came and we had no means of knowing if the messages had got back safely, and if our position was understood. It was so dark and wet, it was very difficult to find out the exact position, but the Colonel and I had been along the whole place, and about 1am he told me to go back and explain the position to the authorities and arrange for us to be supported.[125]

This lack of adequate means of communication was to cost the battalion dearly, as Private Hector Macdonald recalled: 'We got it from the British guns too because the British artillery men didn't know that we were in the German trench at all. That was it. We were shelled from the Germans and from the British guns.'[126]

Although Captain Duff did not know it, one of the messages had gotten through to the British lines. Private

James Gardiner of B Company had succeeded in navigating the 800 yards of broken ground, trenches and ditches in broad daylight under constant heavy fire and had delivered the message for support to Headquarters. For his actions Private Gardiner was awarded the Distinguished Conduct Medal.

The news that the Camerons were holding the Southern Breastwork prompted Headquarters into action. They ordered that the nearest two companies of the 2nd Yorkshires should push forward on the left of the Camerons and link up with them. The artillery was ordered to shell the positions to the left and right of the Camerons' position held by the Germans and the already exhausted 2nd Bedfords were to renew their attack on point K5.[127]

The War Diary of the 2nd Wiltshires records the attempts to support the Camerons.

> During the night a patrol was sent out to try and obtain touch with the Camerons. It failed to find them but found the 2nd Bedfords and reported that the intervening ground was much cut up by wide ditches full of water which were very difficult to cross. Also during the night two companies of the 2nd Yorks came up and proceeded to dig themselves in from about M6 to L9. They also failed to obtain touch with the Camerons.[128]

Captain Duff also made his way back to Headquarters, and finding that the plans for another attack were in hand, decided to set off back through the ditches to rejoin the Camerons. His plans were put on hold as just before dawn the Germans attacked the Southern Breastwork, intent on driving out the Highlanders. Short on bombs and reserve ammunition and with his machine guns unable to be brought up to the trench, Lieutenant-Colonel Fraser had no choice but to order a retreat or face the annihilation of his men. Private Hector Macdonald of B Company described the scene:

> Well, there was a Lieutenant in my Platoon. A Lieutenant Campbell, along with another man. They went along to our flanks and discovered it was German bombers that were on both flanks and they came, my Lieutenant came rushing back and he said, men, its every man for himself and these 2 men jumped out and went across a piece of open ground towards a ditch which was going in the direction which we had come the previous evening and that was the beginning of the retreat and it was every man for himself from that point onwards.[129]

An Inverness man wrote to the *Highland News* of the dilemma facing the battalion:

> We had either to stay and get shot or surrender and either alternative would mean that men as well as rifles would be out of action and lost for the rest of the war. But in any case 'A Cameron can never yield.'[130]

An unidentified member of A Company wrote to the *Inverness Courier*:

> We got the order to retreat and started to do so in as orderly a manner as possible. The Germans had machine guns playing on the parapet and this parapet had to be crossed. Many men were hit in doing so.[131]

As the Southern Breastwork was itself a communication trench leading from the old German front line to its second line, there were no supporting trenches into which the 4th Camerons could escape to make their way back to the British lines. There were only two places where gaps had been made in the parapet which the Camerons could use to make good their retreat. Unfortunately, once on the other side of the parapet the soldiers had to cross a large portion of open ground before coming to a large ditch which would afford them some shelter from the storm of bullets and artillery fire.

The same unidentified soldier of A Company told how he escaped from the trench:

> I leaped the parapet with five others and lay flat on my stomach in the mud as snipers were now at work. The five other fellows started doubling across country but all were hit. I crawled on my stomach towards what proved the salvation of all who escaped, viz. a canal running right up to the British lines and into it I at once jumped.[132]

Private Hector Macdonald continued:

> On our left 150 yards away there was a German redoubt manned by Prussian Guards and they machine gunned the piece of ground between the trench and the ditch and they also had rifles on tripods. Before leaving the trench, I could see the blades of grass jumping up in the air – it was a flat piece of ground and impossible to escape. We were being attacked by German bombers now on both flanks and we had to get out and cross this piece of ground. Three men in front of me jumped

> out and after going about 20 yards, each in turn jumped up several feet and then dropped dead, shot in the left side from the redoubt. I was next and after going about 30 yards I was struck by three explosive bullets simultaneously, the first one hit the centre pouch on my left side, in which there was ten rounds of ammunition, exploded and set my clothes on fire, the second came through my tunic, cut across my abdomen but did not penetrate, the third came through my tunic, hit the buckle on my webbed equipment, exploded and blew it to smithereens. When doubling across no man's land the previous evening, the pouches which should have been at the front moved round to the side and saved my life. I lay unconscious about 30 yards from the ditch and on coming round I felt as if somebody was keeping a red hot poker to my tummy. I couldn't move but shortly afterwards a pal of mine who got into the ditch, though badly wounded in the right shoulder, came out and dragged me into the ditch and out of sight in the water and mud, as my clothes were still smouldering.[133]

Another member of A Company takes up the story:

> I had many narrow escapes while retiring by the deep ditch. When the water got too deep and I felt myself sinking into the mud I got onto the bank and crawled as flat as I could. By this time I had to part with my pack and equipment but stuck to my rifle and bayonet and two bandoliers full of ammunition. I crawled on and on resting where I saw the best cover, many bullets striking the earth under my face. It was a miracle I was not hit. I was leading another five who had no idea where to go. We crawled fully three quarters of a mile as we

> could not go direct back to our own trenches. I got back with nothing but my knee cut slightly from barbed wire and broken glass.[134]

One of the battalion bomb throwers wrote to the *Highland News* of his experiences that night:

> It was pure Hell let loose – shrapnel bursting above our heads, shells dropping alongside of you and German machine guns and snipers picking off the men by scores. It was a pitiable sight to see some of the boys coming down the road without kilts, jackets, haversacks and drenched to the skin. Anyone who came out of it alive should be thankful. You will see it for yourself in the papers. I can't explain it, and what's more, I'm not going to try.[135]

Lieutenant-Colonel Alexander Fraser, as always, was determined to put the safety of his men before his own. In covering the retreat he was shot through the heart and died instantly. Captain Duff wrote to his widow on 20 May:

> Your husband did all that could be done to hold the trench but saw that it was impossible to hold it long so very wisely ordered a retreat. In this we suffered heavily, and it was while superintending and covering this retreat that he was killed. He was shot through the heart and never moved. This is, I think, certain from accounts given me by Lieutenant Ross and one or two men who saw him hit and tried to bring him away. We hoped against hope that they were mistaken and I went all over our trenches to see our wounded, and to try and get information, but in vain. Efforts to find him the next

> night were also fruitless, as he was too close to the trench held now by the enemy. They hold it still, but we hope very soon they may be driven out.[136]

Lieutenant-Colonel Fraser was not the only officer to be killed during the retirement. Captain David F. MacKenzie, who had advanced with the front two platoons of A Company, and had accompanied Colonel Fraser to the Southern Breastwork, also died. His friend and fellow A Company officer, Lieutenant Ian Mackay, wrote of the circumstances of his death:

> The Colonel fell dead and D.F.[137] was badly wounded. Two men, one of them Sergeant Roake who was with me that night at Neuve Chapelle, helped him on and dragged him down to the water, but he was done that they feared they would kill him, so laid him on the bank under cover hoping to return with help. Others, officers and men, saw D.F. as they passed, and offered to take him on, but he would not allow them. He said that he was alright where he was and that they had enough to do to save themselves.[138]

Captain Mackenzie's body was not found until 29 June.

Captain John Campbell, who had commanded C Company in the advance after the death of Captain Allison, was reported missing. Dugald MacEachern in his book *Sword of the North: Highland Memories of the Great War* described Captain Campbell's death:

> Young Captain John Campbell was last seen at the end of the German trench firing his revolver into the Germans, who were close upon him as he covered the

> retiral of his men. Thus did this hero give his life to save others, making his own body the shelter for his men from the storm of bullets.[139]

Private Duncan MacKenzie wrote of his experiences that night to William Mackay over 50 years after the event:

> I clearly remember when day broke and the lads had to vacate the trench and were promptly shot down by a party of the enemy put out on the flank. I lay between two others, Forsyth, shot through the buttocks and Tolmie, shot in the stomach area, the former survived, the latter did not. I can still see the Germans opening up the paybooks of the dead, discarding items and putting other items in their pockets, while others were spitting on the fingers of the dead and pulling off their rings. What was ringing in my ears was what I had previously been told that the enemy bayoneted the wounded, whether true or not, I was able to escape via a water filled communication trench or watercourse which was lapping my mouth. When I got to my feet as I tried to pull myself along by grasping the grass there was a burst of machine gun fire, which detracted from the use of this method.[140]

James Gray of Ardross Street, Inverness, forwarded a letter to the *Inverness Courier* which he had received from his nephew in the 4th Camerons. The latter described the situation in the ditch leading back to the British trenches:

> Once in the ditch we had good cover, but knew not whence it would take us. The ditch was deep enough to give us cover, that average depth being 4 feet and 6 inches

> but every few yards we encountered pools about 6 feet deep. The trip 'doon the burn' will never be forgotten. After going some distance word was passed along that we were safe and that we were going to pass into our own lines. That cheered us up very much. I used my rifle and bayonet as a punting pole and pushed myself over the pools being very frequently out of my depth. After a terrible struggle we reached our lines and what a terrible condition we were in. Drenched to the skin with a few inches of mud and feet etc swollen with water. The majority of the survivors were in a state of collapse.[141]

The survivors of the attack rendezvoused behind the British lines where they waited for instructions from the Brigade staff. Some of the men tried to dry their soaked clothes but as the day was as wet as the previous one, they had little luck. The Camerons were also subjected to heavy German artillery fire which further wounded some of the men who had been hurt in the attack.

> When the greater part of the remains of the battalion came in, we were ordered to return to our former quarters behind the -----.[142] There the various companies lined up for roll call and it was then the havoc wrought by the fight became apparent, not alone in the number of names not answered to, but in the bedraggled appearance of the survivors, for every garment was soaked with dirty water and smeared over with clayey mud.[143]

The exhausted, soaked and broken 4th Cameron Highlanders were ordered to retire back to their old billets in Rue de l'Epinette. Stragglers continued to return until late on in the afternoon of 18 May, each one being greeted, the *Inverness Courier* reported, like he had risen from the dead.[144] The officers and men tried everything they could to try and find information on their friends who had not returned; it was hoped that the Canadian Division, who were to attack over the same ground later that day, would find some of the wounded.

Private Hector Macdonald, wounded in the retreat from the Southern Breastwork, was taken to a Dressing Station for treatment. He then was taken to an empty farm where he spent three days and nights lying on the floor of the granary with no medical help and no means of getting his clothes dry. He was then moved to a schoolhouse some miles behind the line where he lay on the floor for nearly a month before being able to rejoin the battalion. Private Macdonald was one of a number of wounded men who returned to the battalion within a month of receiving very serious wounds. The spirit of the 4th Cameron Highlanders was strong.

At 11.00am on 18 May, battalion doctor Captain Robert Lindsay, and the Chaplain, Reverend J. Campbell Macgregor, set out across no man's land to find Lieutenant-Colonel Fraser's body. They reached a point about 200 yards from the German trench but found no sign of him. Later that day, a search party of 150 men drawn from all companies of the battalion was organised to accompany the battalion bombers and fight their way back to the Southern Breastwork. Orders came from Brigade that the attack should not go ahead and the Camerons were ordered to stand down and return to their billets.

The first mention of the battle in the Highland papers came in the *Inverness Courier* of 25 May. They carried news of the death of Lieutenant-Colonel Fraser, Captain David MacKenzie, Captain Thomas Allison, Captain Ian

Baillie and 2nd Lieutenant James Bookless. The papers of 28 May 1915 reported that the battalion may have received up to 400 casualties but this was downgraded to 13 officers and 212 men killed, wounded and missing.

From a collation of all available sources it appears that Lieutenant-Colonel Alexander Fraser, Captain Thomas Allison, Captain David MacKenzie, Captain John Campbell and 2nd Lieutenant Herbert Kidd died on the field of battle. Captain Ian Baillie, Captain Ronald Macdonald and 2nd Lieutenants James Bookless and Alistair Paterson were to die of their wounds. Captain Nigel MacKenzie and 2nd Lieutenants Cameron Carruthers, Thomas Chalmers and Joshua Thompson were wounded. Of the men, 108 were killed or died of wounds and a further 126 were wounded.

D Company had fared worst, losing two officers killed and four wounded and 46 men killed and 54 wounded. C Company was also badly hit losing three officers and 35 men killed and 29 men wounded. B Company lost 2 officers and 16 men killed and 23 men wounded while A Company, the flank guard for the attack, lost 1 officer and 11 men killed and 19 men wounded.

In addition to the men killed and wounded, four men were taken prisoner at Festubert. Privates James Waugh, Alexander MacPherson, Lowden Hillcoat and John Martin were to see no more fighting with the 4th Camerons and were marched off for three years captivity in Germany.

The loss of these 13 officers and 234 men was keenly felt not just in the battalion but across the Highlands. Lieutenant Ian Mackay was particularly affected by the death of Captain David MacKenzie:

> His loss is one of which we can hardly speak about. He was such a charming little man when one really knew

> him, absolutely worth his weight in gold, and extraordinarily plucky when it came to the real thing.[145]

On 27 May, Inverness Sheriff Court met for business. Before proceedings started, Sheriff J.P. Grant spoke to the audience:

> This court meets for the first time after the terrible losses that the county Territorial has recently met with at Festubert. I am sure you will deem it right if I take notice of what has occurred and briefly express my own feelings (which I am sure are shared by you all) of sorrow and sympathy – a sorrow that is not without pride and rejoicing.[146]

Lieutenant-Colonel Alexander Fraser was spoken of in the highest regard by all who met him. Captain Garden Duff in writing a letter to Fraser's widow in Inverness described his feelings:

> I can hardly tell you how much everyone feels his loss. I knew he was beloved, but was surprised to see how utterly the battalion was devoted to him. The hearts of every officer and man go out to you and your family. For myself, I have lost not only a very dear friend, but a chief, one of the finest gentlemen and most gallant and efficient soldiers I have ever known.[147]

Lieutenant Ian Mackay agreed:

> The Colonel's death is a terrible calamity for the battalion. He had done splendidly here, and he had such a good presence when it came to interviewing Generals

> and such like. Apart from that, he was a gentleman and so pleasant to have anything to do with.[148]

In the first week of June a service was held at the United Free High Church in Inverness to honour the fallen officers and men of the 4th Cameron Highlanders. The Reverend Alfred A. Cooper presided over the ceremony, which devoted a large amount of time to the life and work of Lieutenant-Colonel Fraser. The junior officers were praised for their sacrifice and, after the benediction, the service was closed with the singing of the National Anthem.[149]

Many families across the north of Scotland felt the pain of losing a loved one on the field at Festubert. Two such families had the misfortune of losing two sons with the 4th Camerons. Along with 2nd Lieutenant Alistair and Corporal Donald Paterson of Beauly Acting Sergeant James and Private John MacDonald of Kingussie died. They were aged 28 and 26 years old respectively.

The depleted battalion, billeted in the Rue de l'Epinette, took stock of its losses and licked its wounds. The esteem in which the actions of the 4th Cameron Highlanders at the Battle of Festubert were held was shown by a friend of Lieutenant-Colonel Fraser, Duncan Shaw of Inverness:

> There is always the consolation that these men who commenced simply as citizens and served in the Citizen Army, should have blossomed out into real, good, hard soldiers and that they have died the most glorious of deaths in the service of their country.[150]

For the survivors of the attack on the Southern Breastwork on the night of 17/18 May, questions remained to be answered. Chief in their minds was what went wrong? This was, at least in part, explained by a visit from Brigadier-General G.E. Watts, commanding 21 Brigade. Lieutenant Ian Mackay watched with interest as the Brigadier spoke:

> Yesterday the Brigadier came down specially to inspect us and the whole battalion (or what is left of them) paraded to receive him. He spoke very well, said most flattering things about us and made very nice references to Colonel Fraser. He said that, as often happens in war, we were sent out to attack that trench at a moment's notice without any time for reconnoitring the ground we had to advance over; that nearly everyone he had come across since had made reference to the way we had advanced across the open and the final charge against the trench; that owing to a series of misfortunes such as the failure of the attack on our right, the want of bombs, and clogging of rifles, our position in the trench was untenable; that we did everything that was humanly possible and that our Regiment and Country might be proud of us.[151]

Many of the stories regarding near escapes and heroic deeds appeared in the papers back in Scotland but none can be more heroic than 28-year-old Private Frank Buchanan of B Company. During the attack on the Southern Breastwork, Private Buchanan was shot in the ankle and could not go on. He met two more seriously wounded men in the area round about him and took refuge in a cave where they remained for ten days until found by a party of Canadian soldiers. On their journey to hospital Private Buchanan recounted the tale of his adventure to an Inverness doctor serving with a water ambulance. A week later one of the Canadian soldiers who rescued Private Buchanan was treated by the same doctor. The Canadian spoke of the incident and mentioned how he held Private Buchanan's actions in the highest regard. It transpired that the two wounded men with Buchanan were in a particularly serious condition and although Buchanan's bullet wound was enough to keep him out of the fight he could have made his way back to the British lines. He refused, preferring to stay with his comrades in arms, giving them food and water and tending to them as best as he could. They were so near the German lines that two German soldiers entered their cave and Buchanan thought the British soldiers were about to be killed, but the Germans left them alone. Even though he could have escaped, he stayed with his friends and undoubtedly saved their lives.[152]

Private Buchanan was taken to No.4 General Hospital in Versailles on 28 May to recover from his wounds. He remained there until 8 June, then was transferred to a hospital in England. He was discharged from the British Army on 21 June 1916, unfit for further military service. A medical report in his Pension File stated that the bullet broke his ankle, and another bullet hit him in the thigh. As a result, even after hospital treatment, Private Buchanan experienced pain in his ankle if he walked or stood for any length of time. This severely affected his ability to work as a chauffeur as he could not push the pedals of the car. Sadly, unable to work and probably psychologically damaged from his time in the army, Frank Buchanan died on 24 February 1922, six days after attempting suicide by drinking acid. He was 36 years old.

The last word on the Battle of Festubert, however, should be given to an unnamed member of B Company who wrote home to Nairn on 31 May:

We are very pleased, however, to know that our conduct in that affair gave entire satisfaction to those in command in high places and we received the highest praise. Always proud of being a '4th Cameron', I am prouder than ever now.[153]

7

The Battle of Givenchy, 19 May–30 August 1915

On 19 May, the much depleted 4th Cameron Highlanders were placed into reserve along with the rest of their 7th Division colleagues. At 2.15pm they marched to Robecq, some ten miles distant, for a period of rest and recuperation. They did so without 13 of their officers and 234 of their men.

On the death of Lieutenant-Colonel Fraser, command passed to Major Hector Fraser who had been with the battalion since their arrival in France in February. Due to the severe losses at the Battle of Festubert, officers and men were transferred to other companies to make up numbers and give each company approximately the same strength.

A Company
Captain Murdoch Beaton (in command)
Lieutenant Roderick McErlich
2nd Lieutenant Alexander MacKenzie
2nd Lieutenant Donald Ross

B Company
Captain Frederick Fraser (in command)
Lieutenant Charles Campbell
2nd Lieutenant Max Roemmele
2nd Lieutenant John MacLaren

C Company
Captain Peter Cram (in command)
2nd Lieutenant Andrew Sutherland
2nd Lieutenant Ian Nelson
2nd Lieutenant Hector Morison

D Company
Lieutenant Ian MacKay (in command)
2nd Lieutenant Angus Urquhart
2nd Lieutenant Henry Scott[154]

At Headquarters, Major Hector Fraser commanded, with Captain Garden Duff as Adjutant and Major John Lockie as Quartermaster. Captain Robert Lindsay of the RAMC was Medical Officer, Reverend J. Campbell Macgregor was Chaplain, Lieutenant Harold Law was Machine Gun Officer, Lieutenant John Macpherson was Transport Officer and 2nd Lieutenant Francis Laughton was seconded to 21 Brigade as Brigade Bombing Officer.

In a letter home on 21 May, Lieutenant Mackay described the difficulties of adjusting to his new position:

> I went out that night as a subaltern in command of a platoon and a few hours afterwards I occupied the position of a Senior Captain, as no less than 6 of our Captains were knocked out. I have been put in

> command of D Company, and it is not an easy job. All the old officers of the company, many of the sergeants and about half the men have been knocked out. I have two inexperienced subalterns with me, who will, I think, do well; but neither they nor I know any of the NCOs or men, and it is not easy taking command of an entirely new company with none of its former officers to help me. However, time will put all that right. D Company is made up of the Beauly and Portree boys and includes the Glenurquhart section, so an Achmonie Mackay again goes on the warpath with his ain folk.[155]

Following on from the visit of Brigadier-General Watts on 22 May, several other senior officers and dignitaries visited the battalion to give their thanks for their efforts at Festubert. On 24 May, Major-General Hubert Gough, commander of the 7th Division, inspected the troops and three days later the Camerons marched the five miles to the village of Busnettes where they were inspected by General Joseph Joffre and Field Marshal Sir John French, the commanders of the French and British Armies. On 1 June Sir Douglas Haig and the Prime Minister, Herbert Henry Asquith, drove past the battalion in a motor car.

It was while at Robecq that a further tragedy befell the 4th Camerons. On 23 May, Private Louis Kennedy was swimming in the canal when he got into difficulty. When he sank under the water one of his comrades dived in to help him, but owing to the muddiness of the water, took several attempts to pull him out. His comrades tried to save him, but to no avail. Private Kennedy was only 19 years old. A similar incident happened on 7 June when Private William MacPherson of C Company had a heart attack after swimming in the divisional baths.[156]

Swimming in the canals of the area round Robecq became a feature of the late spring of 1915 for the men of the 4th Cameron Highlanders. Life was getting back to normal, helped by the fine weather. One of the battalion sergeants wrote to the *Inverness Courier* on 2 June:

> Owing to the continued fine weather and the fact that we had a good long rest, the men are in great spirits again. This afternoon we held a water gymkhana in the canal and you can be assured that the usual company rivalry will ensure a high standard of merit in the different events to be decided. They speak also of sports to be held here in a day or two – that is, of course, if we are not shifted in the interim.[157]

The Sergeant also recorded his displeasure at the battalion football team being beaten:

> Our stalwart football team got rather a setback the other day. Up til that time the battalion team, composed of men from Inverness, Glasgow and London, had the enviable record of having played 18 matches and not having been beaten. A team from the Canadian Transport got to hear of this – for the fame of our team has spread far and wide – and invaded the little village in which we are billeted – team, officers and supporters. They succeeded in beating our team and the enthusiasm of the Canadians, officers as well as men was immense. We found a little consolation in the fact,

> however, that half the Canadian team was composed of Scotsmen.[158]

On 6 June, the battalion marched six miles to fresh billets in Locon where they spent six days practising drill and bathing. While at Locon, the battalion supplied working parties of men to assist the Royal Engineers who were making preparations for an attack by the 7th Division at Givenchy. Montague Goodban was one of the men detailed for this task. On 9 June, Goodban mustered with the rest of the working party at 6.15pm and marched to the trenches, only to find that they had been sent to the wrong place. They were forced to spend the night doing nothing before marching back to their billets at 3.30am. The following day, the working party tried again and this time had more success:

> Again marched to trenches at 6.30pm (Givenchy D Lines). On arrival we start to make our communication trench. There are 300 of us and we have to dig a trench 1 mile long and 3 feet deep and also fill 3000 sandbags and arrange them along the top edge. It is pouring with rain the whole time and stray bullets keep whistling through the air, the conditions are hardly pleasant, it is pitch dark and you cannot see where or what you are digging. It is 10 o'clock when we start and our job has to be completed by day break. We do it and arrive back at our billets at 5.15am wet through and pretty tired.[159]

The weather in Locon was glorious with high temperatures and sunshine every day. However, on 8 June a terrific thunderstorm washed many of the men out of their billets in an orchard. The newly promoted Lance Corporal Goodban mentioned in his diary that the thunderstorm dropped hailstones the size of sugar lumps! The men took advantage of the generally fine weather and secured passes to go into the town of Bethune, some two miles away, for a change of scenery and to buy meals in one of the many estaminets in the town. Goodban described one such trip:

> Church parade 10am. Me and another chap paid a visit to a place called Bethune about 4 miles away, the only decent sized place around here. It seems quite civilised, they have a good many quite good shops and some fairly decent people. We had a good 'blow out' and a look round and returned feeling quite cheerful. The Huns put 6 large shells in here regularly every morning and evening but funnily enough never seem to do a great deal of damage.[160]

By the first week of June, the 9th (Scottish) and 51st (Highland) Divisions had arrived in France and many of the officers of these units sought out their counterparts in the 4th Cameron Highlanders for advice, and to renew friendships made in Bedford. Captain D.E.M.M. Crichton of the 1st Camerons, 2nd Lieutenant P.B. Duff of the 5th Seaforths, Captain J. Cameron, and Lieutenants P.B. Macintyre and W. Dewar of the 4th Seaforths all visited, passing on their good wishes from shared acquaintances back in Scotland. Other visitors included Lieutenant-Colonel J. Grant Smith and Major Sinclair Gair of the 6th Seaforth Highlanders, the Morayshire Territorial Battalion who had been with the 4th Camerons in the Seaforth and Cameron Brigade in the pre-war days.

In the evening of 9 June, Major Hector Fraser, Captain Duff and the company commanders rode to Windy Corner near Givenchy where they inspected some reserve trenches in preparation for the battalion taking over that sector. Givenchy was only a mile south of the area over which the 4th Camerons had charged to take possession of the Southern Breastwork the previous month. On 14 June, the battalion paraded at 3.30pm and marched to reserve trenches at Estaminet Corner where they took over trenches from the 6th Gordon Highlanders. Lieutenant Ian Mackay, now in command of D Company, wrote home to his parents:

> We left our billets on Monday evening, and marched about four miles to reserve trenches some 2000 yards behind the firing line. These trenches were protection against artillery fire but had few dugouts, so most of the men slept in the open. We were there all next day. Our guns and some French ones were all round about us and very near, and they kept up a continuous bombardment all night and day. The noise was terrific – nearly blew our heads off.[161]

The British trenches in the Givenchy sector were in very poor condition; the maze of old trenches, shell holes and mine craters made it a haven for German snipers on the higher ground to the east. The time of the attack was set for 6.00pm on 15 June with 21 Brigade being detailed as the assaulting troops. They lined up with the 2nd Wiltshires on the left in front of the German line at points J7 to I4 with the 2nd Yorkshires on their right between I4 and H3 which can be seen on the map on page 135.[162] The Canadian Division was on 21 Brigade's right and the

Grenadier Guards and 51st (Highland) Division on their left. The aim was to take the German trenches on a line running east of Givenchy village to the southern end of the Rue d'Ouvert. The 51st Division in the north was to advance over the same ground the 4th Camerons had attacked at Festubert.

In the morning of 15 June, Lieutenant Ian Mackay had been sent forward with a party of officers and sergeants to reconnoitre the ground over which the attack was to take place. He wrote to his parents of the terrain:

> We got up to the firing line up a long deep communication trench. All the trenches are named, with signboards showing the way and they are all named after the Piccadilly part of London – Piccadilly, Curzon Street, and Oxford Street (which is the firing line) with Bond Street and others running between them. These trenches are on a ridge – the top of a long sloping hill up which the communication trench runs. The trenches run through the village, which of course is in absolute ruins now. It must have been a nice place before the war, as it stands near the top of the hill and some of the houses appear to have been very good ones with nice gardens. The trenches run through the gardens and we could see bits of the dividing railings here and there and all kinds of garden flowers and vegetables growing wild. We passed a very good bed of asparagus![163]

All day on 15 June the British artillery steadily bombarded the German trenches. At 5.30pm the British guns upped their rate of fire and gave the enemy positions everything they had. At 6.00pm, the 2nd Wiltshires and

2nd Yorkshires went over the top. The assaulting battalions had not bargained on the strength of the trenches opposite, nor the amount of German soldiers manning them. Each trench in the Givenchy sector was 9–10 feet deep with protected dugouts buried deep within them, giving the German defenders secure places to sit out the bombardment.

The attacking battalions were hit by a hail of machine-gun and rifle bullets as soon as they tried to leave their trench. Those who got through charged the German wire. Some men of the Yorkshires managed to get into the German trench and bombed their way right and left and along a communication trench. The bombing section of the Yorkshires advanced along a sunken road to the edge of a mine crater and commenced a bombing duel with their German counterparts. In the face of heavy fire, the Yorkshires were forced to retreat. The two companies of the 2nd Yorkshires who attacked on 15 June numbered 10 officers and 350 men before the battle; only 1 officer and 71 men came out unscathed.[164]

The 2nd Wiltshires fared no better. Advancing on the left of the Yorkshires, they had more ground to cross to reach the German line. They were hit by enfilade fire from machine-gun positions on their right in a communication trench leading from the mine crater to the German second line, and on their left from machine guns hidden in long grass. The Wiltshires lost nine officers and 200 men killed and wounded. On returning to their trenches they found orders asking them to regroup and charge again.[165]

Luckily for these battalions the orders were countermanded and the troops pulled out of the front line. The Yorkshires were replaced by the 2nd Royal Scots Fusiliers and the Wiltshires by the 2nd Bedfords, both of whom had been in 21 Brigade support. At 9.00pm the 4th Cameron Highlanders were also ordered forward. A Company took possession of the keeps and redoubts of the Givenchy village defences, and B, C and D Companies moved up to the 3rd line reserve trenches at Windy Corner. The attack had been postponed until the next day.

At 4.00am on 16 June, the Camerons were on the move again. Lieutenant Mackay recalled lying out in the open behind the Windy Corner trenches:

> I was just dozing off when a message came down to fall in at once and we had to turn the men out and move off. We had not gone far when the order was cancelled and we lay down again behind the same trenches and went to sleep. Not long afterwards the order came again to fall in and this time we moved off to other reserve trenches just behind the communication trenches which led up the slope to the firing line.[166]

The time for the attack by the Royal Scots Fusiliers and Bedfords was set for 4.45pm. Like the day before, the British artillery kept up a steady barrage on the German positions but this time the Germans replied like for like. When the orders came for the 4th Cameron Highlanders to move up to the first line reserve trenches in support of the Royal Scots Fusiliers, they had to negotiate a communications trench called the Queen's Road. It proved a terrible journey. Montague Goodban:

> The enemy are shelling this trench for all they are worth, evidently having located it previously by aeroplane. The smoke from the bursting shells is so dense that you can

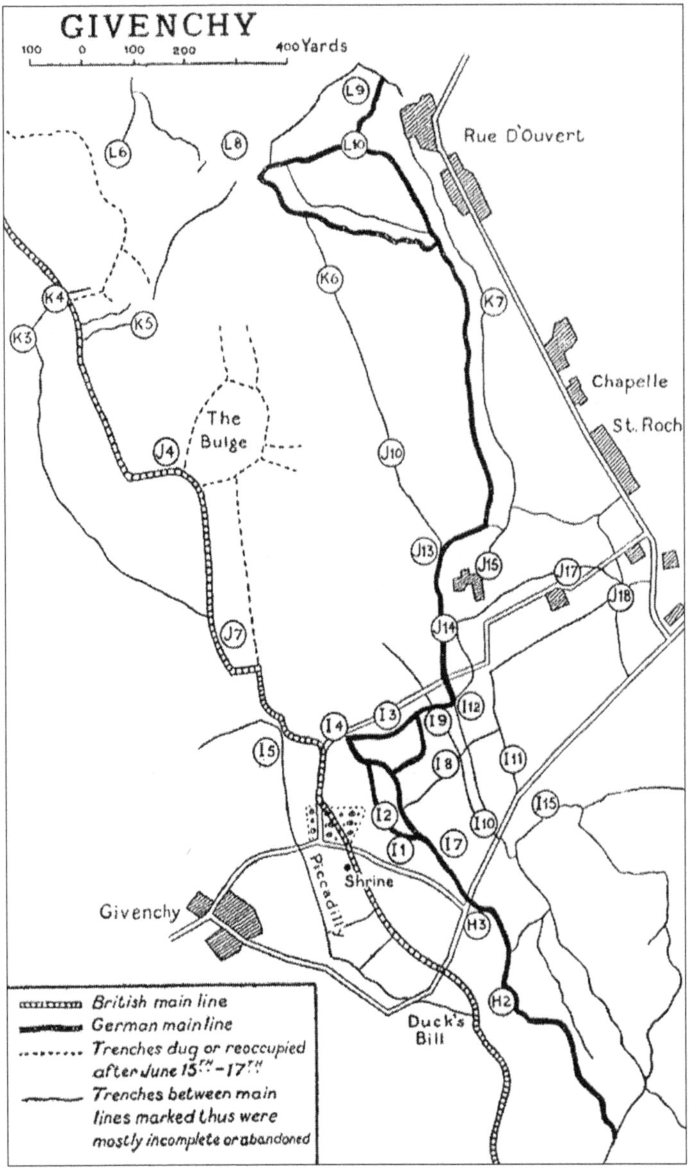

The Battle of Givenchy, 15–16 June 1915. (*7th Division History*)

> only see about 50 yards ahead of you, it looks like certain death to attempt to go down it, however it has got to be done so off we start. Jack Johnsons and Coal Boxes are bursting thick and fast all around, it is a very trying ordeal, every now and then we have to stop and the word comes back 'we cannot get on, the trench is blocked with dead and wounded' – this is when a shell bursts in the trench. I make up my mind that I will be thundering lucky if ever I get out of it alright. However, eventually we get into the 1st Line reserve and take up our positions. This trench too is coming in for a very heavy shelling, this is the worst bombardment I have been in so far and I hope I may not be in for another like it. We are unable to do anything but wait – first a shell bursts on your left and word comes down that it has killed and wounded 18 then one on the left killing 4 and wounded 2 more. One cannot help wondering 'when is my turn coming'. A fairly small shell (about an 18 pounder) dropped in the trench about a yard from me and exploded, there were 3 other chaps standing with me and 2 were wounded, the 3rd man and myself being knocked down by the explosion but fortunately uninjured. Earlier in the day I had another escape, a piece of shell came buzzing through the air and just missed me, it tore a slit in my tunic and shirt and scratched my skin. Another inch and I should have been right for Blighty.[167]

Lieutenant Mackay, with Goodban in D Company, also described the experience:

> We accordingly filed off up the communication trench and then came in for the worst bit of shelling we have

> had yet. There was a furious bombardment going on both sides and when we started we could not see the top of the hill for smoke and dust. All the way up we got it hot and had a good few casualties. You never heard such an inferno in your life. Shells of all kinds were coming thick – shrapnel, high explosives and 'coal boxes'. Many of these fell among the buildings which are of red brick, sending bits flying all over the place, nearly all of us had the most extraordinary escapes. The trench was very narrow and progress was very slow especially as we were often delayed by having to pass wounded men and step over those that had fallen. However, at last we reached Piccadilly and lined it and the other 'streets'. We were grimy looking objects as in addition to the black dust of the shells, the air was full of red dust from the bricks.[168]

Corporal Patrick MacBean wrote of the advance up the communication trench in a letter to his former employer in Inverness that was reprinted in the *Inverness Courier*. He told of his shock of learning of the casualties:

> There are two of our comrades, however, who we shall miss very much. One is the son of Mr Dow, Inverfarigaig, who is killed. He was third from me in the trenches going up, when a shell burst and he was hit with a piece of it. He was killed outright, and suffered no pain whatsoever. I was nearly stunned when I found out it was Dow. I knew him so well! Many a talk he and I had over athletics. He was a fine boy – just manhood at its best. Dow was one of the finest men we had in the battalion – a soldier and a gentleman. Its men like

> him who make a Battalion. It is pretty hard luck to lose them, but what can you do? We are fighting for freedom and liberty and I may tell you that many brave men fell and will yet fall for the cause. The Germans will suffer for every man yet.[169]

B Company took over part of the fire trench in Oxford Street and C and D Companies were one trench further back in Piccadilly. From there they could watch the Fusiliers and Bedfords attack. The artillery bombardment intensified 45 minutes before the assault but the Germans, anticipating a repeat of the previous day's attack, began to man their parapet two minutes before the British went over the top.[170] In the Fusiliers' sector, between points H3 and I4, more than half of the attacking troops were killed or wounded before they reached their own barbed wire defences. The Bedfords on the left succeeded in taking the mine crater but were eventually bombed out. Some of the Bedfords who had got close to the German wire reported that the Germans had been lining the parapet two or three soldiers deep, the ones in the back loading rifles for the ones in front.[171] The British troops did not stand a chance. Lieutenant Mackay wrote of the attack:

> We found that the regiment we were supporting had not taken the German position but were holding the ground they occupied about 30 yards out in front and were digging themselves in there. They had attacked while we were coming up the communication trench and we knew at once as a furious rifle and machine gun fire burst out as soon after we began to meet wounded coming down the trench.[172]

Mackay also reported a close shave in the support trench:

> I met Duff in Piccadilly and had a few words with him en passant. We had just moved off when a shell came through the parapet just where we had been and killed ten of our men and wounded many more. I shall never forget that sight. Six of the killed were of my company. Poor D Company has again lost the most in killed, though C Company had the most wounded.[173]

The shell had killed Sergeant John Cooley, Corporals William Paterson and James Vass, Lance Corporals Harry Locke and William Stacey and Privates Harold Reid, George Hammond and Thomas Stoddart.

The battalion remained in position, not knowing if it would be called on to attack, until 8.00pm when the orders came for C and D Companies to move back to the GHQ line. B Company remained with the Royal Scots Fusiliers in the firing line until relieved by the Warwickshires at 2.00am on 17 June.

The Camerons marched back to billets at Estaminet Corner. Lieutenant Ian Mackay told his parents how he rested after the battle:

> When we were relieved we made our way back, the old Hun sending a few parting shots in the shape of Jack Johnsons after us, quite as if he knew we were on the move. When we got down and under shelter we called a roll and marched off to the reserve trenches we had occupied at the beginning of the show. I and some others slept in a room in a deserted and partly ruinous estaminet. We got hold of some bully beef and a friendly

> motor man who happened to be there produced a loaf and a bottle of vin ordinaire and we had a jolly good meal and then a jolly good sleep after what had been a pretty tiring two days. All the regiments of our brigade came out that night and there were great hob-nobbings going on between our men and theirs. We are always 'Jock' to them.[174]

Once back in the reserve the 4th Camerons could take stock of their losses. Major Hector Fraser – leading the battalion in battle for the first time – and Lieutenant Andrew Sutherland were slightly wounded and Lieutenant Francis Laughton – attached to the Brigade Bombing Company – was seriously wounded in the head and evacuated to England. In total, 15 men were killed and 47 wounded.

In the afternoon of 17 June, the Camerons marched to billets at Le Choquaux, near Locon, where they and the rest of 21 Brigade were given a rest and the opportunity to clean up and refit before moving on to Robecq and the billets they had left on 5 June.

The Battle of Givenchy marked the end of the diary entries of Corporal Charles Bowdery. After the Battle of Festubert he made only one entry, that of 16 June, and his recollection of the fight at Givenchy. The entry is very brief and only mentions that he was with the Bombing Squad in the front line with the Royal Scots Fusiliers. From June onwards there was also a change in the reporting by Scottish newspapers. While descriptions and reports on Festubert had been given pages and pages over a three-week period, for the Battle of Givenchy only a casualty list was published in the *Inverness Courier* and the *Highland News*. There were some things, it appeared, that the public were better off not knowing about.

At Robecq, things started to get back to normal for the 4th Cameron Highlanders. Captain Murdoch Beaton and Lieutenant Ian Nelson went back home for a few days leave and the remainder of the battalion were employed on company route marches. In the evening of 21 June, the Adjutant, Captain Garden Duff, gave a lecture on the progress of the War. Lieutenant Ian Mackay wrote home of being based in the Robecq sector again:

> The country people seem to be very glad to see us back as they gave us a great welcome when we arrived last night. Some of them came sprinting across the fields when they recognised men who had been billeted with them before and shook hands vigorously. My company are not in the same billets this time but are not too badly off. The officers are in a small cottage, the owner of which is a very genial old bird. I am writing this 'at the cottage door' near a small orchard and the sun is very bright.[175]

The rest period in Robecq saw some administrative changes in the battalion. 2nd Lieutenant Donald Ross joined the Brigade Grenade Company in place of Lieutenant Francis Laughton, who had been wounded at Givenchy, and Regimental Sergeant Major Alexander Whitton, twice wounded at the front, left to take up the position of Quartermaster with the 3/4th Cameron Highlanders back in Britain. He was succeeded temporarily by Regimental Quartermaster Sergeant Harry Keates.

Lance Corporal Montague Goodban also got a change of job with the battalion, writing in his diary:

> I am chosen to join the bombers or as they are more frequently called the 'Anarchists' or 'Suicide Club'. I left here about 2.30 and went to the bombers' billets the other side of Robecq.[176]

Word also came through to the battalion that several officers were to be promoted. On 22 June, Lieutenants Ian Mackay, Charles Campbell and John MacPherson were gazetted as temporary captains. Ian Mackay wrote to his mother about what happened during an evening meal in an estaminet for A and D Company officers:

> I forgot if I told you that I am now a Captain, although not officially gazetted (so you can now address me as Captain!) and as it was the first time that I had appeared with three stars on, they drank my health after Beaton had proposed it in a 'touching' speech.[177]

Captain Murdoch Beaton had commanded A Company since the battalion arrived in France in February 1915 and was 45 years old. His coolness in battle won the respect of his men and officers, Lieutenant Mackay in particular:

> Old Beaton is still bullet proof too and it is a funny thing that at the Givenchy show, although we were in different companies, it so happened that we came together frequently. So we have practically been side by side in every action that we have been in.[178]

At 10.45pm on 26 June, the 4th Camerons paraded and marched back to Locon. The following morning Major Fraser and the company commanders rode to near

Festubert and reconnoitred the trenches the battalion were to take over. The trenches in this sector were newly built and lay across the ground over which the 4th Camerons charged during the Battle of Festubert in May.

The Camerons relieved the 7th Gordon Highlanders of the 51st Division at 11.00pm on 27 June, A and B Companies being posted to the firing line, C Company in support and D Company in reserve. On 29 June, the bodies of Captain David F. MacKenzie, Corporal Gordon and Lance Corporal George MacKenzie were found opposite A Company's trench.

Captain Roderick McErlich and Captain Murdoch Beaton decided to set out and retrieve the body of their friend Captain MacKenzie. As German patrols would be in the area at night and thus the Germans would not be expecting it, the men set out in broad daylight. Three Gaelic speaking members of the Camerons volunteered to help: Sergeant Donald MacDonald, Sergeant Duncan MacMillan and Sergeant Malcolm MacLean, all of the island of Raasay.[179] The story is recorded in *The Sword of the North*, by the Reverend Dugald MacEachern:

> Beaton, McErlich and their three stalwart companions girded up their kilts about their waists and moved along the ditch, which contained water, dead bodies, mud and green slime, with rank grass at its lip. When they arrived opposite the body, Captain McErlich and MacDonald, being the best shots, lay on guard with their rifles over the lip of the ditch. MacMillan and MacLean took the spades, and Captain Beaton directed. Through the side of the ditch a sloping avenue was dug up towards the body. Captain MacKenzie lay curled up as if asleep as

> they had often seen him lie curled up in his dugout. Gently the body rolled down towards them. From his tunic pocket they took his New Testament and his paper, and then they dug a grave in the bank and said a prayer over the beloved dust, reverently interring it and raising over it a little cross.[180]

In the evening of 29 June, the Camerons were visited by their Chief, Lieutenant-Colonel Donald Cameron of Locheil, commanding officer of the 5th Battalion, Cameron Highlanders. The following evening, the 5th Cameron Highlanders replaced the 4th Battalion in the Festubert trenches. Amongst the ranks of the 5th Camerons was Private J. B. Mackenzie, whose letters to his wife from the trenches are preserved in the Imperial War Museum. He wrote of the trenches his battalion occupied:

> We relieved our 4th Battalion in here, these are the trenches they lost so many men in capturing and is just one vast dead house, the stench in some places is something awful. The first thing we had to do was to dig the trenches deeper and otherwise repair them and we came across bodies all over the place. You know the Germans occupied these trenches nearly the whole winter and have been losing heavily and have had to bury their killed in the trenches, there were legs and arms sticking out all over the place when we arrived but we have buried most of them properly now. The ground behind us is now covered by dead Camerons and Germans who fell on the 17th May and we go out at night and bury them. It is a rotten job as they are very decomposed but it has got to be done and then one feels to have one's own countrymen lying out like that and we

> think it is only right to relatives at home to put their poor bodies under the ground properly.[181]

Lance Corporal Montague Goodban, now of the Brigade Bombers, missed the last tour in the trenches. He made a discovery:

> I undergo an examination and test in bombing which I passed successfully. I am now a full blown 'Anarchist'. While digging up some potatoes today in an old ruined farm (we were going to have them with our bully) I hit something hard and going deeper down found it was a wooden box which the people who left the farm had evidently buried for safety before leaving. Inside the box was a large crucifix about 2 foot high made of oak and white metal – a number of photographs both framed and unframed, a rosary and several other several small Altar Ornaments. The folks would never find them again I think for the farm is now a heap of bricks.[182]

On leaving the trenches at Festubert, the 4th Camerons marched to a position in the rear at Ham-en-Artois where they would remain for eight days to recuperate after their time in the trenches. While there, Captain Duff and Lieutenant Harold Law went home on leave and Lieutenant Alexander MacKenzie went to hospital sick. This countryside was much more to the liking of the troops:

> This is a cushy spot, don't mind how long we stay here. Plenty of cherries knocking about, but we are not supposed to take these as were are now outside the 2 miles radius – however we chance our arm and tuck into

> them. The penalty by the way is to be shot for looting – but there is one satisfaction, we shall be shot (if caught) on a full stomach – it must be very unpleasant to be shot on an empty stomach.[183]

For the next three days Montague Goodban and some of his companions gorged themselves on some of the finest food in Artois. Goodban's diary for the first week in July recorded:

> Have a good clean up – a bath in a pail and do some washing, shirt, towel, kerchiefs, socks etc. Then go to a little farm (3 of us) which we discovered and have a jolly good feed of eggs, potatoes, strawberries and cherries. Fine old girl here, we are going tomorrow and she is going to get some food for us.[184]
>
> Usual parades. We go and have our feed which consisted of roast pigeon, green peas, chipped potatoes, salad, strawberries, cherries, bread and butter, biscuits, coffee and white wine. We only wanted a string orchestra and we might have shut our eyes and thought we were in the Iroc. And it only cost us 2 francs 50. Bon n'est ce pas.[185]

On 6 July, the battalion was treated to an open air concert in the evening during which men of the 4th Camerons showed off their various talents with the mouth organ and concertina, solos, songs and recitations, accompanied by music from an officer's gramophone.[186] Two days later the battalion was ordered to parade for an inspection by Lord Kitchener and the Prince of Wales. The men lined up either side of a road at five-pace intervals as the Secretary for War and the heir to the throne drove past.

The following day, the 4th Camerons were on the move again, this time via Robecq, Hinges and Locon to a position near the trenches at Vieille Chapelle. The battalion spent a rain soaked night bivouacking in a muddy field and an orchard before falling in at 8.00pm and marching to the trenches at Richebourg, on the extreme south of the Neuve Chapelle battlefield. Lance Corporal Goodban described this new sector, which the Camerons took over from the 3rd Ghurkas:

> This is a piece of trench recently captured, the Germans are in the same trench as ourselves, only a double block made of earth 15 paces wide separating them from us. Of course me being a bomber I get the job of guarding this piece together with 3 other 'Anarchists'.[187]

During this tour in the trenches Lance Corporal Montague Goodban was wounded in the leg by a rifle grenade while guarding the section of the trench mentioned above. His diary entry for 12 July described the incident, which sent him back to Blighty:

> A little shelling going on, nothing very great. 1.30pm I clicked and stopped about 20 pieces of a rifle grenade with my leg. Am bandaged up and taken to the advanced dressing station, where I arrived about 8.30pm. Here I am redressed and taken to the dressing station at Vieille Chapelle by motor ambulance. Here I am examined by doctors and dressed again. Spend the night here on a stretcher in a barn.[188]

At 11.00am the following day, Lance Corporal Goodban was taken by a motor ambulance to Number 7 Casualty

Clearing Station at Merville. His wounds were dressed and he spent the rest of that day lying on a stretcher. The following morning he embarked on a 24-hour journey onboard a Red Cross train to Rouen where he was taken to Number 12 Stationary Hospital. He was posted to Surgical Hut Number 2 and got the luxury of a bed with clean sheets where his wounds were dressed again. In the afternoon of 15 July, three days after being wounded, he was operated on, the surgeons removing several pieces of shrapnel from his head and hand. Goodban spent the next few days being x-rayed and operated upon to remove further pieces of shrapnel stuck in various parts of his body. On 22 July, he got the news most wounded soldiers dreamed of:

> Doc comes round and puts a 'B' on my board which I find stands for boat – not blighty although it is the same thing. Well of course my spirits rise to boiling point. At 12.30am I leave here and am put on the RX train for Havre, we left at 1.30pm and arrived at 6.30pm but we remain on the train all night in a siding and we are taken on the hospital ship 'Carisbrook Castle' of the Union Castle Line at 8am on Friday, 23 July. Was put in a nice little cot down in the saloon and had my leg dressed. Then each of us were given a pipe, 1/4 lb of tobacco and 20 cigs, a book to read and a gramophone playing. We sailed at 8.30am and arrived at Southampton at 3pm. On arrival I was taken by Ambulance to Highfield Hall Red X hospital, Southampton and again put to bed.[189]

Goodban was generous in his praise of the treatment he got both in the field and at hospital in England:

> [Regarding] practical experience of the Red Cross methods I have nothing but admiration for them. Everyone I came into contact with was exceedingly kind and everything seemed to be worked on through business like lines. The red cross trains are very fine bordering on the luxurious. The hospital ships are equally well fitted up. And a wounded Tommy has the very best of attention once he is off the field.[190]

In total, Lance Corporal Goodban spent four months in hospital. When he was released he applied for and received a commission as a Second Lieutenant in the East Surrey Regiment on 22 January 1916. Lieutenant Goodban was seconded to the 22nd Squadron of the Royal Flying Corps where he learned to fly a Caudron Biplane. He graduated from the Ruffy-Baumann Flying School in Hendon on 8 December 1916. Second Lieutenant Montague Goodban was killed in action on 19 May 1917. He was buried in Plot VIII.K.6 in Fins New British Cemetery at Sorel-le-Grand between Cambrai and Peronne.

Back with the 4th Camerons in the trenches at Richebourg, a draft of eleven replacement officers joined the battalion from the 2/4th Cameron Highlanders in Scotland. Lieutenants Neil McArthur, James A. Symon, James R. Park, William E. Cattanach, George C. MacMillan and Charles C. Douglas joined along with 2nd Lieutenants Donald J. Maciver, Archibald A. Macdonald, Donald Morrison, Charles S. Powell and William S. Valentine and were posted to their companies. The new officers were much appreciated by the battalion who had been reduced to only ten officers spread over the four companies.

The Battalion remained in the Richebourg trenches until midnight on 17/18 July when they were relieved by the 6th Gordon Highlanders. Seven men, including Montague Goodban, had been wounded during their eight-day tour.[191] The only event considered worth recording by Captain Ian Mackay was the battalion having to stand to on the night of 16/17 July due to an attack made on the battalion's right flank at Givenchy.

The 4th Cameron Highlanders arrived at Calonne after a ten-hour march. Here the battalion spent three days resting and cleaning up after their tour. On 19 July word was received that Major Hector Fraser – who had commanded the battalion since the Battle of Festubert in May – was promoted to Lieutenant-Colonel. At this time Lieutenant-Colonel Fraser and Lieutenant John MacLaren proceeded back to Britain for a well deserved rest, their first since arriving in France in February. Further changes to the personnel of the battalion were made at Calonne when 2nd Lieutenant A.W. Hughes joined from the 2/4th Cameron Highlanders and Captain Frederick Fraser – commander of B Company – and Lieutenant Alexander MacKenzie became ill and had to be taken to hospital.

The organisation of the officers in the battalion had changed completely since coming out to France in February. When 2nd Lieutenant Hughes joined the 4th Camerons at Calonne the officers were posted as follows:

Lieutenant-Colonel Hector Fraser	in command
Major Murdoch Beaton	second in command
Major Garden Duff	Adjutant
Major John Lockie	Quartermaster

Captain J.W. Wood	Medical Officer
Captain Reverend J. Campbell MacGregor	Chaplain
Captain John D. MacPherson	Transport Officer
Lieutenant Harold B. Law	Machine Gun Officer

A Company

Captain Roderick McErlich	in command
Lieutenant Donald Ross	
2nd Lieutenant A.W. Hughes	
2nd Lieutenant Donald J. MacIver	
2nd Lieutenant Donald Morrison	

B Company

Captain Charles Campbell	in command
Captain John F. MacLaren	
Lieutenant James R. Park	
2nd Lieutenant Max A. Roemmele	
2nd Lieutenant Archibald A. MacDonald	

C Company

Captain Peter M. Cram	in command
Captain Andrew Sutherland	
Lieutenant Ian T. Nelson	
Lieutenant Hector M. Morison	
2nd Lieutenant William S. Valentine	
2nd Lieutenant Donald Finlayson	

D Company

Captain Ian Mackay	in command
Lieutenant Angus Urquhart	

Lieutenant Neil McArthur
Lieutenant George MacMillan
Lieutenant Henry J. Scott
Lieutenant Charles C. Douglas

On 22 July, the 4th Camerons marched to Vieille Chapelle and took over the 21 Brigade reserve trenches from the Royal Welch Fusiliers. Their time in Vieille Chapelle was spent building trenches near the firing line and helping the front line battalions repair their parapets. On 30 July, the officers of the 4th Camerons took on their counterparts in a nearby battery of the Royal Garrison Artillery at cricket. They lost.

On 1 August, the battalion marched to billets in Busnettes along with the rest of the 7th Division. High Command had decided to give the Division a rest in recognition of its exertions in the four engagements that year: Neuve Chapelle, Aubers Ridge, Festubert and Givenchy. A further reason for the rest was to blood newly arrived Territorial and New Army Division men in the front line trenches in quieter sectors to give them time to acclimatise to their new surroundings. The battalion spent two weeks resting and training in Busnettes where the highlights were a regimental concert held in a local schoolhouse and sports days held at Gonnehem where the relay team of the 4th Camerons came in second.

At Busnettes the training programme focused primarily on bombing. On 11 August, Major Bidder, 21 Brigade Machine Gun Officer, gave a lecture on the art of bombing which was followed by the regimental bombers giving a demonstration of a bombing attack. As bombing was now part of ordinary battalion drill as opposed to being a specialised discipline, many of the men sought to become experts. As there was a shortage of rifle ranges at Busnettes that discipline did not receive as much focus.

As part of the build up of strength in Busnettes a draft of 55 men were sent from the 3/4th Camerons in Inverness, 22 of whom had already seen service with the battalion in France. They were commanded by Lieutenant William Mackay who had been wounded with the battalion in April. Lieutenant Mackay was not able to stay with the battalion long, however, as his orders required him to hand over the recruits at the base and proceed back to the depot in Inverness.

His brother, Captain Ian Mackay, commanding D Company, wrote home to his sister Kathleen on 8 August, describing his time in Busnettes:

> Beaton and self and some others went to a town not far off and did some shopping and had dinner at a restaurant. Yesterday afternoon McArthur, MacMillan, and I rode over to Robecq and Calonne where we were formerly billeted and called on old friends at both places and got a great reception. We had a most delightful ride through pretty country, mostly harvest fields with the corn in stooks. We said if war was always like this we could do with a good lot of it.[192]

It was not just the officers who enjoyed the rest period. The *Inverness Courier* of 13 August reproduced a letter written by a member of the battalion to a friend in Inverness.

> The only things that trouble us are the endless swarms of flies, wasps, mosquitos and other insect nuisances. The mosquitos are the worst by a long chalk. They fasten on every exposed part of the body and raise

> some big blisters, and we decent Highlanders come in for a heavy share of the attacks. We get some amusements provided for us occasionally, especially when we get away back from the firing line. For instance, a concert was got up by the — Division and a couple of waggon-loads from this mob went to the place about three miles away. We were just like a lot of bairns on a Sunday school trip – sang and shouted and behaved in a general daft sort of style the whole time. The concert was jolly good. You have no idea how much real talent there is out here. Our pipers came up and played a selection and had quite a royal reception. It is so different from home, where a pipe band hardly ever gets a decent clap, far less a rousing round of cheers. Of course, our regiment has a very good name, even among the regiments of a glorious Division and the pipers seem to appear as our representatives. I know that sounds 'braggan' so you can put it down to my inordinate pride in my regiment.[193]

At 8.00am on 16 August, the battalion fell in and marched to Locon where they bivouacked for the day before relieving the 8th Gordon Highlanders in the C2 subsection of the Festubert trenches. A, B and D Companies took over the firing trench with C Company in reserve, the position being slightly to the north of the positions occupied by the 4th Camerons at the battles of Festubert and Givenchy and close to the orchard in the middle of the Festubert battlefield.

The trenches in the sector had been strengthened since the battalion's last visit, but still further repairs had to be carried out. Every night the 4th Camerons were in the C2 trenches they had working parties in front of their trenches, thickening the parapet to a distance of 15 feet. The Germans opposite them were approximately 300 yards away and they too were busy repairing their trenches. On the night of 18 August, the Germans suddenly downed tools and opened up with rifle fire on men of the 2nd Bedford Regiment, who were repairing the trenches to the right of the Camerons. Sergeant James MacBean of Achnabeachan, in a listening post in no man's land, reported back to headquarters that the German fire had been preceded by the faint sound of a whistle. This information was relayed to Brigade headquarters and the other battalions were notified. Armed with this information, Headquarters devised a series of signals to be relayed between listening post and working parties which forewarned the troops. In the seven nights the brigade had working parties in front of the trenches, not one man was hit by German fire. The only casualty of the tour was 2nd Lieutenant Charles Powell, recently arrived from home.

After ten days in the trenches the 4th Camerons were relieved by the men of the 9th Devon Regiment and marched to Les Choquaux where they entered billets. While there, each of the companies restructured their ranks as every company was to have a dedicated Grenade Platoon. At 9.00pm on 28 August the battalion took over the B3 subsection trenches from the 2nd Worcester Regiment, with B and C Companies in the firing line, D Company in support and A Company in reserve.

While in these trenches, word was received that Captain Murdoch Beaton – who had commanded A Company since the battalion embarked for France in February – was promoted Major and left to take up position as second in command of the 4th Cameron Highlanders. His promotion left a vacancy in A Company, which was filled by Captain Roderick McErlich.

On 31 August, the 4th Camerons were again pulled from the line and placed in reserve in Le Preol where they cleaned up and had a rest. They would need it. Army High Command was planning the last of the summer offensives in the Artois region – the Battle of Loos.

8

The Battle of Loos, 1 September–10 October 1915

At Le Preol, the 4th Cameron Highlanders' only duty was to supply working parties to assist with mining operations in the Givenchy sector. On 3 September, the battalion marched to Bethune where the officers had a regimental dinner in the Hotel de France, the first time since leaving Bedford that all the officers had had a regimental mess. After dinner the battalion pipers played for the assembled officers.

From Bethune the 4th Camerons marched the six miles to Busnettes where they occupied their old billets. On 6 September, the battalion fell in and marched ten miles south to La Bourse where they heard the news that Adjutant Captain Garden Duff was to be promoted to the rank of Major. Five battalions of the Cameron Highlanders were based in that district at the time: the 1st, 4th, 5th, 6th and 7th.

The 4th Camerons were still moving farther south, towards the village of Vermelles where D Company occupied Chapel Keep and Junction Keep just behind the firing line with the rest of the battalion in dugouts in Vermelles. The task of the 4th Camerons at Vermelles was to build communication trenches connecting the British front line trenches with the reserve lines. On 11 September, the Camerons were relieved by the 23rd Battalion, Yorkshire Regiment, before moving to Noyelles followed by La Bourse and Busnettes. Five days later they marched back to the Loos sector, going into billets in Fouquereil where a draft of 117 men joined from the 2/4th Camerons in Inverness, 33 of whom were wounded men returning to the battalion.

On 17 September, on their way to taking over front line trenches just south of the Hohenzollern Redoubt, the 4th Camerons passed through the village of Verquin. There, they met the 7th Cameron Highlanders who were billeted in the village and gave the 4th Battalion a cheer, lining the streets as they passed. The 7th Camerons' pipe band piped the 4th Battalion through the village and Lieutenant-Colonel Sandilands of the 7th rode alongside Lieutenant-Colonel Hector Fraser. On leaving their regimental companions, the 4th Camerons took over the Y2B subsection trenches from the 2nd Border Regiment where they remained with A and B Companies in the firing line, C Company in support and D Company in reserve.

During this seven-day tour the battalion was employed assisting members of the Royal Engineers in laying gas canisters in the front line trenches. This was to make the trenches suitable as a jumping off point for the battalions who were to go over the top in the first wave during the forthcoming Battle of Loos.

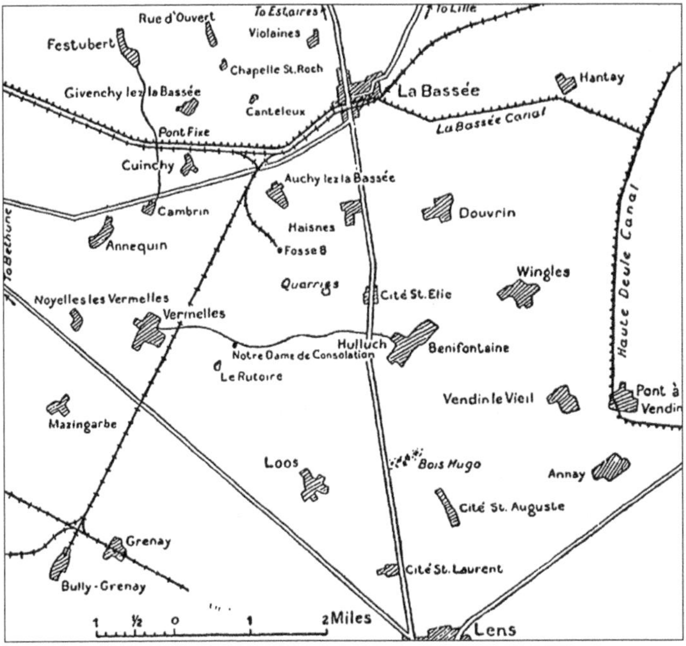

The area of the Battle of Loos, September 1915. (*7th Division History*)

The Loos battlefield was in a sector to the south of the battlefields of Neuve Chapelle, Aubers Ridge and Festubert, on the southern side of the La Bassee Canal. The terrain differed from the marshy grounds over which the 7th Division had fought with such distinction in the summer of 1915. The ground was drier, with chalk ridges sloping down towards the canal to the north of the British position. In the Loos sector the British and German lines were a considerable distance apart and needed to be closed up to reduce the distance the attacking troops would have to cross in the open. When the 7th Division arrived in the sector on 17 September the majority of the work had been completed and the troops were employed deepening the trenches and creating dugouts in communication trenches.[194]

The 4th Cameron Highlanders, in trenches near the Hohenzollern Redoubt, had a quietish time of it in the run up to the battle. On the morning of 21 September, the 4th Camerons were ordered to shoot five rounds of rapid fire four times at the Germans. A Nairn man in B Company wrote to the *Inverness Courier*:

> The enemy, thinking we were to attack, sent over a large number of 'coal boxes' to the first line trench. It was terrible for a time. Nothing could be seen of the German trenches for dust and smoke and the noise of the bursting shells was deafening.[195]

On 22 September, a German shell exploded in the doorway of one of B Company's dugouts, killing Privates William MacLeman, Duncan MacIntyre and Roderick MacKenzie and wounding Private Alexander Menzies in the foot. At 10.00pm on 23 September, the 4th Cameron Highlanders were relieved by the 2nd Warwickshire Regiment and marched back to billets in Verquin where they fitted out for the battle.

The German shelling was in retaliation for the commencement of the pre-battle artillery bombardment by the British forces. The First Army, consisting of I and IV Corps, had managed to obtain 919 artillery pieces for the battle, including 594 field guns, 132 field howitzers, 76 counter-battery artillery guns and 69 heavy howitzers with approximately 1000 rounds per gun for the field artillery and 400 rounds per gun for the howitzers and heavy guns.[196] The guns were to be used over a frontage of 11,200 yards, substantially larger than that of Festubert (5080 yards) and Neuve Chapelle (1450 yards) which led to a lower concentration of artillery fire than at those earlier battles; this artillery shortage would cause the same problems as it had done at Festubert and Neuve Chapelle.

I Corps went into the battle with the 2nd Division holding the northernmost sector, guarding the northern flank on both sides of the La Bassee Canal from a German counterattack. To their south came the 9th (Scottish) Division, a New Army division which included the 5th Cameron Highlanders, whose task it was to take the sector from the Vermelles-Auchy road in the north to the gap between the villages of Haisnes and Cite St Elie and incorporating the strong points of the Hohenzollern Redoubt, the Dump, the Colliery and the newly constructed German trenches Big Willie and Little Willie. The 7th Division was on the left of I Corps' front. Their northern boundary was the gap between Haisnes and Cite St Elie, and on the south the boundary between them and the 1st Division of IV Corps was the Vermelles-Hulluch Road.[197]

Directly opposite the attacking troops of the 7th Division was Quarry Trench to the north and Breslau Trench to the south, with the Pope's Nose Redoubt in the centre. The German communication trenches St Elie Avenue and Breslau Avenue linked these front line trenches with a further line consisting of Gun Trench and Stone Alley protecting the main feature of the 7th Division's front – the Quarries. The German main second line trench system, 1500 yards further back, protected the village of Cite St Elie in the centre of the divisional front and Hulluch on the right, to be assaulted by the 1st Division. The main trenches in the second line were, from north to south, Pekin, Puits and Hulluch Trenches. The terrain over which the 7th Division attacked between Vermelles in the British rear and Cite St Elie in the German second line was made up of relatively flat grasslands gently sloping up to Grenay Ridge, on the German side of which lay the Quarries.

The British IV Corps were detailed to assault the southern sector of the battlefield. The 1st Division was on the left of their attack, facing Hulluch, with the 15th (Scottish) Division in the centre facing Loos village and Hill 70, and finally the 47th Division on the southern extremity of the attack facing the Double Crassier. The scene was set for the largest British battle of 1915.

The German trench systems in the Loos sector were formidable. The trenches were built on areas of the battlefield which gave not only the best vantage points but also had the best drainage system. The fronts of the trenches were covered in a thick blanket of barbed wire designed to impede the British troops and give the well placed German machine guns time to pour enfilade fire into the mass ranks of the attackers.[198] In order to give the infantry a fighting chance of overcoming these defences, the artillery set about bombarding the German trenches on 21 September; it lasted for four days.

After nightfall on 24 September, the assaulting brigades of the 7th Division – 20 Brigade on the right and 22 Brigade on the left – assembled in their trenches and formed up for the attack. Facing them were two companies of the 11th Reserve Infantry Regiment of the German Army in the front line with additional companies in the Quarries and garrisoning Cité St Elie.[199]

At 5.50am on 25 September, the artillery bombardment intensified and troops in the British front line released a potent mix of smoke and chlorine gas from the canisters laid by the troops, including the 4th Camerons, in the preceding days. The wind blew from the southwest, the desired direction for the gas to disperse over the German lines, but was not strong enough to carry the gas properly, in places blowing back over the assaulting troops and causing casualties in their ranks.[200] At 6.30am, the assaulting battalions went over the top.

21 Brigade were detailed to be the divisional reserve, and in the hours preceding the battle were based in Verquin, several miles behind the British lines. Captain Ian Mackay wrote to his mother after the battle, describing the trouble involved in getting to the town:

> The day we were relieved was very wet and as the trenches were hard, the water remained in them and we had to wade down over a mile of trenches with water over the ankles. We arrived at this town at 2am and rested for some hours and then had a busy day getting instructions and outfitting for the coming fray. That evening we D Company officers had a good dinner together.[201]

The battalions of 21 Brigade moved off at half hour intervals from their positions around Verquin, starting with the 2nd Yorkshires at 11.30pm, followed by the 2nd Royal Scots Fusiliers and the 2nd Bedfords at midnight, the 2nd Wiltshires at 12.30am with the 4th Camerons bringing up the rear at 1.00am on 25 September. The battalions arrived at reserve trenches southeast of Noyelles between 3.00am and 3.30am where they waited to be ordered forward.

In the front line of the 7th Division trenches, 22 Brigade started the battle with the 2nd Royal Warwickshire Regiment to the north and the 1st South Staffordshire Regiment to the south. The 1st Royal Welch Fusiliers were in support with the 2nd Queens in brigade reserve. 20 Brigade took up position to the south of 22 Brigade. They employed the 8th Devon Regiment in the north of their attack and the 2nd Gordon Highlanders in the south, advancing up the Vermelles-Hulluch Road. The 2nd Border Regiment and 6th Gordon Highlanders were in support and the 9th Devons in reserve.[202]

The troops had 400 yards of open ground to cross before reaching the German lines. The aim of the 22 Brigade assault was the capture of the Quarries and Cité St Elie. Their colleagues in 20 Brigade aimed for Cité St Elie and the northern end of Hulluch.[203]

At 6.30am on 25 September, the four infantry battalions went over the top and advanced in four waves. The men began the advance at a walk as it was deemed that they would be tired out if they had to cross the 400 yards between trenches at a run. It took them twelve minutes to cross no man's land under heavy rifle, machine-gun and artillery fire.[204] All battalions suffered heavy losses. The battalion war diary of the 1st South Staffords recorded the scene presented to the battalion:

> The line occupied by the battalion was about 300 yards long and facing nearly due east. The German line we were tolled off to attack was about 450 yards long and strongly fortified, powerfully strengthened with flank defence wire in front of exceptionally thick wire and strong posts. There were small redoubts

The 7th Division Front at the Battle of Loos, 25 September 1915. (*7th Division History*)

> manned with numerous machine guns at intervals and the left flank was enfiladed by a variety of fire from Hohenzollern Fort and Fosse 8.[205]

By 9.30am, three hours after going over the top, the four assaulting battalions had taken the German front line and support trenches. The 1st South Staffords and 2nd Warwicks had advanced as far as 50 yards from the German position at Cité St Elie. The 2nd Royal Welch

Fusiliers had advanced in support of the two battalions, with the 2nd Queens slightly behind them. These two battalions had advanced furthest and had troops in Puits Trench in front of Cité St Elie, in touch with the 9th (Scottish) Division on their right. By 6.00pm, the four battalions had made repeated attacks on the German second line defences but were repulsed by heavy fire from Cité St Elie.

On the 20 Brigade front the 8th Devons and 2nd Gordons faired similarly. Emerging from the smoke and gas cloud the British soldiers made clear targets for the German machine gunners. The troops, heading for gaps in the German barbed wire made by the artillery bombardment, faced a bottleneck, and as a result bunched up and sustained severe casualties. The two battalions doggedly advanced and reached the Lens to La Bassee Road where they awaited reinforcements. The 2nd Borders and 6th Gordons came up and occupied the German positions in Gun Trench in support. The 9th Devon Regiment, who were brigade reserve at the start of the battle, were decimated before even reaching Gun Trench. At 8.30am, the 2nd Gordon Highlanders reported that they had seen a column of German infantry entering Cité St Elie. This was the reserve battalion of the 11th Infantry Regiment; the Germans were reinforcing.[206]

As the attack was progressing, 21 Brigade came up from their assembly positions. The 2nd Yorkshires and 2nd Wiltshires in the Noyelles Lines, the Royal Scots Fusiliers in Noyelles village and the 4th Camerons and 2nd Bedfords a mile back in the Labourse Lines began their advance. At 6.00am, the Bedfords and the Wiltshires advanced up Chapel Alley Communication Trench and the Yorkshires and 4th Camerons advanced up Gordon Alley.

After the battle, the *Inverness Courier* produced a souvenir booklet commemorating the actions of the five Cameron battalions at Loos. Entitled *The Cameron Highlanders at the Battles at Loos, Hill 70, Fosse 8 and the Quarries* it detailed the advance of the 4th Camerons to the communication trench:

> Along the road we marched with buoyant step by platoons, A Company leading, B following, then D and C. The two last were to act as supports to A and B respectively when the battalion came into action. By-and-by we entered one of those long tortuous communication trenches which led right up to the front line. Heavy guns cracked at our ears as we went along and two squadrons of cavalry which passed on ahead received a cheer. At the village of ---- we emerged from the trench under shelter of the ruined houses and made our way to where, on all previous occasions, we had of necessity to enter the communication trench. Just when we were to enter we were told we could advance over the open, and up went our spirits with a bound, for it meant that the Huns, who hitherto had been established within rifle shot of where we stood, must have been routed from their dens.[207]

The advance over the open was made necessary because the communication trenches had become clogged with wounded men returning from the front. The 4th Camerons formed up in artillery formation and proceeded to advance under enemy shellfire. It had been decided that 21 Brigade was to be split to assist the attack of 20 and 22 Brigades. The Yorkshires and Camerons would go to the left to help 22 Brigade at Cité St Elie and the

Quarries while the Wiltshires and Bedfords would make for the ground held by 20 Brigade in front of Hulluch. The advance over the open was not easy, nor was it quick. Captain Ian Mackay, of D Company, 4th Cameron Highlanders, described the advance:

> At one point we had to lie down in extended order for nearly two hours. We had a few casualties there but it was miraculous how we did not suffer heavily as shells and bullets were absolutely flying about. One shell landed in my Company and knocked out several Beauly boys though not seriously I hope. A fellow lying next to me got a bullet, whack on his entrenching tool, which saved his life. McErlich's Company[208] was in front of me and at one time I went forward to speak to him and while we were standing together a bullet ploughed up the ground between us. Bullets were going pat into the ground all round about. At last we got the order to move on and this advance was the finest thing I have seen here yet.[209]

The 4th Camerons had been detailed to support the Yorkshires but in their eagerness to advance had gone ahead of the other battalion. The 4th Cameron Highlanders' war diary recorded that up until this point the battalion had received about twelve casualties and had not yet reached the old British front line trenches. By 10.30am, the Camerons and Yorkshires took up positions in the old British front line and support trenches with the Bedfords and Wiltshires on their right. The order to advance was received at 11.30am.

> Over our own old parapet we went, and through our wire, across to the front German trench. What a

> forest of fierce looking wire and what cavernous dens of trenches they had! We marvelled as we hurriedly passed these how we were ever able to expel the occupants of such strongholds. On every side we came across dead and wounded, British and German, and every yard of ground bore the marks of war – shell holes, tangles of wire, broken shells in hundreds, rifles with fixed bayonets etc, etc.[210]

Captain Mackay wrote of the advance:

> It was a battle picture of the good old kind. We were advancing up an immense plain which sloped upwards to the ridge beyond which lay the village of Hulluch which you will have seen mentioned in the papers. All across the plain our troops were advancing in long lines. The air was dense with smoke and shells, and the row was awful. On our right our artillery were galloping furiously into action in an advanced position, and on our left I saw through the smoke a party of horsemen riding across the plain. I think this was the General of our Division, Sir T. Capper, and his staff. By degrees line after line was absorbed into the firing line, and we swept over the old British trench and into the German trenches which had been captured that morning.[211]

The 2nd Yorkshires were making for the Quarries but again the 4th Cameron Highlanders overtook them and had to mark time in the open ground once more. While there, they saw a spectacle which filled them with regimental pride. The 5th Cameron Highlanders, part of the 9th (Scottish) Division on the left of the 7th Division, had attacked the Fosse 8 and Hohenzollern Redoubt positions. In the course of the attack, the telephone wire connecting the battalion with Brigade Headquarters was cut and communication lost. A lance corporal signaller, John Gilchrist of the 5th Camerons, climbed to the top of a slag-heap and used flags to relay a message. The story was reported in the *Inverness Courier*:

> Fosse 8 was some distance away on their right[212] front and as they lay waiting they saw a figure appear on a slag-heap near Fosse 8 and wave a white flag. Thinking this was a token of surrender hoisted by the Germans occupying Fosse 8, the 4th Camerons burst into a loud cheer. In a moment or two, however, it became apparent that the solitary figure on the slag-heap was signalling, and presently one of the 4th signallers spelt out the words 'Seaforth and Cameron Brigade'. The 5th Camerons and 7th Seaforths had captured Fosse 8 and other means of communication gone a heroic signaller was risking his life in order that this important news reach headquarters. The admiration of the 4th Camerons for the gallant act was unbounded, and it was with great regret they learned later that the daring signaller had paid for his bravery with his life.[213]

The 2nd Yorkshires soon caught up with the Camerons and the attack continued on towards the Quarries, which they reached at midday. 22 Brigade had dug in round the eastern edge of the Quarries with the 2nd Queens at the northern end, the South Staffords on their right, followed by the Warwicks. The Yorkshires tried to advance on Cité St Elie but were stopped by fire from Puits Trench and Puits 13. They retired to the Quarries and also dug in. At 1.30pm, the Camerons came up in support and extended the left of the Yorkshires along the eastern edge of the Quarries, and deployed two platoons to the right of the Yorkshires to get in touch with the Wiltshires in Gun Trench.

Captain Ian Mackay did not enjoy the time spent in the Quarries. He wrote to his mother after the battle:

> We spent two or three hours in those Quarries and it was not a pleasant spot as the Germans were shelling it heavily and in addition there was a perfect deluge of rain which wet us through. Scott, one of my officers was hit here and we are very sorry to see that he died of his wound. He was a delightful fellow whom I got very fond of. Macmillan was hit here too, but as a matter of fact he was doing duty with A Company at the time. We were in these old Quarries until after dark and were tired and wet and preparing for a miserable night.[214]

The men of the 4th Camerons – along with the Yorkshires and the three battalions of 22 Brigade – lined the side of the Quarries. The position was described by the author of the *Inverness Courier* souvenir booklet:

> The Quarries are in form like a flat bottomed square basin, 300 to 400 yards wide, the sides some 30 feet high and very steep and the bottom severely dented into lumps and cavities, especially at one corner, which contained not only pits 100 feet deep but had subterranean tunnels connecting these. Their own length from the

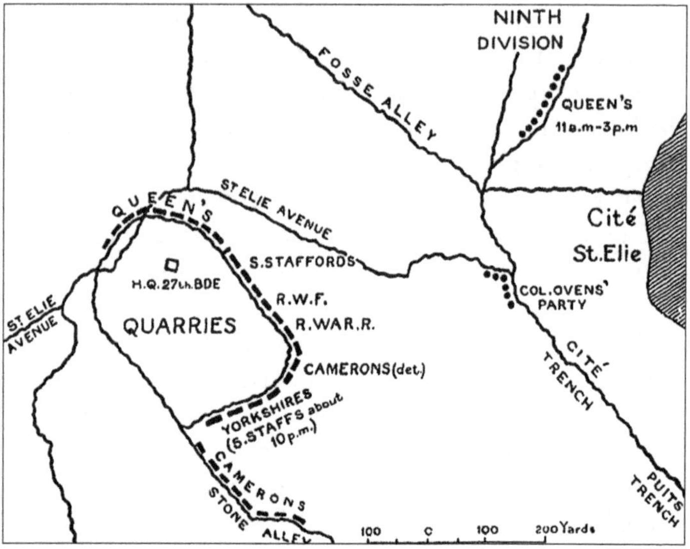

The Quarries Position at the Battle of Loos, 26 September 1915. (*7th Division History*)

> brim, our men cut a bankette on which they could stand and sweep the plain in front with their eyes and, if necessary, their fire.[215]

On the right of the attack, the 2nd Bedfords and the 2nd Wiltshires had advanced to support 20 Brigade in front of Hulluch. By the time they reached the weakly held Gun Trench, the Wiltshires had lost seven officers and 200 men and the Bedfords had lost their commanding officer, adjutant and all four company commanders, along with over 200 men.[216]

After nightfall, 21 Brigade reorganised and stabilised the line. The 2nd Royal Scots Fusiliers crossed from the old British front line trench where they had been kept in reserve and took up a position in the old German front line. The 2nd Wiltshires and 4th Camerons were withdrawn to Breslau Trench in reserve to the 2nd Bedfords in Gun Trench and the 2nd Yorkshires in Stone Alley. The commanders of the 7th Division had decided that Cité St Elie was too well defended by Puits Trench for another attack to be successful, and had instead decided to push east past Hulluch in conjunction with the 1st Division on their right.[217] Captain Ian Mackay told of the reorganisation:

> Suddenly we got the order to go back to the old German trench for the night, as we were to attack a village the next day. We had only just got back to the old German trench when the Germans attacked the Quarries and bombed out the regiment holding them. We tried to get some rest as we were all pretty done, but about 2am we got orders to go back and recapture the Quarries. We fell in and were just starting off when the order was again cancelled and we spent the night in the old German trench.[218]

In the withdrawal from the Quarries the sector vacated by the Camerons was not properly covered by the 22 Brigade troops and the 2nd Yorkshires. The Divisional History suggests that the reason for this was the 7th Division command not realising that the 4th Camerons were covering front line positions in the first place, so when the Camerons were ordered to retire to Breslau Trench, no further orders were given to cover the gap. It suggests further that the view of the Camerons moving back under orders prompted some of the leaderless groups of men holding the Quarries to think that the order had been given for a general retirement, leaving a gap in the British line the German troops were bound to exploit.[219]

The Germans recaptured the Quarries and in the process captured Brigadier-General Clarence Bruce, commander of 27 Brigade of the 9th Division, and fortified the position with machine guns. The right hand sector of the 7th Division's front, held by 20 Brigade in front of Gun Trench, was also attacked. The Gordon Highlanders and the Devons fell back on Gun Trench and re-established a new front line. The 7th Division had no reserves with which to mount a counter attack, so First Army sent the 9th Norfolks from IV Corps to take charge of the assault. They attacked at 6.45am and lost over 400 killed and wounded.

Before leaving the Quarries, the 4th Camerons had sent a ration party back to the British lines to bring up supplies. A detail of men were posted to watch the kit of the ration party and when the orders came to retire these men were left behind. When the Germans counterattacked the men – Privates Patrick Fleming, Peter Ross, Walter Cassingham, Kenneth Sutherland, William Haslam and Allan Cameron – were taken prisoner. Evidence suggests that they may have been wounded when the Germans attacked. Certainly Private Haslam received a pension after the war for gunshot wounds to the right forearm and shoulder and the left hand. Captain Mackay wrote of the capture:

> When we got the orders to leave the Quarries that night we had to leave a few men behind in charge of some equipment. Some of these fellows are missing and I think must have been taken prisoner when the Germans retook the Quarries later on. Two fellows in my Company were taken prisoner but escaped. One of

> them was being escorted off by two Germans but came across two Yorkshires who were on patrol. These chaps attacked the Germans and put them to flight, leaving their prisoner.[220]

In the morning of 26 September, the 7th Division was ordered to stay put and consolidate the gains they had made. Captain Mackay wrote to his parents in Inverness:

> Next day [Sunday] we spent in that trench, or rather in a comfortless trench in front of it, and from this we saw a spirited attack on the Quarries by fresh regiments brought up. The machine gun fire they had to face was terrific and we had to 'duck our heids' to avoid it. Donald Ross came along the line and he and I had a little reconnaissance as we suspected Germans being in a communication trench quite near. While on this job a shell burst near to us and a bit landed on the top of his head and cut it, although not badly. I bound him up and he remained on duty. Next day he had one finger and a half blown off by a bullet and I expect he is now in England. He passed me as he was going back – quite cheery. I am very sorry he is gone as he was an excellent fellow.[221]

That same day, Lieutenant Angus Urquhart, second in command of A Company, was killed. Thus far, the 4th Cameron Highlanders had lost five officers: Lieutenants Henry J. Scott and George MacMillan of D Company, Lieutenant Archibald MacDonald of B Company and Lieutenants Donald Ross and Angus Urquhart of A Company. In addition, over 70 men lay dead and wounded on the field.

In the evening, the 4th Camerons relieved the 2nd Wiltshires in Breslau Avenue and Stone Alley with the Wiltshires moving to support them. The 2nd Yorkshires were on the battalion's left towards the Quarries and the Royal Scots Fusiliers were on the right in Gun Trench. Captain Ian Mackay was not impressed with the standard of the Camerons' new position:

> The trench we occupied was of course a mere scrape in the ground and we worked hard all night to improve it and get deeper in. There were of course no dugouts and we had to lie in the open trench and to add to our discomfort it rained incessantly and was bitterly cold at night. The Germans were continually making counter-attacks – not across the open but down communication trenches with bombs.[222]

Every one of the German counterattacks were repulsed by the sharp shooting and bravery of the men of the 4th Camerons. In this battle, as in all of the battalion's actions, the men looked to the example set by James MacBean of Achnabeachan.

The *Inverness Courier's* souvenir booklet described the attack before MacBean's intervention:

> The most determined attack along this sap was made on Wednesday morning. Just after 'stand down' when all seemed quiet, and the men were being detailed for various duties, there was a tremendous din all along the enemy front, and the sap was practically hidden from view by the smoke of bursting bombs. The Huns apparently thought they could overwhelm our men

> by mere force of numbers, and they rushed along, literally sowing bombs, forward and to the right and left. A Company's bombers had been happily reinforced by their comrades in D and C Companies, and the little party on guard stood their ground without flinching, and threw their bombs with coolness and precision. Those men would not have budged an inch even if the Huns succeeded in getting right up to them.[223]

Captain Mackay told of Sergeant MacBean's actions:

> Our fellows were hard pressed and the Germans got up to our block and two of them were scrambling over, but both were shot by MacBean. This gave our fellows time to rally and they bombed the beggars back.[224]

MacBean in turn scrambled over the block in the trench and even though he was wounded, aided with the defence and killed several more of the German snipers who were lying in long grass covering the attack.[225] For his gallantry, Jimmie MacBean was awarded the Distinguished Conduct Medal. In this German attack the Grenade Officer, Lieutenant Morrison, was wounded and all his non-commissioned officers in the grenade platoon were either killed or wounded.

On 27 September, the Germans opened up a furious artillery barrage on the 4th Cameron Highlanders in Breslau Avenue and Stone Alley, supported by rifle fire from the Quarries. The enemy massed in front of Stone Alley and attacked that trench at a position called Point 54, located at the extreme southern end of the Quarries.[226]

The commanding officer of the 2nd Wiltshire Regiment, in support, thought the Camerons were being overwhelmed and sent two companies over the top to assist the Highlanders. Together, the men of the two battalions fought off the German assault. The Wiltshires remained in the Camerons' trench which made the position much stronger. After dark the Wiltshires reorganised and took over the part of the line on the left of the Camerons formerly held by the 2nd Yorkshires.

All the next day the Germans repeated their attacks on the 4th Camerons' position, particularly that of B Company holding the left portion of Gun Trench. One enemy shell exploded in the doorway of the German dugout being used as B Company Headquarters, killing Captain John F. MacLaren, in temporary command of the Company, and eight of his men. Lieutenant James Park and Lieutenant Harold Law, in command of the Machine Gun Section and six other men were wounded. While tending to the wounded from the shell explosion, snipers picked off members of B Company. One such man was Lance Corporal Duncan MacDonald who was carrying a wounded man to safety when he was killed.

B Company was particularly badly hit during the battle. A Nairn soldier, recently arrived with the August draft of replacements, described the period spent in Gun Trench:

> We were shelled continually, often with very large shells, and it is regretted that many Nairnshire lads were killed or wounded, as it was B Company that was in that particular part of the trench. The enemy on four or five occasions attacked us from a sap with bombs, but every time they were driven back,

> suffering a good many casualties, whereas we had only two slightly wounded.[227]

On 29 September, the Germans again tried to bomb their way up communication trenches leading from the Quarries and Cité St Elie to the 4th Camerons' trenches between Points 39 and 54 in Stone Alley. Again they were repulsed. Captain Ian Mackay, writing to his mother after the battle, described the time in these trenches:

> We spent three days and nights in this trench and were pretty fed up with it. All the time attacks were going on all round about and the Germans were always hammering away at our line. On the third night we were relieved and went back to the old German trench and remained there one day.[228]

The 4th Cameron Highlanders were taken out of the front line at Gun Trench and Stone Alley and relieved by the 2nd Bedfords at midnight on 29 September. During the relief, 2nd Lieutenant Donald John MacIver from Stornoway on the Isle of Lewis was shot in the thigh by an explosive bullet. At first his wound was not thought to be serious, but there were complications and he died on 14 October 1915.

The 4th Camerons spent the following day in the old German front line and support trenches awaiting the order to get back into the thick of the action. The order came quickly as the Germans had recaptured a 100-yard stretch of Gun Trench at Block 39, to the north of the Hulluch Road. The Camerons readied themselves and set off to support the 2nd Bedfords in expelling the Germans from the position. The *Souvenir Booklet of the Inverness Courier* described the 4th Camerons' advance:

> As cool and steady as if it were merely a 'night operation' on the Morrich Mhor or in the bracing hills of Badenoch, our men went forward, ready for whatever was required of them. The front line was, however, able to deal with the enemy and the Camerons spent that night and the next day in a shallow trench, which afforded neither proper sitting nor standing room.[229]

Writing to the *Inverness Courier*, an unidentified Nairn soldier was keen to heap praise on his colleagues:

> Since we were relieved we hear that the Germans have captured by bombing a small portion of the trench at that particular part, so it says a lot for the Cameron bombers, most of whom were in action with bombs for the first time, that they were able to hold them back.[230]

One section of the 4th Cameron Highlanders' bombers was seconded to the 2nd Royal Scots Fusiliers and the commanding officer of that battalion reported that they had done good work in removing the Germans from Gun Trench. Their work on this occasion must have been as successful as their conduct during the rest of the battle. For their efforts at Loos, three of the battalion bombers were awarded the Distinguished Conduct Medal for their bravery. The medal citation for Private Donald Henderson reads:

> Private Henderson accompanied a non-commissioned officer in an attack on an enemy communication trench,

> driving back the enemy, and capturing a supply of enemy bombs, which he used to pursue the enemy. Throughout the operations he displayed the most fearless courage and devotion to duty.

Thirty-five-year-old car driver Lance Corporal John McDonnell was the non-commissioned officer mentioned above. His medal citation reads:

> For conspicuous bravery on the 27th September 1915 in front of Hulluch. Our bombing party having been temporarily withdrawn from our block in the communication trench near Point 39, and the bombardment suddenly ceasing, the Germans captured the block. Lance Corporal McDonnell at once led a determined attack, drove the Germans back, recaptured a supply of our own bombs, and using these, pursued the enemy back beyond their own block, killing several of them. His bravery and leadership were most conspicuous throughout the operations.

Private Charles Nightingale, one of the London Scots, also received the Distinguished Conduct Medal:

> For conspicuous gallantry when he crossed our block and advanced along a sap to the enemy block, which he discovered was held by one man and one bomber, at whom he threw a bomb. He was able to make a useful report.

On the night of 1 October 1915, the 4th Cameron Highlanders were relieved from their position by the 2nd Worcesters and retired to the village of Vermelles to take stock.

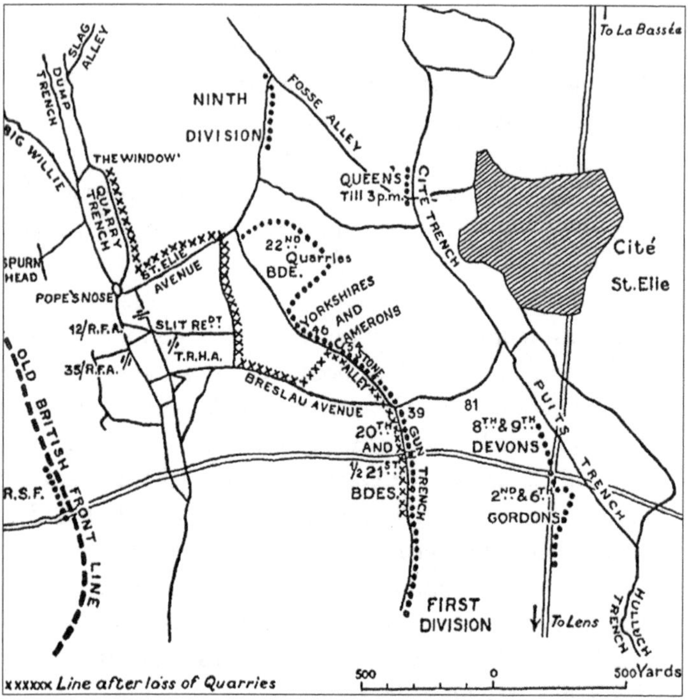

The Situation at the Battle of Loos after the loss of the Quarries, 26 September 1915. (*7th Division History*)

At the end of seven days in the front and support line trenches during the Battle of Loos, the 4th Cameron Highlanders had suffered two officers killed – Captain John MacLaren and Lieutenant Angus Urquhart – and Lieutenant Henry Scott and 2nd Lieutenant Donald MacInver would die of their wounds. Seven more – Captain Peter Cram, Lieutenants James Park, Harold Law, Donald Ross, George MacMillan and Donald Morrison – were wounded. The men faired equally badly.

The Regimental Journal of the Cameron Highlanders, the *79th News,* published casualty lists from the Battle of Loos in the January 1916 issue. It is unique amongst the other casualty lists as it describes the nature of wounds inflicted upon the men of the 4th Camerons. From these lists it can be ascertained that, in terms of wounded men, A Company lost 26 men to gunshot wounds, eight to unknown injuries, five to shrapnel wounds, one with a crushed back and one with bruising. The Nairn men of B Company lost 19 men to gunshot wounds, 7 to unknown injuries, 3 to shrapnel wounds, 2 to bruising and 1 from shell shock. C Company lost 17 men to gunshot wounds, 4 to unknown injuries, 3 to shrapnel wounds and 1 to bayonet wounds. The Skye and Beauly men of D Company lost 18 to gunshot wounds, 10 to unknown injuries, 2 to shrapnel wounds and 1 with cuts. In addition to these men, four men of B Company, and three each in C and D Companies were sent back suffering from the effects of poison gas.

In total, the battalion had lost 4 officers and 48 men killed or died of their wounds and 7 officers and 139 men wounded, as well as 6 men captured. The 4th Cameron Highlanders had made their way through another tough battle, the last of 1915 for the British Army, but at a price. The 7th Division as a whole had lost 227 officers and 5199 men killed, wounded and missing.[231]

In the evening of 1 October, the battalion marched back to their previous billets in Le Preol, arriving about 5.00am on the following day. They remained there until the night of 4 October when they received orders to relieve the 2nd Warwickshire Regiment and the South Staffordshires in a position from the sap R1 to the Vermelles to Auchy road, in front of the village of Cambrin. The 4th Camerons remained here in the front line trenches, but not under fire, until 11 October.

This was to be the 4th Cameron Highlanders' routine until the end of the year, as the onset of winter stopped any further meaningful attacks in 1915. They were not to be idle, however, as preparations had to be made to renew the fighting in 1916.

9

The Winter Campaign, 11 October 1915–31 March 1916

On 5 October, at Le Preol, Lieutenant John Clift joined the 4th Cameron Highlanders with a draft of 50 replacements from the 3/4th Camerons back in Scotland. They did not make up one third of the number of men the battalion lost at the Battle of Loos.

While at Le Preol, a Court of Enquiry was ordered by Lieutenant-Colonel Hector Fraser to find out the truth of the circumstances of the wounding of 19-year-old Private Edwin Middlecote on 6 October. Captain John MacPherson, Lieutenant Neil McArthur and 2nd Lieutenant Max Roemmele made up the panel that would judge whether his wounds were self-inflicted. Middlecote had claimed that the Corporal of Number 3 Machine Gun Team had sent him to Cambrin for water. While going down a communication trench he thought he would take a shortcut over the open ground. As he was doing so he sustained a gunshot wound to the hand.

Middlecote scrambled back into the trench and ran to get help. He stated that the first soldier he met told him to abandon his rifle, which he did and proceeded to a dressing station. Before he could get there he met an officer, Lieutenant Frederick Hobson, the 21 Brigade Signals Officer, who bandaged his wounded hand.

Hobson later reported that he became suspicious of the whereabouts of Middlecote's rifle and went to investigate. Farther up the trench, close to a recently opened cover of a field dressing, was a rifle lying in a recess in the trench beside a spent cartridge. Both Lieutenant Hobson and one of his men were of the opinion that the bullet had been recently fired and they also noticed some spots of blood on the barrel of the rifle. This, and Private Middlecote's agitated manner when he met him, led Lieutenant Hobson to gather up the rifle, cartridge and field dressing and report the incident to Major Garden Duff of the 4th Cameron Highlanders.

The first person to testify at the Court of Enquiry was Lieutenant William Baird of the Royal Army Medical Corps, attached to 21 Field Ambulance. He gave evidence that, in his opinion, the bullet that wounded Middlecote had to have been fired from long range, as one fired from close-up would have caused significantly more damage.

Private Middlecote himself came to testify before the Court of Enquiry. He claimed that the rifle found was indeed his rifle but that he had only just received it, his usual rifle having been taken by a colleague. Middlecote swore that he had not looked at the rifle since he received it and did not know if it had been fired before he got it. He also stated that during his period of training in Inverness he had been stationed in the Orderly Room and had not received much actual training.

Could this explain his agitated state and abandoning of his rifle? The Court of Enquiry thought so, and so did Lieutenant-Colonel Hector Fraser who agreed with the medical opinion that Private Middlecote's wound was caused by a long distance rifle shot. Private Edwin Middlecote was admonished and evacuated on account of his injury.

The 4th Camerons were relieved by the 2nd Wiltshire Regiment on 11 October and marched to billets in the nearby village of Annequin. Two days later, the 12th and 46th Divisions attacked the German trenches to the south of the Camerons' position. The men of 21 Brigade were readied to support any breakthrough in the German lines but in the end were not called upon. On 14 October, the 4th Camerons were again relieved from their supporting role and marched back to the reserve billets at Le Preol before marching to Cense La Vallee where they took on an intensive training programme, focusing particularly on bombing. From there, it was on to Bourecq and Bethune, where the battalion attended lectures by the company commanders on signalling, bombing and machine gunning, and spent their time on route marches, running parades and drill.

On 24 October 1915 a further batch of officers joined the 4th Camerons from the second line battalion back in Scotland. They were Captain Alexander MacBean, Lieutenants Alfred W.H. Cooper, George Johnson, Alfred Calder and Alistair Birnie, and 2nd Lieutenants James Smith, Archie Macrae, Benjamin Bartholomew, Hugh Henderson and Archibald R. Mackenzie. They were joined on 29 October by 2nd Lieutenant David Melville, recently promoted from the ranks. These officers were desperately needed to replace the eleven officers who had been killed or wounded at Loos. The composition of the battalion had completely changed since leaving Bedford eight months previously and the majority of the original Territorial Force officers had been killed, wounded or evacuated sick. The new make up of the battalion was as follows:

Lieutenant-Colonel Hector Fraser	Commanding Officer
Major Murdoch Beaton	Second in Command
Major Garden B. Duff	Adjutant
Major John Lockie	Quartermaster
Captain J.W. Wood (RAMC)	Medical Officer
Captain Rev. J. Campbell MacGregor	Chaplain
Captain John D. MacPherson	Transport Officer
Lieutenant A.W. Hughes	Machine Gun Officer

A Company

Captain Roderick McErlich	in command
Captain Ian T. Nelson	
Lieutenant John Clift	
Lieutenant George Johnson	
Lieutenant Alfred Calder	
2nd Lieutenant Hugh Henderson	

B Company

Captain Charles Campbell	in command
Lieutenant Max A. Roemmele	
Lieutenant William S. Valentine	
2nd Lieutenant James Smith	

C Company
Captain Alexander MacBean in command
Captain Hector Morison
Lieutenant William Cattanach
2nd Lieutenant Alistair Birnie
2nd Lieutenant Archibald R. Mackenzie
2nd Lieutenant David Melville

D Company
Captain Ian Mackay
Lieutenant Charles Douglas
Lieutenant Alfred W.H. Cooper
2nd Lieutenant Benjamin Bartholomew
2nd Lieutenant Archie J. Macrae

On 24 October, the 4th Cameron Highlanders marched to their old fighting ground at Givenchy, and took over trenches from the 2nd Border Regiment. Their front line was from the Shrine to Grenadier Road with A Company on the right front and B Company on the left. C Company was in support in New Cut and Poppy Redoubt and D Company was in reserve in Windy Corner. The trenches in this sector were in a very poor state and the Camerons had to work round the clock to repair them. This work had to be done in particularly trying conditions, as not only were the German snipers in the Crater position only a few yards from the Cameron lines, but the weather took a turn for the worse with frequent rain and sleet. The men who had arrived in the August, September and October drafts were most affected by the conditions, with over 20 of them being sent to hospital sick between 24 October and the end of the year. The majority of the men of these drafts had come from the towns and cities of Yorkshire, the 3/4th Cameron Highlanders' recruitment areas, and were clearly not as used to inclement weather as their Scottish colleagues.

Despite the best efforts of the 4th Camerons, the trenches remained in a fairly bad state during the tour and the constant wet weather not only hampered the men's progress, but also caused the collapse of several parapets in the Camerons' area. In some areas of the Givenchy sector they reported that there was several feet of water at the bottom of the trench. The enemy, for the most part, were quiet, except on 25 and 27 October when they launched twelve shells each day into the Camerons' support trenches. The battalion had orders not to return fire, so the situation soon returned to normal. On 28 October, German snipers destroyed nine of the battalion's periscopes, used to survey the German trenches, and this time the Camerons did respond, causing an equal amount of damage to their enemies' periscopes.

On 29 October, the 4th Cameron Highlanders were relieved by the 2nd Battalion of the Queen's Regiment and marched back to billets in Hinges, a distance of seven miles. While there, Lieutenant-Colonel Hector Fraser, who had been with the battalion since 1899, was ordered home on special leave. He would not return, instead being given command of a reserve battalion of the Argyll and Sutherland Highlanders. Command passed to Major Murdoch Beaton who was promoted Temporary Lieutenant-Colonel and Captain Ian Mackay was promoted second in command of the battalion, with the temporary rank of Major. The 4th Camerons received more bad news on 30 October when the Adjutant, Major Garden Duff, left to take up a new position as the commanding officer of the 8th Black Watch. He was succeeded as Adjutant by 29-year-old solicitor Captain Neil McArthur. Major Duff in particular was a severe loss to the 4th Camerons. The *Regimental History of the Queen's Own Cameron Highlanders* described his leaving:

> All ranks regretted very much the departure of Major Duff. In the two and a half years he had spent with the 4th Battalion he had taken a firm grip of their affection and esteem; and it was generally recognised that the high state of efficiency attained by the battalion was not a little due to his energetic devotion to its interests.[232]

The 4th Camerons remained at Hinges until 1 November, supplying a working party of 250 men for employment with the Royal Engineers before marching to Les Harisoirs, two miles away. There they undertook another training programme in signalling, machine gunning and bombing. The Camerons stayed in Les Harisoirs until 4 November when they went back to alternative billets in Le Preol. In the meantime, further drafts arrived from the 3/4th Cameron Highlanders: 26 men on 29 October and another 84 on 14 November.

The intensive programme of training the previous week was in preparation for an attack on 7 November at Givenchy, in which the 4th Cameron Highlanders were to be one of the leading battalions. The preparations were almost complete when the attack was called off. Instead, on 5 November, a composite company of 130 men under Captain Charles Campbell went to Givenchy to support the 2nd Bedfords in anticipation of a German counter-attack on the explosion of a British mine in the area. In the event, the Germans did not attack following the explosion and the Bedfords occupied the mine crater with few problems. Captain Campbell and his men rejoined the battalion on the following day.

From 6 to 11 November, the 4th Camerons supplied men for working parties every day. On one of these they sustained their only casualties of the tour when 2nd Lieutenant Donald Finlayson was seriously wounded along with two of his men. On the same day Lieutenant Archibald R. Mackenzie managed to injure himself when he fell off a baggage wagon.

On 12 November, the battalion was again quartered in Les Harisoirs, where the latest draft of reinforcements was inspected by Brigadier-General Berners. That week, the battalion war diary, written for the first time by Captain Neil McArthur, started giving weekly statistics of the men coming and going from the battalion, as well as a weekly total of men currently serving with the 4th Camerons. For the week ending on 13 November, the war diary shows that twelve other ranks had proceeded to hospital sick and eight had returned. In addition to these, one officer, Lieutenant Finlayson, had been wounded and another, Lieutenant Mackenzie, had been injured, and one man had been sent to the base to be discharged and another to be commissioned. The total strength of the battalion was 28 officers and 545 other ranks. This low strength was to cause problems for the battalion in the future.

At 8.30am on 15 November, the battalion paraded and marched five miles to billets in Essars and Ferme Duroi, where the men got the chance to have a much needed wash. The following day the battalion took over trenches to the south of Givenchy from the 6th Gordon Highlanders, with A Company in the front line between points Willow RA and Willow RH, B Company in Strathcona Walk and Orchard Redoubt and C and D Companies in Windy Corner. During this tour of the Givenchy trenches every man in the battalion was issued with thigh-high gumboots, which gave some protection against the horrible weather conditions and the flooded trenches. The 4th Camerons also supplied four officers and 100 men to assist the Royal Engineers and 36 men working to keep the Glasgow Street, King's Road and Herts Avenue trenches in repair. The battalion remained in these trenches until 20 November. The only action during this tour was on the night of 18/19 November when patrols from the 4th Camerons heard German working parties outside the enemy trenches repairing the barbed wire. They reported this to headquarters and the battalion opened fire, causing several casualties. That week the battalion lost 15 men to hospital, 2 with trench foot, and 1 man was sent to the base as he was underage. Only one man was wounded during this tour. The weekly statistics in the battalion war diary record the addition to the strength of the last draft of 84 men, which gave the battalion an effective fighting strength of 27 officers and 618 men.

The 4th Camerons were relieved by the 7th King's Liverpool Regiment on 21 November and marched to billets in Essars, where Captain Archibald Fletcher – who had been invalided sick earlier in the year – rejoined the battalion, along with the newly commissioned 2nd Lieutenant Illytd Mackintosh. Captain Fletcher was posted to D Company. Major Mackay described Captain Fletcher's readjustment to life back in the trenches:

> I am very glad to have him, the day we arrived we went into the trenches and he was very miserable in the wet and cold and wished he had come out for the summer

> campaign. I had a good laugh at his expense one night. We were spending the night in a broken down house behind the firing line. We occupied what was the kitchen, I had a little room off it with a straw bed in it. When I went to turn in I found a large cat on the bed. I pursued it out and it went bounding past Fletcher who was lying down in the kitchen, with its tail well in the air. Fletcher was just dozing off but he saw the apparition in the dim light and jumped up and said 'Good heavens, what's that![233]

On the following day, C and D Companies marched back to the trenches to take possession of keeps at Le Plantin, with the remainder of the battalion joining them at 5.00am the next morning. C Company took over the front line trenches from Grenadier Road to Fife Junction and D Company moved into support in George Street while A Company garrisoned Grouse Butts and the Lees Redoubt. B Company was in reserve in Le Plantin and Redoubt B. Again the battalion had to carry out repairs to the trenches, but this had to be done mainly at night as the position was overlooked by the German trenches on Givenchy Ridge. Captain Neil McArthur, writing in the war diary, described the poor state of the trenches:

> Excepting the portion of Fife Road between Grouse Butts and George Street all trenches were found all fallen in unserviceable. Long stretches of the front line trench had also been allowed to fall into disrepair and become waterlogged, only a few isolated parts being capable of occupation. The unoccupied parts were patrolled at night. The George Street support trench was also in disrepair and waterlogged and only a few of the dugouts

> were serviceable. Only 2 dugouts in the front line. All relief and fatigue parties had to move across the open to the front line and only at night except by portion of Fife Road above mentioned.[234]

Major Ian Mackay wrote to his mother on 2 December of the trials of this latest tour:

> We went into trenches on Givenchy Hill and had a spell of it there getting out for one night. Next day we went back again to trenches a little further north. The trenches were in a very bad state, and it was awfully cold. We had reliefs amongst ourselves, the companies not in the firing line being in support trenches behind. Except for the vigilance required in the front trenches, there is not much different as the support trenches are often nearly as wet and muddy as the firing line, and are often shelled as much or more than the front line. Altogether we were in 16 days with one night out, and we had our clothes off only once during that time, and although not actually in the firing line all the time we were always within rifle and shell fire.[235]

The men worked for over a week trying to improve the trenches in the Givenchy sector. The days and nights were freezing cold, with snow and hard frost. By 28 November it seems some progress had been made as the battalion war diary recorded that the front line now had a continuous parapet except for a 50-yard section on the right of the battalion. The whole of the George Street trench and the majority of the old British front line trenches had been laid with floorboards and the water level was lowered by pumps and a new drainage system.

On 29 November the Germans began to shell the 4th Cameron Highlanders' position, resulting in four casualties. In addition 2nd Lieutenant Hugh Henderson was taken to hospital with an injured leg and 2nd Lieutenant Archibald R. Mackenzie went to hospital sick.

The only death of the tour was 22-year-old Private Roderick J. Mackenzie. Private Mackenzie worked as a Headquarters Orderly and was killed while taking a message along a road some distance behind the firing line. Major Ian Mackay described his burial:

> We sent for our padre and as my company were in one of the back trenches at the time I went to the funeral in a little British cemetery near a ruined farm not far from the firing line. It was a regular Sir John Moore burial as our guns were thundering at the time and while we were at the grave the Germans sent over several shrapnel and high explosives into a field near us, which burst unpleasantly near us.[236]

Major Mackay also described the problems with the newly issued gumboots:

> On going into trenches we are now equipped with long waders – every officer and man as they are needed, as one is frequently up to the middle in mud and water. I wore riding breeks which are more convenient for the waders than the kilt, but our fellows invented an ingenious idea of sewing two sandbags together like trousers and tucking the kilt into them. The effect was very amusing as it gave them all enormous posteriors!! To get to the front line we had to go over the open and it was an awful

> journey as the nights were pitch dark, ditches and shell holes numerous and the mud deep and clinging and one could hardly move one's legs at all. Fellows often got absolutely stuck and had to be hauled out, often leaving their waders in the mud behind them. They would also sometimes disappear in a shell hole and get drenched to the skin up to the neck.[237]

This ten-day spell in the trenches was described by Major Mackay as being the most difficult time the battalion had had since arriving in France in February, with the exception of the week spent in front of Hulluch during the Battle of Loos. Even though no major battle was being fought, the general conditions made for a miserable time. And, of course, the Germans were not idle:

> During the time we were in we had all kinds of weather, rain first of all, then one night a fall of snow, from that it turned into keen frost and then to a rapid thaw. The artillery of both sides were very active, especially ours and they gave the Germans a great pounding every day. The Germans occasionally landed a shell in our trench, and while my company were up we twice had our parapet blown in. Another day our doctor was doing a round of the trenches and was in a dugout when a shell blew the whole thing in and buried the medical man, he was after some time extricated declaring he was dead![238]

The Medical Officer in question was Captain J.W. Wood of the Royal Army Medical Corps, who had joined the battalion in August when Captain Robert Lindsay was transferred to Number 11 General Hospital in Camiers. Captain Wood spent six days in hospital before rejoining the battalion. He was none the worse for his experience.

On 30 November, three mines were exploded in the Givenchy sector, two British and one German.

> They were about 600 yards from us but I thought we were going up too as there was a rumble under us and a terrific tremble of the earth. The last one to go off was after daylight and we had an interesting view of what went on. The mine went off on the ridge on our right and against the skyline we could see our troops running up to occupy the crater and digging themselves in. A little in front of them we also saw in the skyline the Germans. They were quite near each other but not in full view of each other owing to the mounds thrown up by the explosions. We however could see both sides in profile on the skyline. We saw the Germans raising their rifles to shoot at our men when they could see them and we started peppering them from our trench down below and we made them keep their heads down, later on we saw a stretcher party leaving that part. Whether it was due to our fire or to the mine I cannot say. The incident relieved the monotony of trench warfare and our men got very excited over it.[239]

On 1 December 1915, the 4th Cameron Highlanders were relieved by the 18th Royal Fusiliers after nine straight days in the most trying of conditions, and marched four miles to billets in Bethune. The battalion war diary entry for that day recorded that during the last tour the battalion had used 10,000 sandbags, 300 floorboards, ten coils of trench barbed wire and 40 riveting frames to shore up the leaking trenches. The following day the 4th Camerons marched nine miles to the village of Busnes where the battalion bathed in the 7th Divisional baths. The move to Busnes was as a result of the 7th Division being pulled out of the fighting line. It was to be transferred to the Third Army area of operations in the south, around the River Somme.

Major Ian Mackay was glad to be leaving the Nord Pas de Calais battlefields for the Somme:

> We hear that things are less active there, and the country more interesting, and trenches better. We have made a lot of friends round about here and are sorry to leave them, but are glad to be finished with these trenches here, which are bad ones and have unsavoury recollections for us.[240]

Whilst writing to his parents in Inverness, Major Mackay told them of the last time they passed through the village of Le Preol, where they had been billeted for much of the time in this sector:

> When on the march here the other day we passed through a village we were billeted in for a fortnight in the summer and where we had a royal procession through the village, all the people coming out to see us. They got very excited when they recognised and shouted out the name 'Ha Alastair', 'Jackie', 'Monsieur le Capitaine'. I was riding at the end of the battalion and when we got near the yard the horses had been in I let the reins hang loose on my horse's neck to see if she would remember the place. As soon as we came up to it she broke away from the column and wanted to turn in,

> which I thought very remarkable considering the billets she has been in since then.[241]

At 12.30pm on 6 December, the 27 officers and 611 men of the 4th Cameron Highlanders boarded trains at Lillers station which they left at just before 4.00pm. The journey took them through Chocques, Doullens, St Pol and Hangest sur Somme before arriving at Saleux and marching eight miles to their new billets in Saisseval. The arrival in Saisseval marked the end of Major Ian Mackay's letters home from the front line. He developed pneumonia and was invalided to hospital on 7 December. Major Mackay spent two months in hospital in France before being transferred back to the 3/4th Cameron Highlanders in Yorkshire to regain his strength. Whilst there he was reunited with his brother William, who was serving as Signals Officers for the Reserve Highland Division.

Major Ian Mackay served with the 3/4th Camerons until August 1917 when he was posted to the 6th Cameron Highlanders in France. He was killed in action on 28 March 1918, during the Battle of Arras. *The Regimental Records of the Cameron Highlanders* described his last moments:

> Above all others Captain Ian Mackay of the 4th Battalion, who was unfortunately killed in the fighting, performed such valorous services that his name was put forward for a posthumous award of the Victoria Cross. The award, however, was not granted. The particular act for which the award was sought was witnessed and testified to by several of the NCOs. About 1pm on the afternoon of March 28th the enemy were attacking the sunken road when Captain Mackay

> discovered a Vickers gun set in position in front of a trench, its officer and team lying around, helpless casualties. Without considering possible cost, he rushed across the open, and, managing to reach the gun, he operated it single handed. Although the enemy infantry were only some thirty yards away, Captain Mackay succeeded in holding them up until his company retired to their new position. When he saw his men in their line he destroyed the gun by firing two shots through its mechanism before leaving the post. In addition to being a splendid leader of men, Captain Mackay had those sincere qualities that endear one to all, and his death was consequently deeply felt in the battalion. His gallant action on the afternoon of the 28th was undoubtedly the means of saving the lives of many of the men in his company. In the midst of the turmoil, and in the face of heavy odds, he steadied the men with the remark 'We are Highlanders; no retiring.'[242]

On 19 December 1915, 21 Brigade left the 7th Division, their place being taken by 91 Brigade from the 30th Division. It had been decided that whole brigades of New Army troops fresh from home would be attached to Regular Army divisions like the 7th, and the New Army divisions would get a brigade of battle hardened veterans. Once a few administrative changes had been made, 91 Brigade was composed of the 21st and 22nd Battalions of the Manchester Regiment fresh from England, and the 2nd Queen's Regiment and 2nd South Staffordshires from 22 Brigade.

The 4th Cameron Highlanders, however, were not to leave the 7th Division and were temporarily attached to the incoming 91 Brigade. It had been decided that, for the campaigns of 1916, all infantry brigades in the British Army were to be reduced to a strength of four battalions. For 91 Brigade, this meant the removal of their only Territorial Force battalion, the 4th Battalion Cameron Highlanders, who were ordered, along with the 6th Gordon Highlanders, also of the 7th Division, to rejoin their old comrades in the Highland Division.

At Saisseval, the 4th Cameron Highlanders embarked upon yet another rigorous programme of training, recorded in the war diary. From 9.00am to 11.15am, the men practised close order drill and handling of arms, while the subaltern officers and non-commissioned officers were drilled by the Regimental Sergeant Major, Joseph Price. From 11.30am until 12.30pm, the battalion was paraded by the Adjutant, Neil McArthur. After a break for lunch, they spent their time either on route marches or improving their fitness through a programme of athletics. The officers passed the afternoons by going on rides through the Somme countryside. In the evenings, the men attended lectures by their company officers and, on 14 December, the battalion took part in night operations over cross country.

While at Saisseval, several officers who had been sick or wounded returned to the battalion. Lieutenants Archibald R. Mackenzie and Hugh Henderson rejoined the battalion from hospital and Captain Angus Ross, the brother of the late CSM William Ross who died at Festubert, returned after being wounded at the Battle of Neuve Chapelle in March.

New Year 1916 was seen in by the 30 officers and 589 other ranks of the 4th Cameron Highlanders at their billets in Saisseval. New Year's Day was given as a day off, before the battalion assembled on 2 January for church services. On 7 January, the 4th Camerons completed their move back to the 51st (Highland) Division. They were posted to 154 Brigade, the old Argyll and Sutherland Brigade, alongside the 4th Seaforth Highlanders and the 4th and 5th Black Watch, based in the village of Rainneville, just north of Amiens. The 4th Camerons were finally back serving with Territorial Force troops in the Highland Division.

December 1915 and January 1916 saw Lieutenant-Colonel Murdoch Beaton, commanding the 4th Cameron Highlanders, make appeals to the 2/4th and 3/4th battalions back in Britain to send more recruits to the front. The 1/4th Battalion had been under strength for a front line unit since the Battle of Loos, but had received fewer replacements than some of its colleagues in the old 21 Brigade. The 4th Camerons received 15 officers and 146 other ranks between 1 October and 31 December 1915, which was comparable to the 2nd Battalion, the Royal Scots Fusiliers but far short of the 529 and 430 men received by the 2nd Battalion, the Yorkshire Regiment and the 2nd Bedfords respectively. Rumours were circulating that under-strength Territorial Force battalions were to be broken up or given tasks such as guarding the lines of communication, a fate which had befallen another Highland battalion, the 6th Gordons.

Historical Records of the Queen's Own Cameron Highlanders gives the impression that the 4th Camerons had been operating at a strength of under 500 men for some months, but this was not the case. Captain Neil McArthur's weekly statistical account of the strength of the battalion, enumerating the exact number of personnel, shows that in November 1915 the strength of the

4th Camerons fluctuated between 553 and 618 men, and in December between 591 and 611 men.

For the men of the 4th Cameron Highlanders, their time spent with 154 Brigade consisted of yet more training, and assisting with menial but necessary tasks, such as the detachment of three officers and 164 men to the Royal Engineers, making horse standings at Argoeuvres on 12 January. Although this detachment was temporary, there were many which were not, placing the battalion in even more danger of being withdrawn as a fighting force. It seemed the 4th Cameron Highlanders were to be a victim of Army administration rather than a lack of strength.

On 12 January 1916, while the battalion was training, they received word to send a party of 20 men to be permanently detached for work under the Royal Engineers, building accommodation billets. The Army High Command was also looking at ways of unifying the machine-gun sections of each battalion in a brigade into one company, and as a result Lieutenant A.W. Hughes, 2nd Lieutenant William S. Valentine and the Machine Gun Section along with the battalion transport personnel left to join 154 Brigade Machine Gun Company. This was a loss of 31 men which the 4th Camerons could ill afford. Lieutenant Charles Douglas was also soon to leave the battalion, being appointed to the newly created position of 154 Brigade Grenade Officer.

New officers were still joining the battalion, however. Second Lieutenants James MacDonald, Harold White, Charles MacGillivray, Charles H.S. Hunter and Harry A. Mackintosh all arrived in the last week of January and joined their companies. They were joined by 2nd Lieutenant Donald MacDonald, raised from the ranks of A Company, on 19 February. As of the middle of February, the officers of the battalion were as follows:

Lieutenant-Colonel Murdoch Beaton	in command
Captain Neil McArthur	Adjutant
Major John Lockie	Quartermaster
Captain J.W. Wood	Medical Officer
Captain J. Campbell Macgregor	Chaplain

A Company

Captain Roderick McErlich	in command
Captain Ian T. Nelson	
Lieutenant Alfred G. Calder	
Lieutenant John Clift	
Lieutenant George M.W. Johnson	
2nd Lieutenant Hugh F. Henderson	

B Company

Captain Charles Campbell	in command
Captain Hector M. Morison	
Lieutenant Max A. Roemmele	
Lieutenant Harry A. Mackintosh	
2nd Lieutenant James Smith	
2nd Lieutenant Illtyd Mackintosh	
2nd Lieutenant James MacDonald	

C Company

Captain Alexander H. MacBean	in command
Captain Angus Ross	
Lieutenant Alastair Birnie	
2nd Lieutenant Archibald R. Mackenzie	
2nd Lieutenant David Melville	
2nd Lieutenant Harold M. White	

D Company

Captain Archibald M. Fletcher in command
Lieutenant Alfred W.H. Cooper
Lieutenant William E. Cattanach
2nd Lieutenant Benjamin J. Bartholomew
2nd Lieutenant Archie J. Macrae
2nd Lieutenant Charles MacGillivray
2nd Lieutenant Charles Hunter

The new officers replaced ones who had to be evacuated due to illness and some, like Transport Officer James D. MacPherson, were struck off strength while sick on leave in England. According to the battalion war diary, in the first two months of 1916, the 4th Cameron Highlanders lost 21 men to hospital sick, 16 men came to the end of their Territorial Force service, six men were evacuated, five men commissioned from the ranks, two men discharged underage, one sent home to England, two transferred to the Machine Gun Corps and one man, Private Alfred Marshall, was killed as the result of an accident. Their total strength stood at 529 men. In order to have any chance of survival the battalion had to be reinforced, and to do that they had to turn to their 3/4th Battalion.

From November 1915, the third line of the 4th Cameron Highlanders had been based in the town of Ripon in Yorkshire as part of the 3rd Line Training Centre of the Highland Division, based in South Camp. As wounded officers and men of the 1/4th Camerons recovered they were posted to the 3/4th Battalion in various capacities. In early 1916, officers of the 4th Camerons were serving in a disproportionate amount of senior training positions in the Division: Major Peter Cram, who had been wounded leading C Company at Loos, was the Divisional Entrenching Officer; Captain William Mackay was employed as Divisional Signalling Officer; and Lieutenant Francis Laughton was the Divisional Grenade Officer. Other training positions were occupied by Captain Nigel Mackenzie, Lieutenant Alexander Mackenzie, Lieutenant John Black and Lieutenant William Shaw, all of whom had been wounded in service with the 1/4th Battalion.

The 3/4th Cameron Highlanders sent drafts of 77 men to the 1/4th Battalion on 24 February and a further 100 men on 7 March 1916. Even with this reduction of strength, the 3/4th Camerons numbered some 72 officers and 1001 men when reviewed by Field Marshal Lord French in April. With this type of reinforcement ready to bolster the 4th Camerons in the field, what happened next shocked all ranks of the 4th Cameron Highlanders to the core.

The rumours which had been circulating since the end of 1915 came true. The Imperial Chief of Staff, Sir William Robertson, and the War Minister, Lord Kitchener, paid a visit to the Army Adjutant General in St Omer on 9 February. They informed him that all battalions of the army which were under strength, and had no adequate prospect of reinforcement, would cease to exist as front line fighting forces, their men sent to serve in other battalions of their regiment. Three Highland Division battalions were chosen: the 4th and 5th Battalions of the Black Watch, and the 4th Cameron Highlanders.

The commanding officers of those three battalions were summoned to General Headquarters in St Omer on 16 February. Here, Lieutenant-Colonel Murdoch Beaton, commanding officer of the 4th Camerons, pleaded with the

Adjutant General to save his battalion. It was to no avail. The *Historical Record of the Queen's Own Cameron Highlanders* state that as the 4th Camerons were the only Territorial Force Battalion of the regiment in France, they were to be amalgamated with the only battalion of the regiment senior to them: the 1st Battalion, Cameron Highlanders. The 4th Cameron Highlanders were to be disbanded.

This was, however, not the full story. Lieutenant-Colonel Beaton's protestations did meet with some success, as he managed to ensure that a battalion nucleus of three officers and 100 men would be retained at the base to await reinforcements from home, which, when combined with the 4th Cameron Highlanders men already in France, would be enough to reconstitute the battalion. Headquarters also announced that if no reinforcements were forthcoming, the battalion would be built from scratch in Inverness, but only once the war was over.

This was not a popular decision in the Scottish Highlands. The Member of Parliament for the Inverness Burghs, Annan Bryce, raised the question of the future of the 4th Camerons in Parliament. An article appeared in the *Inverness Courier* of 24 March which summarised Mr Bryce's statement.

> Mr J. Annan Bryce (Inverness Burghs) said he wished to call attention to an action of the War Office which was in violation of the law. Under the Territorial Forces Act 1907, it was provided that the regulations and orders to be issued by the War Office should not, when the corps command of the Territorial Force included any battalion or other body of the Regular Forces, authorise a man to be posted without his consent to that battalion or body.[243]

It was an interesting point. Mr Bryce continued:

> The 1/4th Cameron Highlanders Battalion of the Cameron Highlanders, which had won deathless renown on the fields of Flanders, had now, under orders from the War Office, been merged into the Regular regiment of that corps, the 1st Cameron Regiment. This action of the War Office has excited great indignation in the county of Inverness because that county and the burgh of Inverness took an immense pride in the performance of that Territorial Regiment, and it grieved them to think that its identity should disappear, and that it should be merged in this other regiment, however brilliant the 1st Camerons might be. No consultation appeared to have taken place by the War Office authorities with the County Association, which had represented their case to the War Office so far without success. It appeared that the 1/4th Camerons were to be used purely as furnishing drafts for the 1st Camerons, and that he did hope, even at this late date, it might be possible for the War Office to change its view and re-establish the identity of the regiment.[244]

In a response from the government, Walter Long, Under-Secretary for War replied:

> Mr Bryce was quite right when he said that the question raised a general principle. His objection was that the Territorial Cameron Battalion had been absorbed into the Regular Battalion, the 1st Battalion of that famous Regiment, but he (Mr Long) found it rather difficult to appreciate the grounds of the complaint, because, after all, if it had finally been absorbed into

> a battalion so famous, its fate was nothing to grumble at. But it was not a question of the extinction of the Territorial Battalion; it was not a question of absorption in such a way that the battalion would never be heard of again. This particular battalion had been so reduced in numbers by gallantry that, in the opinion of the Commander-in-Chief at the front, it was desirable, for the present, to merge the Territorial Battalion in the 1st Battalion in order that, for the time being, they might form one strong battalion. There was no intention, however, of destroying the Territorial Battalion, and in due course its identity would be restored and he ventured to believe that its future would be none the less satisfactory or less glorious that for a time it had formed part of one of the most famous battalions of the famous Army of the King.[245]

In the end, the men of the 4th Cameron Highlanders were not to be sent as drafts directly to the 1st Cameron Highlanders. On 26 February 1916, the 4th Camerons left 154 Brigade and proceeded by train from Corbie station to the 51st (Highland Division) Base Depot at Étaples, on the northern French coast, before moving to permanent quarters in L Camp two weeks later. Two days before they left for Étaples, the battalion received orders from Brigadier-General C.E. Stewart, commanding officer of 154 Brigade.

> Thursday, 24th February 1916, on the departure of the 1/4th, 1/5th Battalions the Black Watch and 1/4th Queen's Own Cameron Highlanders, the Brigadier-General Commanding desired to place on record his appreciation of the high standard attained by these three distinguished Battalions during the past

> seven weeks in which all ranks have worked so well in the 154th Infantry Brigade as well as his full recognition that they, whether individually or collectively, may be depended on to help most effectively in some material objects. The maintenance of civilization against and the subjugation of the common enemies of humanity who have broken every law, just and divine, in their mad quest for power. The Brigadier-General thanks all ranks of these three Highland Battalions for their loyal and cordial co-operation with him in the all too short time they and he have been together and trusts it may be his good fortune to serve with them again.[246]

The 4th Cameron Highlanders were being broken apart. Even though five officers and 177 men had joined the battalion between the start of the year and the first week of March, during that time the more experienced officers had been posted elsewhere. Lieutenant-Colonel Murdoch Beaton, part of the contingent which left Bedford a year before, was evacuated to England sick, along with Captain Charles Campbell, Captain Hector M. Morison and Lieutenant Illtyd Mackintosh. Captain Ian T. Nelson was sent home to the Reserve of Officers. Some officers would remain in France, transferred to administrative appointments. The first week of March saw Captain Archibald Fletcher appointed Adjutant of the Machine Gun Base Depot in Camiers, Major John Lockie was given the job of Quartermaster of the Machine Gun Corps Base Depot, and Captain Neil McArthur became the Adjutant and Quartermaster of Number Two Training Camp in Étaples.

It was a different story for the men. The battalion war diary recorded that on 10 March 1916, orders were received to send 350 men to a holding unit called Number 1 Entrenching Battalion. The Entrenching Battalion was based near Poperinghe in Belgium and the draft from the 4th Camerons began their journey there on 12 March. The men were commanded by Captain Angus Ross and included Lieutenant Max Roemmele, Lieutenant Alfred W.H. Cooper, Lieutenant George Johnson, and 2nd Lieutenants Hugh Henderson, James Smith and Alistair Birnie, who were also to be attached to the Entrenching Battalion. On 26 March, orders were received to send a further six officers and 250 men to Number 1 Entrenching Battalion. Accordingly, Lieutenant Alfred G. Calder and 2nd Lieutenants Archibald MacDonald, Charles MacGillivray, Charles Hunter and Benjamin Bartholomew travelled north to Belgium with their men.

The battalion war diary recorded a total strength of 32 officers and 731 men on 8 March. After the 550 men left for Number 1 Entrenching Battalion, this left 181 men left in Étaples, almost all of whom were pre-war Territorial Force soldiers and those who had worked at Battalion Headquarters. Around this time news was circulating that a further draft of 300 men would soon be embarking from the 3/4th Camerons. It raised the hopes of the men in France that this would be enough to save the stricken battalion, but it was not to be.

The 3/4th Cameron Highlanders, with their pool of 1001 men eager to get to the front, were unable to send any further drafts of reinforcements to France. Since 2 March, the rifle ranges at the Reserve Highland Division Base at Ripon had been unavailable, so the men of the 4th Cameron Highlanders could not train. The *Historical Record of the Queen's Own Cameron Highlanders* states that the shortage of rifle ranges was no fault of the Cameron

Highlanders; but the problem would not be resolved until three months later, by which time it had been decided that a draft of 187 men of the 3/4th Camerons were to be transferred to the 2/4th Gordon Highlanders. Soon after, orders were received that the 3/4th Camerons were also to be disbanded, the men being absorbed by the 3rd (Special Reserve) Battalion, Cameron Highlanders based in Invergordon. The first party left Ripon for Invergordon in July 1916 under Major Ian Mackay, with the rest of the battalion following in September. Twelve officers who were deemed surplus to requirements were transferred to the Liverpool Scottish battalion in France.

Back in Étaples, command of the battalion nucleus was passed to Captain Alexander MacBean, with 2nd Lieutenants David Melville and Donald MacDonald as his assistants, both of whom had been promoted from the ranks of the 4th Camerons. The men of the nucleus must have still retained some hope of the battalion being resuscitated, as while at Étaples, they continued their programme of training, taking instructions from Regimental Sergeant Major Price in the mornings and learning signalling in the afternoons.

The daily duties of the men at Number 1 Entrenching Battalion are not known. No contemporary records about this battalion survive but we can get some idea of their work from other sources. Between 12 March and the end of June 1916, some 39 men were wounded and six sent to hospital suffering from illness. The service or pension records of eight of these men survive, and from those the precise location of the battalion can be identified.

Norman Mackenzie enlisted at Inverness on 7 August 1914, the week war was declared. He had spent four years in the 4th Cameron Highlanders, resigning his appointment in March 1914, before returning to the colours in the time of need. Private Mackenzie was transferred to Number 1 Entrenching Battalion on 12 March 1916 and only five days later, received a gunshot wound to the knee. He was evacuated to Number 5 Canadian Field Ambulance, which was based near Poperinghe at the villages of St Remy and La Clytte, now called De Klijte, to the southwest of Ypres. This Field Ambulance was attached to the 2nd Canadian Division, based in March 1916 around the village of Westoutre in Belgium.

Other casualties from Number 1 Entrenching Battalion were also treated by the 2nd Canadian Division. Private Harry Clough was wounded on 29 March and was evacuated to Number 4 Canadian Field Ambulance at Westoutre. The three Field Ambulances of the 2nd Canadian Division were concentrated around a small area to the immediate north of the French border: the 4th in Westoutre, the 5th in La Clytte and the 6th in Locre. Therefore, in March 1916 in can be assumed that Number 1 Entrenching Battalion was based in the same vicinity, around Kemmel, to the southwest of Ypres. In the spring of 1916 this area was the scene of sporadic actions by the 2nd Canadian Division and the 3rd British Division.

On 2 May 1916, Private Albert Warrior Bainbridge was shot in the thigh while serving with Number 1 Entrenching Battalion. He was taken to Number 142 Field Ambulance, attached to the British 3rd Division. On 19 May, Private James Stephen was wounded. He was treated at Number 8 Field Ambulance, also attached to the British 3rd Division. Clearly the entrenching battalion remained in the Ypres area for a prolonged period and was close enough to the firing line to lose almost 40 men, nearly all of whom suffered gunshot wounds. Four men transferred from the

4th Camerons to the entrenching battalion were killed. Private Angus McMaster was wounded in action on 28 April 1916 and died at Number 13 Stationary Hospital in Boulogne two days later. Private Andrew Hunt died on 22 May and Private John Wrightson died on 26 May; both men are buried at La Laiterie Military Cemetery. 2nd Lieutenant Archibald MacDonald was shot while commanding a digging party on 17 April. He was evacuated to a field ambulance but died some hours later.

As previously stated, the day-to-day activities of Number 1 Entrenching Battalion are not known, but records of other entrenching battalions in the area do survive. Private Stanley Bradbury enlisted into the 3/4th Cameron Highlanders at Ripon, arriving there on 1 April 1916. After being absorbed into the 3rd Cameron Highlanders at Invergordon, Private Bradbury was selected to travel to France on 12 December 1916. After a month at the depot in Étaples, Private Bradbury was drafted into Number 2 Entrenching Battalion, also in the Ypres sector. He described the work he had to do:

> Our Company was split up into two parties, one party proceeding to Dickebusch to dig trenches, and the other party proceeding to Vlamertinghe to work at an RE dump. I drew a lucky ticket by forming one of the latter party and had a very cushy day as our 'work' consisted of threading wire netting with canvas strips to form camouflage. This occupation would have suited me until the termination of the war. We also scrounged some grub from the RE's. The Dickebusch party had been shelled and received several casualties.[247]
>
> ...It appeared that there was not a proper drainage from the trenches and higher ground and the water

> had overflowed the banks of the narrow beck running along one side of the field we were in and had flooded the whole of the land, therefore our work was to bank up the inner side of the beck with mud so as to confine the water within its proper channel. Our immediate task then was to carry large shovels full of sloppy mud from the centre of the field to the beck side and deposit them there. We had been provided with shovels at the entrance to the trench.[248]

There were more problems in Bradbury's entrenching battalion than simply the monotony of the work:

> The food we were receiving at this time was most wretched and greatly insufficient to keep any warmth in our bodies. We had one loaf of bread between eight men and a tin of marmalade (I do not like this stuff) between eleven. Each morning our bread was frozen so stiff that only a hatchet would break into it. For dinners, we had either a Dixie of watery soup or tea and a tin of bully. Tea was the same as breakfast although the loaf referred to had to last the whole day. During this keen frost it was impossible to obtain any cold water as all water carts were frozen and fires had to be placed underneath to melt the water when the latter was required for meals. A sentry was on guard to keep men from taking water for drinking or other purposes.[249]

Stanley Bradbury's time with Number 2 Entrenching Battalion seems to have been a thoroughly horrible experience and in his diary he mentions his and his comrades' excitement at being transferred to a front line unit and no longer having to work like navvies.[250] It seems reasonable to infer that this type of labouring work was done by the 4th Cameron Highlanders men while at Number 1 Entrenching Battalion in the spring of 1916. Some of the 4th Camerons would not have to put up with it for long. They were about to go back into action.

10

The Camerons on the Somme and the Battalion Nucleus, 1916–1917

When the orders were given in February 1916 for the battalion to be broken up, it had been decided that the officers and men of the 4th Camerons would provide drafts of men for the 1st Cameron Highlanders when required. The transfer started with the officers. On 27 April, Captain Max Roemmele, Lieutenants Alfred Calder and George Johnson, and 2nd Lieutenants Alistair Birnie, James Smith, Hugh Henderson, Benjamin Bartholomew, Archie Macrae, Charles MacGillivray and Charles Hunter were attached to the 1st Cameron Highlanders for administrative purposes. They all joined the 1st Camerons at the heads of drafts of men from Number 1 Entrenching Battalion throughout the next two months.

On 4 May, the first 4th Cameron Highlanders officers began their service with the 1st Battalion. Lieutenant John Clift and 2nd Lieutenant Harold White were attached to A Company, 2nd Lieutenant Harry A. Mackintosh to B Company, 2nd Lieutenant James MacDonald to

C Company and 2nd Lieutenant Archibald R. Mackenzie to D Company. They came not from Number 1 Entrenching Battalion, but direct from the 4th Cameron Highlanders' battalion nucleus at Étaples. Four days later, 48 4th Cameron men were sent from the Number 1 Entrenching Battalion to join the 1st Camerons at Les Brebis.[251] That same week, Captain Roderick McErlich transferred from the battalion nucleus and Captain Harold Law – who had been wounded at Loos in September 1915 – joined the 1st Camerons from the 3/4th Battalion in Ripon. Over the next two months 2nd Lieutenants James Smith, Charles MacGillivray and Archie Macrae were posted for duty with the 1st Camerons, taking with them drafts of 70 and 58 men on 2 and 12 June respectively.

These men brought the strength of the 1st Cameron Highlanders up to 1033 men, a good strength for a battalion on the front line during the First World War. It meant that ten officers and 174 men of the 4th Cameron Highlanders were now serving with the 1st Battalion. They were to pay a heavy price. By the time the 1st Cameron Highlanders moved to the Somme sector on 6 July, they had lost one man killed and ten wounded who had just transferred from the 4th Camerons from total casualties of 19 dead and 63 wounded.

The 1st Camerons took over front line trenches the day after arriving at Albert in the Somme sector. The trenches, called Scott's Redoubt, were an old German trench system between the villages of Becourt and Contalmaison. Their first tour in the region was in support of the battalions that were attacking Contalmaison between 10 and 14 July. During the tour 21 men were killed and 76 were wounded, including four 4th Camerons men killed and 15 wounded, two more of whom would die of their wounds within a week. 4th Camerons officers Captain Alexander MacBean and 2nd Lieutenant James MacDonald were wounded.

On 21 July, the 1st Camerons took over front line trenches at Bazentin Le Petit Wood. On the morning of 23 July, the 1st Camerons and the 10th Gloucester Regiment launched an attack on the road from Bazentin Le Petit to Martinpuich from trenches just north of the former village. C Company led the way and reached the German lines, but were repulsed by bombs, rifle and machine-gun fire. The attack had failed and they dug in until they could be relieved. The 1st Cameron Highlanders lost 65 men killed and 129 men wounded, including 15 men of the 4th Camerons killed and 20 wounded.

While on the Somme more 4th Cameron Highlanders officers joined to bolster the ranks. On 15 July, Captain Max Roemmele, Lieutenant Alfred Calder and 2nd Lieutenants Charles Hunter and Alastair Birnie proceeded for duty, and 2nd Lieutenant Benjamin Bartholomew joined up on 26 July.

On 11 August, the 1st Cameron Highlanders received a draft of 65 men from the Cameron base depot in Étaples, all of whom were recently arrived men from the 3/4th Camerons. They were soon to get their first taste of action. The 1st Cameron Highlanders were in action from 16 to 20 August. Fifteen men of the 4th Camerons were killed and 20 wounded in heavy German shelling out of a total of 42 killed and 80 wounded for the battalion.

On 3 September, the 1st Cameron Highlanders launched their largest assault of the Somme battles. The battalion advanced on a 500-yard front from Worcester Trench on the south side of High Wood to Wood Lane Trench about 250 yards to the east. The 1st Camerons attacked with the rest of 1 Brigade at 12 noon. After brisk hand-to-hand fighting they easily carried their objective and advanced past Wood Lane to occupy a semi-circle of shell holes. The Germans counterattacked from northeast of High Wood and drove the Camerons back to Worcester Trench at 3.30pm. Half an hour later, A and C Companies on the right of the attack were almost surrounded by the enemy and ordered to withdraw. The 1st Cameron Highlanders had lost 100 men killed and 137 wounded, many of them ex-4th Camerons men.

When the roll call was called on the evening of 3 September 1916, A Company consisted of 2 officers and 23 men, B Company had only 12 men, C Company had 1 officer and 36 men and D Company had 2 officers and 42 men. The battalion which, on moving to the Somme sector two months previously, had 1033 men on strength was now down to 132 men. Clearly more reinforcements were needed.

The 1st Cameron Highlanders again took their replacements from the men of the 4th Camerons still working in Belgium with Number 1 Entrenching Battalion. Accordingly 200 men were sent to the 1st Camerons on 12 September, with a further 94 being sent on 15 September. This would only just make good the casualties sustained on 3 September.

The men of the 4th Cameron Highlanders fought on in the actions of the 1st Camerons until the end of the war, sustaining many casualties. By the end of 1916, 88 members of the 4th Cameron Highlanders had died during the Somme campaign.

Back in Étaples, the battalion nucleus was still in operation. On 1 April, the men were formed into one company, predominately pre-war Territorial Force soldiers and those who had served the 4th Camerons in administrative capacities, such as the Orderly Room and Shoemaker Sergeants. The non-commissioned officers were retained at the base as instructors to train the new recruits passing through the depot.

On 9 July, the men attached to the battalion nucleus over the permitted number of 100 other ranks were transferred to Number 19 Infantry Base Depot, the Cameron Highlanders Depot, in Étaples. Three days later a draft of 197 men arrived as the final draft of the 3/4th Cameron Highlanders before their disbanding, and on 30 July the depot received 403 men from the 2/4th Cameron Highlanders. The 4th Cameron Highlanders now had over 1000 men fit and present for France. By the end of August, a further 631 men had arrived. Rumours began to circulate that the 4th Battalion was to be brought back up to strength and retake its position in the field, but it was not to be.

These last drafts of men were broken up and transferred to the 1st, 5th, 6th and 7th Cameron Highlanders. With their new battalions they took part in some of the hardest fighting of the Somme battles. By the end of 1916, 621 men had been transferred to the 1st Cameron Highlanders, 242 to the 5th Camerons, 557 to the 6th Camerons and 325 to the 7th Camerons. If a roll call had been taken on 12 November 1918, it would have found that 293 4th Cameron Highlanders died on service with the other Cameron battalions. When added to the 257 men who died of measles in Bedford and on active service with the 4th Camerons in 1915, the battalion's butcher's bill was 550 officers and men.

Captain Roderick McErlich, in command of the 4th Cameron Highlanders battalion nucleus from July 1916, wrote to the Regimental Journal, the *79th News,* of the unit's time at the depot in Étaples:

> The 1/4th is still in the wilderness. But, scattered as it is, it is doing its bit in different parts of France. Its members – officers and men – form not an inconsiderable part of the 1st Battalion; drafts have been sent to other battalions of the Regiment; a few still remain with the Entrenching Battalion; while the nucleus plays an important role at the Base. This last mentioned part of the battalion recently took over on of the IBDs and has had a very busy time. Nearly 2000 troops have at times to be accommodated and catered for, and this is no trifling task where drafts come and go at all hours, every man of the nucleus has some task or other allotted to him. Thanks, however, to the experience and capabilities of these, everything goes smoothly, and all ranks seem happy to have something tangible to do. It is a gratification to them that all troops passing through this depot belong to kilted Highland regiments – many of them Camerons, including the 4th Battalion.[252]

On 26 December 1916, the battalion nucleus received orders for Captain McErlich, 2nd Lieutenant Donald MacDonald and 49 other ranks to take over the guard of ammunition dumps at Dannes. The remainder of the nucleus was employed at the BB Camp in Étaples, with the non-commissioned officers as instructors at the Étaples training camps. On 15 February 1917, orders were received from the Adjutant General that the 4th Cameron Highlanders' battalion nucleus was to cease to exist, its men being examined for service at the front with other Cameron Highlanders battalions. The first draft left for the 7th Camerons in March, and the second draft reached the 6th Camerons in June 1917.

The men of the 4th Cameron Highlanders, pre-war Territorials, veterans of the battles of 1915, and new recruits who never saw service with the 4th Battalion, were spread across the army. The fought through the horrors of the Third Battle of Ypres, the Battle of Arras in 1918 and the Second Battles of the Somme before marching on to victory.

The 4th Cameron Highlanders had paid the ultimate sacrifice. Their bravery at Neuve Chapelle, Aubers Ridge, Festubert, Givenchy and Loos had counted for little as the army administrators proved more destructive to the battalion than the Germans. This, however, was not the end for the 4th Cameron Highlanders.

Epilogue

On 19 July 1919, the Colours of the 4th Cameron Highlanders were paraded through the streets of London alongside Colours of other British battalions who had won honours on the Western Front. Captain William Mackay – wounded in the trenches at Fauquisart on 16 April 1915 – carried the King's Colour, and Captain Donald Ross – wounded at Loos in September 1915 – carried the Regimental Colour.

In 1920, the 4th Cameron Highlanders were rebuilt from scratch in Inverness with many of the officers and men who had seen service in France in 1915 as part of the new battalion. In command of the new battalion was Lieutenant-Colonel Francis Laughton MC who had gone to France in February 1915 and had commanded the 21 Brigade Bombers at the Battle of Givenchy. He served in this capacity until 1927 before being succeeded by Lieutenant-Colonel Neil McArthur who commanded until 1933. Lieutenant-Colonel James Symon DSO, another veteran of the 4th Cameron Highlanders, commanded the battalion until 1937.

When the Second World War broke out in September 1939, the 4th Cameron Highlanders were again mobilised and proceeded to France for the second time in 25 years. This second visit also ended poorly for the Highland men, sacrificed along with the rest of the Highland Division at St Valery-en-Caux in June 1940, while protecting the Dunkirk beaches.

This book has been a labour of love for me for the past three years. My aim in writing it was to tell the story of this gallant battalion from their mobilising for war in August 1914 until their demise in 1916. Where possible, I have let the men of the battalion tell the story themselves, in their letters and diaries.

The story of the 4th Cameron Highlanders, while almost a century old, is still constantly evolving. New information is continually being found and the author would appreciate any information readers could provide on either the battalion or individual members. Additionally, the author is pleased to answer any queries on the 4th Cameron Highlanders. They can be emailed to 4thCamerons@gmail.com.

I hope this book goes some small way to making people aware of these men, who volunteered to serve their country and sacrificed so much in the French mud almost a century ago.

Presentation of Colours to the 4th Camerons Highlanders, London, 1909.

Training camp at Dornoch, July 1913.

4th Cameron Highlanders in Bedford, September 1914.

Inspection of the 4th Cameron Highlanders, Bedford, 18 February 1915.

Officers of the 4th Cameron Highlanders, Bedford, February 1915.

Officers of the 4th Cameron Highlanders, Corbie, February 1916.

Warrant officers and non commissioned officers at Corbie, February 1916.

Lieutenant-Colonel Ewan Campbell.

Lieutenant-Colonel Alexander Fraser.

Lieutenant-Colonel John Campbell.

Lieutenant-Colonel Hector Fraser.

Major Murdoch Beaton.

Lieutenant-Colonel
Garden Duff.

Major Ian Mackay.

Captain David F. MacKenzie.

Captain James MacPherson.

Captain Roderick McErlich.

Clockwise from top left: Captain Thomas Allison, Captain Ian H. Baillie, 2nd Lieutenant Archibald F. Paterson and 2nd Lieutenant James Bookless.

Clockwise from top left: Captain John F. MacLaren, Lieutenant Henry J. Scott, 2nd Lieutenant Donald J. MacIver and Lieutenant Angus Urquhart.

Lieutenant-Colonel Peter M. Cram.

Lieutenant-Colonel Neil MacArthur.

Lieutenant-Colonel Francis E. Laughton.

Private (later Lieutenant) Montague Goodban.

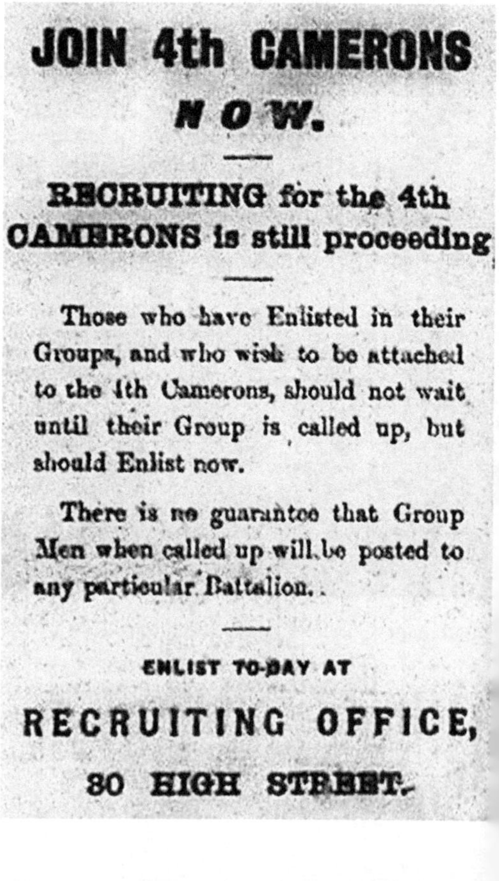

Recruiting advertisement from the *Inverness Courier*.

Captain Max A. Roemmele.

The Officers of the 3/4th Cameron Highlanders.

An unknown Cameron Highlander.

Appendix 1

Order of Battle

The Order of Battle for the brigades in which the 4th Cameron Highlanders served.

24th Brigade, 8th Division (19 February–8 April 1915)
1st Battalion, Worcester Regiment
2nd Battalion, East Lancashire Regiment
1st Battalion, Notts and Derby Regiment (Sherwood Foresters)
2nd Battalion, Northamptonshire Regiment
5th Battalion, Black Watch
4th Battalion, Cameron Highlanders (TF)

21st Brigade, 7th Division (8 April 1915–19 December 1915)
2nd Battalion, Bedfordshire Regiment
2nd Battalion, Yorkshire Regiment (Green Howards)
2nd Battalion, Royal Scots Fusiliers
2nd Battalion, Wiltshire Regiment
4th Battalion, Cameron Highlanders (TF)

91st Brigade, 7th Division (19 December 1915–7 January 1916)
2nd Battalion, Royal Scots Fusiliers
1st Battalion, Queen's Regiment
21st Battalion, Manchester Regiment

22rd Battalion, Manchester Regiment
4th Battalion, Cameron Highlanders (TF)

154th Brigade, 51st (Highland Division)
(7 January–25 February 1916)
4th Battalion, Black Watch (TF)
5th Battalion, Black Watch (TF)
4th Battalion, Seaforth Highlanders (TF)
4th Battalion, Cameron Highlanders (TF)

Appendix 2

Officers and Men of the 4th Battalion, Cameron Highlanders

List of the officers and men of the 4th Battalion, Cameron Highlanders departing for France, published in the *Inverness Courier*, 23 and 26 February and 2 and 5 March 1915.

Commanding Officer	Lieutenant-Colonel Alexander Fraser V.D.
Major	Major Hector Fraser T.D.
Adjutant	Captain Garden B. Duff
Quartermaster	Honorary Major John Lockie
Machine Gun Officer	Lieutenant Harold B. Law
Transport Officer	Lieutenant John D. MacPherson
Medical Officer	Captain Robert Lindsay
Chaplain	Captain Reverend D. Macfarlane

A Company (Old A (Inverness) and D (Broadford) Companies)

Officers

Captain Murdoch Beaton
Captain David F. MacKenzie
Lieutenant Ian Mackay (Assistant Adjutant)
Lieutenant Charles Campbell
Lieutenant William Mackay (Signals Officer)
2nd Lieutenant Francis E. Laughton
2nd Lieutenant John D.M. Black

Roll of A Company in Order of Seniority

2348	RSM Alexander Whitton
186	CSM John A. Macinnes
24	CQMS John Macrae
27	Drummer Sergeant John Matheson
39	Machine Gun Sergeant Robert D. Chisholm
56	Pipe Sergeant John S. Ross
25	Sergeant Alexander MacDonald
358	Sergeant Jacob Matheson
1378	Sergeant Roderick McErlich
970	Sergeant Duncan MacMillan
5	Sergeant John A. MacVinish
2039	Sergeant Arthur E.T. Robinson
1297	Sergeant John MacLeod
2077	Sergeant John Roake
522	Lance Sergeant Donald MacKinlay
1161	Corporal George W. Munro
1278	Corporal Athole G. MacKintosh
1268	Corporal Duncan MacPherson
835	Corporal Farquhar Nicholson
1711	Corporal John Gordon
545	Corporal Roderick J.M. Ross
2041	Corporal George Gordon Anderson
827	Corporal John MacDonald
115	Lance Corporal Charles MacBean
133	Lance Corporal James MacBean
528	Lance Corporal George Forsyth
1052	Lance Corporal Alistair MacLennan
1155	Lance Corporal John M. Hutcheson
1280	Lance Corporal Charles MacLean
1286	Lance Corporal Roderick McKinnon
1456	Lance Corporal John Macinnes
602	Lance Corporal Duncan MacKay
826	Lance Corporal Donald MacDonald
2670	Lance Corporal Thomas D. Mackay
1154	Lance Corporal George F. Mackenzie
1212	Lance Corporal Alistair Mackenzie
1243	Lance Corporal James Jack
1253	Lance Corporal William Morrison
1269	Lance Corporal John B. Stewart
1420	Lance Corporal Andrew S. Williams

1421 Lance Corporal Colin H. Forbes
2224 Lance Corporal Walter S. Jenkins
2228 Lance Corporal John U. Fraser
968 Lance Corporal Malcolm MacLean
1325 Drummer Hugh MacLennan
1090 Piper Alexander Fullarton
1849 Private William B. Allan
1982 Private E.T. Allen
966 Private James Aird
2007 Private William Alexander
2088 Private Charles Anderson
1457 Private James Anderson
2166 Private Henry H. Beeson
1986 Private Alexander P. Boswall
2221 Private Charles Bowdery
2013 Private John E. Brister
2005 Private Charles G. Brown
2085 Private William Beard
1741 Private Norman Beaton
1298 Private William Beaton
2065 Private Eric H. Belk
2134 Private Francis G. Blake
2092 Private Frederick J. Blake
3010 Private Edward J. Blake
2033 Private Charles W. Bradley
2089 Private William T. Bryant
2032 Private Harold C. Bushell
1605 Private Frederick A. Cameron
2254 Private Robert A. Cameron
1459 Private Robert M. Cameron
1950 Private Frank G. Chamberlain
1911 Private James Clark
1847 Private John Charles
2087 Private Geoffrey Corbett
1416 Private Albert J. Corner
2069 Private Edwin H. Chase
2066 Private John Coggins
2078 Private John Cooke
2025 Private Ernest G. Cripps
2072 Private Bernard S. Cumming
2047 Private George J. Davey

2220	Private Layton A. Davey
31	Private Thomas H. Douglas
1890	Private James D. Davidson
1909	Private Francis Deans
1892	Private James G. Dickson
1247	Private Robert Dingwall
1441	Private Frank Dougherty
2081	Private E. Davies
2742	Private Douglas H.T. Drummond
1985	Private Robert Evans
2694	Private Victor Edwards
2037	Private Thomas Elliott
2076	Private Charles F. English
2009	Private Leonard E. Entwistle
1412	Private Donald M. Finlayson
2225	Private Thomas Finlayson
2218	Private John M. Fisher
1822	Private Alexander Fraser
1844	Private Alfred G. Fraser
1542	Private Frederick Fraser
1295	Private Roderick Fraser
1496	Private Fergus Ferguson
1319	Private Kenneth Ferguson
2012	Private William R. Fleming
2149	Private James H. Forbes
2030	Private Alfred S. Fyfe
2144	Private Sidney R. Gardener
1906	Private John Gibb
2146	Private Montague S. Goodban
1910	Private A. Gray
1594	Private James T. Gray
2143	Private Gerald D. Green
2068	Private John Goulding
1288	Private Neil Grant
2083	Private Thomas Gurney
1980	Private William S. Harris
1949	Private William Hislop
2004	Private Frank Hoyle
2034	Private Leslie Hammerton
2139	Private George W.B. Hampton
2038	Private Thomas Hansford

2082	Private George Hart
2091	Private Thomas Henderson
2035	Private Charles A. Jackson
1891	Private Thomas Kennedy
2045	Private William H. Kennedy
2094	Private Charles Keane
2018	Private Ruthven W. Kerr-Smith
2043	Private Malcolm P. King
2028	Private Charles D. Knox
1988	Private Thomas Laidler
1846	Private Harry Logan
2080	Private Francis W. Lambert
1413	Private Alistair K. Maben
1433	Private Lachlan G. Maben
1690	Private David Melville
2165	Private Donald C. Melvin
2141	Private Duncan M. Miller
2552	Private James G. Miller
1894	Private Norman Morrison
2142	Private Cecil C. Mott
1810	Private Ranald C. Munro
1841	Private William Munro
1954	Private William J. Murray
2036	Private Alfred Marshall
2022	Private Joseph G. Martin
1979	Private Edward McBath
1588	Private Robert MacBean
2145	Private Julian A. McBride
1772	Private Duncan MacDonald
2237	Private John MacDonald
1907	Private Peter MacDonald
1235	Private Rae MacDonald
1395	Private William F. MacDonald
1582	Private John M. MacIntyre
2090	Private George MacIntyre
1589	Private Farquhar M. MacKenzie
1777	Private Donald McKenzie
1947	Private Simon J. MacKenzie
1853	Private James MacKintosh
2361	Private J.J. MacKintosh
1848	Private William MacKintosh

1775	Private Frederick MacLaren
1707	Private Alexander F. MacLean
1583	Private Alexander J. MacLean
2535	Private John MacLean
1976	Private Duncan M. MacLeay
1774	Private John C. MacLennan
2253	Private Malcolm MacLennan
1318	Private Alexander MacLennan
1411	Private Duncan MacTavish
162	Private Colin MacInnes
881	Private Malcolm MacInnes
1419	Private Laughlan McInnes
1075	Private John MacKinnon
2350	Private Ian J. MacKinnon
972	Private William MacLeod
1458	Private Alexander J. McPhee
1522	Private A. MacQueen
1494	Private Peter MacQueen
1493	Private Duncan MacRae
1495	Private John MacRae
2074	Private John F.N. MacRae
963	Private Thomas MacRae
1709	Private Archibald P. Nisbet
2147	Private Reginald J. Nixon
1294	Private Donald Nicolson
1893	Private James R. Park
2017	Private Sydney Parker
2016	Private Alfred G. Perry
1417	Private Harold W. Reid
2223	Private Max A. Roemmele
1953	Private Allan Ross
2864	Private William Ross
2008	Private Frederick C. Robertson
2014	Private Harold L. Robertson
2073	Private Robert C. Robertson
1842	Private Robert Sievwright
1983	Private Walter L.J. Smith
2024	Private Charles S. Smith
1905	Private Albert Stanley
1078	Private Adam Stoddart
1083	Private Alexander Stoddart

2046	Private A.C. Sutherland
1955	Private David Suttie
2031	Private Archibald W. Sergeant
2026	Private Henry L. Sherwood
2026	Private Lowton H. Sheppard
2064	Private Alexander J. Simons
2021	Private Frank A. Snelling
1851	Private Bertram W. Tawse
2044	Private Harold P. Tozer
2011	Private Christopher N. Temple
2093	Private James W. Thorburn
2219	Private Reginald W. Unwin
1981	Private Ralph F. Watson
2084	Private Lawrence G. Watson
2079	Private William Watson
1978	Private Tom Watts
1989	Private Thomas R. Wilson
2006	Private George G. Wilkins
1998	Private Stanley E. Winn
2023	Private William G. Wither

B Company (Old B (Nairn) and C (Inverness) Companies)

Officers

Major John Campbell T.D.
Captain James MacPherson
Captain Frederick W. Fraser
Lieutenant William J. Shaw
2nd Lieutenant John F. MacLaren
2nd Lieutenant Frederick J. Kelly

Roll of B Company in Order of Seniority

50	CSM Donald MacLennan
3	CQMS Kenneth MacKenzie
1650	Cook Sergeant Charles K. Blake
506	Orderly Sergeant James MacDonald
724	Shoemaker Sergeant Peter Bruce
272	Sergeant Alexander Johnston
362	Sergeant Alexander J. Fraser
1006	Sergeant Kenneth MacLennan
428	Sergeant Thomas Polson

899	Sergeant Harry Dennis
453	Sergeant Hugh Fraser
1881	Sergeant Magnus Gibson
1115	Sergeant Ronald R. MacDonald
1326	Lance Sergeant David MacKintosh
1204	Lance Sergeant Edward W. Fox
1125	Corporal Gilbert Falconer
1339	Corporal Alexander H. Falconer
1791	Lance Corporal William Gardener
2531	Lance Corporal Neil Grant
1205	Lance Corporal Alexander Robertson
1205	Lance Corporal Hugh Tyronney
454	Lance Corporal John Hossack
627	Lance Corporal William Grant
1324	Lance Corporal William McGregor
1399	Lance Corporal Duncan Mackenzie
275	Lance Corporal John U. Shirran
583	Lance Corporal William MacPhee
943	Lance Corporal John MacNeill
1503	Lance Corporal Hugh S.F. Munro
1644	Lance Corporal Hugh Tulloch
1699	Lance Corporal Archibald Munro
1785	Lance Corporal James Leighton
1807	Lance Corporal Murdo Laing
1812	Lance Corporal Alastair Fraser
1960	Lance Corporal William Grant
1969	Lance Corporal Donald J. MacLeod
1450	Lance Corporal James Robertson
2384	Lance Corporal Alfred Hannan
2530	Lance Corporal Alexander Sutherland
1642	Drummer James Bell
34	Drummer Alexander Campbell
1698	Drummer Archibald MacDonald
466	Drummer Angus McKinnon
44	Piper William Fraser
53	Piper Kenneth Logan
1718	Private James J. Alexander
2058	Private Harold W.R. Banting
1717	Private William Baxter
933	Private Alexander A. Beaton
1604	Private George Beattie

2173 Private Arthur Berk
2052 Private Robert A. Berry
2051 Private Frank Bevis
2048 Private Henry F. Buckby
2049 Private Charles W. Buckby
1627 Private Joseph Batters
1961 Private Donald Bremner
1919 Private Frank D. Buchanan
2425 Private John Bell
1782 Private Colin Cameron
1273 Private David S. Cameron
1916 Private Duncan Cameron
2056 Private Walter J. Campion
2050 Private John C. Chalmers
955 Private James A. Chapman
1786 Private Evan R. Clark
1265 Private Allan Campbell
1653 Private Charles J. Campbell
2554 Private Charles Cochrane
2054 Private Robert T. Drever
1000 Private John B. Duff
1437 Private George Dallas
2256 Private William A. Dick
1896 Private Donald Dingwall
1883 Private Alistair Dow
1882 Private David Dunbar
1174 Private James Elder
2176 Private George W. Pratten
1962 Private Alexander Ewan
1691 Private David Forbes
2180 Private James A. Forbes
1233 Private Alick Fraser
1784 Private Charles Fraser
1303 Private David J. Fraser
1341 Private George Fraser
1809 Private George Fraser
1766 Private John Fraser
1783 Private Norman Fraser
1008 Private William Fraser
1917 Private Duncan Fraser
1261 Private James Fraser

1579	Private John Fraser
1737	Private James Fraser
1956	Private James Fraser
1750	Private George Findlay
1719	Private Peter Gordon
995	Private Hugh Grant
1340	Private James Grant
1731	Private John Grant
1966	Private Angus Grant
1921	Private Peter Grant
2441	Private James Gardner
1260	Private Alexander Gollan
1831	Private Donald Henderson
1171	Private James Hopkins
2167	Private John H. Hubbard
2355	Private Matthew Hoggan
2356	Private James Hoggan
2529	Private Alexander Howie
1713	Private Bertie Hudson
1270	Private Thomas Johnstone
1184	Private Donald G. Kennedy
1593	Private Malcolm Lamont
1309	Private David Logan
1665	Private Donald Longmuir
2171	Private George H. Lovell
1712	Private Robert Lipp
1790	Private William Long
1436	Private Kenneth MacAskill
1726	Private Robert McCook
1724	Private Thomas McCook
1957	Private John McAdam
1914	Private Patrick MacBean
1728	Private Donald MacDonald
1532	Private Frederick W. MacDonald
893	Private Donald MacDonald
1742	Private Duncan MacDonald
1926	Private Duncan MacDonald
1899	Private Francis MacDonald
1952	Private Hector MacDonald
1402	Private Duncan MacDonald
755	Private John MacDonnell
1259	Private William MacDougall

1975	Private Malcolm MacFarlane
1729	Private James MacGregor
1401	Private Duncan MacIntyre
2502	Private James MacIntyre
1186	Private Andrew D. MacKechnie
2525	Private George MacKay
1079	Private John MacKay
2524	Private William MacKay
1312	Private Alick Mackenzie
1852	Private Duncan Mackenzie
1449	Private George Mackenzie
1723	Private Robert Mackenzie
1207	Private Thomas Mackenzie
1755	Private Alexander Mackenzie
1759	Private Alick Mackenzie
2227	Private Angus Mackenzie
2336	Private D. Mackenzie
1746	Private Hector Mackenzie
1974	Private James Mackenzie
1262	Private Kenneth Mackenzie
1738	Private Norman Mackenzie
1972	Private Roderick J. Mackenzie
924	Private William Mackenzie
1725	Private Alexander MacKinnon
1133	Private Robert Mackintosh
1836	Private William MacIntosh
1964	Private Douglas D. MacLachlan
1968	Private Alexander MacLachlan
1632	Private John MacLean
1898	Private Donald MacLean
2421	Private Donald MacLean
2375	Private Charles MacLean
1823	Private William MacLennan
1070	Private George MacLennan
1612	Private Donald MacLeay
1124	Private William MacLeay
1751	Private Angus MacLeod
1792	Private Duncan MacLeod
1958	Private Robert J. MacLeod
2244	Private George MacLeod
1721	Private James E. MacLeod
1422	Private Norman MacLeod

1608 Private Thomas McNair
1756 Private Donald MacPhail
2062 Private A. MacPherson
1471 Private Donald MacPherson
1145 Private John MacPherson
1146 Private William D. MacPherson
1923 Private Donald MacRae
1736 Private Hugh MacRae
1779 Private David Mair
1645 Private Donald Matheson
2175 Private Alexander Menzies
2170 Private George W. Mills
1631 Private Alexander Moir
2454 Private William Martin
1837 Private Hugh Mason
1765 Private Robert G.O. Melville
1927 Private Alexander H. Mitchell
2426 Private Thomas Morgan
1531 Private John Munro
1781 Private James S. Munro
1250 Private Donald Munro
1267 Private William C. Munro
1749 Private William Munro
2179 Private Reginald Murray
1832 Private William G. Nicolson
2178 Private Alfred Ogilvie
2177 Private David G Peattie
1732 Private Henry J. Pickersgill
1595 Private Roderick Ramsay
2481 Private Alexander F. Ramsay
1722 Private Angus Reid
1634 Private James Reid
2377 Private George Robertson
2059 Private Wilfred Rogers
1922 Private Charles E. Ross
1606 Private Harry Ross
1068 Private John Ross
1748 Private James Ross
1032 Private Archibald M. Smith
1727 Private Duncan Smith
1523 Private James B. Smith

2555	Private Duncan Smith
1713	Private Robert Simpson
1754	Private Thomas Sinclair
1924	Private Daniel Stanger
2458	Private Thomas W. Stark
1694	Private William C. Stewart
2526	Private William Stewart
1175	Private John Stephen
1967	Private Finlay Sutherland
1080	Private Roderick Sutherland
1971	Private Robert Sutherland
2055	Private Alexander S.M. Till
2174	Private Harold A. Tompkins
2168	Private James Trotter
1918	Private Harry Thomson
1920	Private Robert Tolmie
1793	Private Donald Urquhart
1743	Private John Vass
1129	Private John M. Watson
2053	Private G. Whitton
1443	Private William Wilson
2459	Private John Wilkie
1965	Private John Williamson
501	Private William Wells

C Company (Old E (Fort William) and F (Kingussie) Companies)

Officers

Captain Thomas Allison
Captain John Campbell
2nd Lieutenant Andrew Sutherland
2nd Lieutenant William Calder
2nd Lieutenant N.J. Mitchell-Innes
2nd Lieutenant Ian T. Nelson

Roll of C Company in Order of Seniority

3012	RQMS Harry Keates
93	CSM William A. Macintyre
1511	CQMS James Stott
691	Signals Sergeant Duncan MacKintosh

258	Sergeant Andrew Robertson
656	Sergeant Donald P. Fraser
368	Sergeant Alexander Macintyre
771	Sergeant Kenneth K. Cameron
1039	Sergeant Duncan Cameron
833	Sergeant Donald MacLeod
134	Sergeant Henry Lawson
237	Sergeant William Munro
505	Sergeant Peter MacDonald
473	Lance Sergeant Duncan Mackenzie
1139	Corporal Alistair MacDougall
114	Corporal Alexander D. MacLean
320	Corporal John MacEachen
1475	Corporal Alexander MacRae
1215	Corporal James A. MacDonald
2101	Corporal Ernest W. Macnamara
1333	Corporal Henry Adamson
420	Lance Corporal Alexander MacPhee
82	Lance Corporal Donald MacKinnon
913	Lance Corporal Alexander M. Macintyre
855	Lance Corporal Alexander MacKintosh
592	Lance Corporal Donald J. Paterson
772	Lance Corporal Henry A.W. MacDonald
1178	Lance Corporal William Paterson
1167	Lance Corporal Beveridge Matthewson
229	Lance Corporal William S. Macintosh
252	Lance Corporal John MacPherson
776	Lance Corporal Angus MacLachlan
1047	Lance Corporal William Beattie
1063	Lance Corporal Robert Macnab
1098	Lance Corporal James MacBain
1182	Lance Corporal Henry R. Munro
1214	Lance Corporal James MacDonald
1332	Lance Corporal Robert J. Cooper
1796	Lance Corporal Donald Grant
2000	Lance Corporal William Waterston
2284	Lance Corporal John Black
2230	Lance Corporal Ewen Cameron
2267	Lance Corporal Robert K. Davidson
1253	Lance Corporal Lachlan Gillies
988	Piper Charles Milne

1928	Private Duncan Allan
2117	Private Thomas J. Ault
639	Private J. Anderson
2103	Private George E. Baker
2115	Private John A. Brown
1994	Private Peter D. Brown
1999	Private Frederick T. Burrows
1334	Private Alexander Black
1444	Private Allan Cameron
1760	Private Alexander Cameron
480	Private Duncan Cameron
1478	Private Ian D. Cameron
1156	Private John A. Cameron
1486	Private William Cameron
1740	Private Donald Cameron
872	Private William Cameron
1762	Private Colin R. Campbell
1048	Private Henry H. Campbell
1466	Private Alexander Cattanach
2258	Private Malcolm Cattanach
1120	Private John T. Cheyne
1348	Private William Cowie
981	Private John Curley
657	Private William Curley
1761	Private Hugh Carmichael
1970	Private John H. Clyne
2098	Private Arthur J. Collins
2113	Private Thomas W. Cundle
1992	Private E.A. Downs
2105	Private Cecil C. Druery
1465	Private Alistair Dallas
215	Private William Dott
3003	Private Alexander Dott
1572	Private John Dunbar
1379	Private Alexander Dunbar
1664	Private John R.D. Durrant
930	Private Patrick Fleming
1384	Private William Fleming
1106	Private Robert Ferguson
1336	Private Colin Fraser
1797	Private Hugh Fraser

2424	Private William Fraser
1455	Private Adam R. Fraser
1534	Private Hugh Fraser
1663	Private Alexander Fraser
2099	Private Morris W.J. Furniss
1996	Private Alexander D. Gavin
2097	Private J. Goulding
1445	Private Ian A. Gray
864	Private John George
448	Private David G. Grant
1524	Private Donald Grant
1535	Private James Grant
1313	Private Charles Geddes
2970	Private William Gorrie
2121	Private Colin M. Henderson
980	Private George E. Hossack
1889	Private James Herd
1180	Private George W. Jack
2111	Private Frank M. Johnstone
865	Private James Johnstone
2109	Private Arthur J. Kelleher
1383	Private Donald Kennedy
1407	Private Neil Kennedy
1507	Private Louis Kennedy
1508	Private John Kennedy
2164	Private William King
2002	Private Robert M. Law
1991	Private Percy A. Lorkin
2107	Private Charles M. Lubbock
249	Private James Logan
2518	Private Angus MacDonald
927	Private Alexander MacDonald
1382	Private Alexander MacDonald
1937	Private Charles MacDonald
1104	Private Angus MacDonald
1693	Private Angus MacDonald
1763	Private Alexander MacDonald
1596	Private Ewen MacDonald
777	Private John MacDonald
1103	Private John MacDonald
1661	Private John MacDonald

1197 Private William MacDonald
1769 Private Daniel MacDonald
1757 Private John MacDonald
1753 Private William MacDonald
513 Private John C. MacDonald
1885 Private Duncan MacDonald
2983 Private Donald MacDonald
1951 Private Duncan MacDonald
1257 Private Archibald McDonnell
1995 Private Charles E. McDermott
1409 Private John MacEachen
1107 Private Alexander MacBain
1597 Private Alexander MacBean
1237 Private John MacBain
1112 Private Joseph McCook
1490 Private William MacGillivray
1337 Private Dugald McGregor
829 Private Robert J. McGregor
1943 Private Christopher McGregor
2510 Private Duncan Macinnes
1380 Private Donald Mackenzie
1452 Private Archibald Mackenzie
662 Private John Mackenzie
2266 Private Ewen Mackenzie
1838 Private Charles J. Mackintosh
1840 Private James D. Mackintosh
2181 Private James G. Mackintosh
1451 Private Alexander Mackintosh
1060 Private James Mackintosh
1274 Private John Mackintosh
702 Private William Mackintosh
1061 Private William Mackintosh
1658 Private Lachlan Macintosh
1662 Private James Macintosh
1802 Private Henry D. Mackintosh
1850 Private Alistair D. Mackintosh
1938 Private Alexander Mackintosh
2231 Private D.D. Mackintosh
1630 Private William MacLean
452 Private Angus MacPhee
1406 Private Duncan McPhee

2001	Private Gerald F. Marshall
1485	Private John Moran
2096	Private Frederick Mott
2118	Private Gordon C. Muirhead
1182	Private Henry R. Munro
2382	Private John Munro
519	Private Robert A. Munro
1100	Private James C. Munro
677	Private Alexander Mackay
1770	Private Christopher McErlich
1799	Private George McKillop
1111	Private Donald MacKinnon
1826	Private George M. MacLeod
759	Private Allan MacLachlan
815	Private Ewan MacLachlan
1798	Private Alexander MacLachlan
1201	Private Alexander MacPherson
516	Private Ewan MacPherson
1302	Private James MacPherson
1202	Private William MacPherson
1530	Private John MacPherson
1611	Private John MacPherson
1614	Private Lachlan MacPherson
1758	Private John S. MacPherson
1767	Private William MacPherson
1806	Private Angus MacPherson
2556	Private William MacPherson
1473	Private James Macrae
1475	Private Alexander Macrae
1939	Private John M. Matheson
1512	Private William Mellis
2003	Private John Neilson
2120	Private George Nicol
2102	Private William E. Oakley
1827	Private Ewan Ormiston
2110	Private Frank Padden
1198	Private Neil Paterson
789	Private John Reid
1181	Private Alexander B. Robertson
1199	Private John Robertson
979	Private Peter Robertson

1993	Private Frederick A. Robertson
1820	Private Henry Ross
1306	Private Lewis Rose
1768	Private James Rennie
1405	Private Charles Sampson
2282	Private William Sim
2095	Private George Smart
869	Private James Scott
1997	Private Alexander Smith
2106	Private Edgar S. Smith
2163	Private Frederick Smith
1014	Private Hugh Smith
1839	Private John A. Stewart
1200	Private Donald Stewart
2116	Private Douglas B. Spurr
1256	Private Walter Thompson
1099	Private Angus Taylor
1944	Private John Tulloch
2112	Private Alexander R. Wallace
1448	Private Andrew E. Watson
917	Private Daniel Watson
2229	Private James Waugh
1618	Drummer John Waugh
2222	Private William Whittingham
2119	Private Thomas F. Woodhouse
2104	Private Leslie G. Workman
2114	Private Lawrence H. Worrall

D Company (Old G and H, Beauly and Portree Companies)

Officers

Captain Ronald MacDonald T.D.
Captain Nigel B. Mackenzie
Lieutenant Angus Ross
Lieutenant Archibald M. Fletcher
2nd Lieutenant Joshua C. Thompson
2nd Lieutenant Cameron R. Carruthers

Roll of D Company in Order of Seniority

402	CSM William Ross
302	CQMS Alistair F. Paterson

721	Pioneer Sergeant John Willox
334	Sergeant Roderick Kemp
173	Sergeant Alexander Mackenzie
295	Sergeant John MacDonald
2158	Sergeant Archibald D. MacAfee
457	Lance Sergeant Duncan Graham
555	Lance Sergeant Donald Macleod
517	Lance Sergeant Alexander MacLeod
1556	Lance Sergeant Donald MacDonald
937	Corporal William Fraser
496	Corporal W.J. Fraser
2162	Corporal John R. Cooley
1042	Corporal Alexander McCallum
1164	Corporal Simon Campbell
192	Corporal James Beaton
1488	Corporal Donald Beaton
1394	Corporal Duncan Fraser
1023	Corporal Thomas MacDonald
630	Lance Corporal Donald MacCrimmon
492	Lance Corporal John Beaton
1356	Lance Corporal John A. Morrison
1322	Lance Corporal Evan J. Macnab
175	Lance Corporal Charles Sinclair
1152	Lance Corporal William Fraser
1088	Lance Corporal Murdo Ferguson
1194	Lance Corporal Angus R. Campbell
1216	Lance Corporal William MacDonald
1118	Lance Corporal Hugh Fraser
2252	Lance Corporal John MacLeod
2234	Lance Corporal Charles Winstone
1117	Lance Corporal Kenneth MacDonald
2184	Lance Corporal Ernest Brodie
2154	Lance Corporal Ernest W. Nightingale
2546	Lance Corporal James Vass
1116	Lance Corporal Robert Munro
1425	Lance Corporal Charles Hercher
1393	Lance Corporal Alexander Munro
645	Lance Corporal Donald Paterson
2198	Private Alfred Akehurst
2511	Private James Baker
2136	Private Charles Barnard

2194 Private Douglas Berg
2211 Private Lawrence P. Bevan
2133 Private George N.T. Boots
2199 Private Horace Blore
2138 Private Geoffrey Bowles
2190 Private James Bruce
1845 Private Angus C. Baxter
2671 Private George M. Cameron
2127 Private Walter Cassingham
1886 Private Alexander Clark
2182 Private Alexander H. Clark
2202 Private Arthur F. Coates
2213 Private Ernest Cooper
1296 Private John A. Cumming
1398 Private Patrick Dailly
1929 Private William Dingwall
1934 Private David Drennan
2108 Private Alexander A.J. Duff
2500 Private Thomas J. Davies
2193 Private George W. Emery
2207 Private William Feiling
1484 Private James Fitzgerald
2467 Private Donald Forsyth
2468 Private Stuart Forsyth
1142 Private Harry Fraser
1222 Private John Fraser
1901 Private James W Fraser
717 Private Thomas Fraser
1933 Private William Fraser
1434 Private Donald Finlayson
1371 Private Ronald Ferguson
2367 Private George Forbes
2547 Private Robert Forbes
2471 Private Edward Fyfe
2137 Private Leonard Gable
1195 Private Thomas Gallacher
1141 Private Edward Gallacher
2155 Private John Glossop
2188 Private Frederick H. Gooch
2206 Private Alfred W. Gray
2195 Private Gordon A. Gray

2191	Private Edwin J. Green
2122	Private Robert Green
2123	Private George Grist
2201	Private Joseph A. Grist
2140	Private David Gunn
1479	Private John K. Gillies
1564	Private John Grant
2131	Private Sydney E. Hands
1543	Private John J. Hercher
2205	Private Thomas Hislop
2186	Private Walter R. Hislop
2214	Private Leonard Higgins
2126	Private James B. Jackson
1300	Private Samuel Johnstone
174	Private William Kemp
2197	Private Herbert D. Kidd
2209	Private John Kowin
1561	Private John Kennedy
2216	Private Harry Locke
2448	Private James Little
2364	Private Francis Lowe
1683	Private John Macaskill
1680	Private Ewan Macaskill
1391	Private Donald W. Macaskil
1549	Private John Macaskill
1897	Private Thomas W McCallum
1414	Private Murdo McDermid
1043	Private Alexander MacDonald
1592	Private Norman MacDonald
1209	Private John MacDougall
1092	Private John MacDougall
1239	Private John MacFarlane
2210	Private Frederick McGowan
1603	Private William McGregor
1147	Private John Macinnes
1599	Private Donald MacInnes
1720	Private John Macinnes
1463	Private Thomas McKenzie
197	Private John Mackenzie
1153	Private James Mackenzie
742	Private Donald Mackenzie

2255	Private John McKay
1211	Private John A. McKinnon
2124	Private Robert F. MacLaren
1888	Private Alexander MacLennan
1246	Private Donald MacLennan
2557	Private James MacLennan
2553	Private Duncan MacLennan
1547	Private Donald MacLennan
1375	Private Hugh MacPherson
1540	Private Hugh Macrae
1903	Private John MacLean
408	Private Donald MacLean
736	Private John MacLean
1166	Private John MacLean
1563	Private Murdo MacLean
1558	Private Donald MacLean
1089	Private Donald MacLeod
1238	Private John MacLeod
1151	Private Lachlan MacLeod
883	Private Murdo MacLeod
1590	Private Donald A. MacLeod
2542	Private Duncan MacLeod
1560	Private Roderick MacNeill
2548	Private James Mackintosh
2445	Private John Mackintosh
2135	Private Ernest G. Major
2215	Private Llewellyn Marsh
2208	Private Cyril H. Matthews
2160	Private Walter S. Matthews
1744	Private Alexander Montgomery
2196	Private Hector M. Morison
1251	Private Alick Murray
2150	Private Charles G. Nightingale
1150	Private Alexander Nicolson
795	Private John Nicholson
1342	Private Murdo Nicholson
1435	Private William Nicholson
1480	Private John W. Nicholson
1570	Private John Nicholson
1566	Private Murdo Nicholson
2159	Private James R Penn

2217	Private Gerald W. Pilon
2480	Private Alexander Petrie
2233	Private James Philip
2128	Private Charles Risley
1584	Private Duncan Ross
1932	Private Peter Ross
1377	Private Richard G. Ross
1030	Private Alexander Ross
2192	Private Albin F.L. Rous
2203	Private William A. Row
2351	Private John C. Robertson
2537	Private Edward Rowles
2161	Private William C.H. Sadler
1930	Private Henry Scott
1469	Private William Scott
2125	Private Eric H. Simpson
2185	Private Francis E. Smith
2212	Private Arthur Southcott
2200	Private William M. Stacey
1887	Private David Stewart
2452	Private Alexander R. Stewart
1577	Private John Stewart
1977	Private Duncan Strachan
2187	Private Stuart E. Sturgeon
2484	Private Kenneth Sutherland
2365	Private George Sinclair
2232	Private Robert Skinner
2362	Private Phillip Sheddon
2189	Private Arnold Theobald
1904	Private Reginald Thirtle
2183	Private T. Thorn
1931	Private William Tolmie
2278	Private Donald Tait
2451	Private William Tweedie
2523	Private Alexander Whiteford
1140	Private Andrew White

Appendix 3

Men Not Mentioned

List of men who travelled to France with the battalion 19 February 1915 but who are not mentioned in the Personnel Rolls in the *Inverness Courier*.

734	Sergeant Alexander Campbell
172	Sergeant Finley Kemp
95	Sergeant Alexander MacPhee
39	Acting Sergeant Lachlan Macintyre
307	Acting Sergeant Duncan Mackenzie
1935	Corporal William A. Barnett
349	Corporal Dugald Beaton
149	Corporal Alexander Fraser
1196	Corporal William G. Fraser
1317	Corporal Kenneth MacDonald
147	Corporal Donald Mackenzie
1819	Lance Corporal Alexander Fraser
1252	Lance Corporal William Morrison
1652	Drummer William Campbell
651	Private John Anderson
2117	Private Thomas S.J. Ault
933	Private Alexander Beaton
1617	Private Donald Cameron

1735	Private David Cooper
2774	Private Horace H. Dukes
2086	Private Ralph Edwards
2600	Private Robert Eglinton
750	Private George Findlay
2434	Private William Fraser
1136	Private James Fraser
1739	Private Bertie Hudson
1155	Private John M. Hutcheson
841	Private Ewen C. MacDonald
1596	Private Ewen MacDonald
2567	Private James MacDonald
3042	Private John McEwan
1236	Private John MacIntosh
1359	Private John MacKay
1787	Private Kenneth MacKay
1710	Private John MacKenzie
2236	Private Donald Mackenzie
1364	Private Duncan MacKinnon
1231	Private Donald MacKinnon
1948	Private William MacKintosh
1747	Private John R. MacLean
435	Private Alexander MacPhee
1370	Private Hugh MacPherson
2326	Private A. Mitchell
1915	Private Donald J. Munro
1242	Private U. Nicholson
1651	Private George W. Oliver
3009	Private William Sharp
2010	Private Lowton H. Sheppard
2482	Private Francis Skiffington
2071	Private Richard C.J. Smith
871	Private Alexander Stewart
1695	Private William C. Stewart
2204	Private Thomas Stoddart
3001	Private Charles Taylor
1502	Private Hugh Tyronney
2219	Private Reginald W. Unwin

Appendix 4

Reinforcements

List of reinforcements to the 4th Cameron Highlanders taken from lists published in the *79th News* and from the Soldiers Medal Index Cards held in the National Archives in the series WO/372.

25 February 1915 (Officers Promoted from the Ranks on Departure from Bedford on but Joining the Battalion at Unknown Dates)

Lieutenant Roderick McErlich (formerly 1378, Sergeant in A Company)
Lieutenant Alexander R. Wallace (formerly 2112, Private in C Company)
Lieutenant James R. Park (formerly 1893, Private in A Company)
2nd Lieutenant Max A. Rommele (formerly 2223, Private in A Company)
2nd Lieutenant Alistair F. Paterson (formerly 302, CSM in D Company)
2nd Lieutenant Herbert D. Kidd (formerly 2197, Private in D Company)
2nd Lieutenant Hector M. Morison (formerly 2196, Private in D Company)

22 March 1915 (Replacement Officers from 2/4th Cameron Highlanders)

Captain Ronald Macdonald T.D., D Company
Captain Peter M. Cram, C Company
Captain Ian H. Baillie, B Company
2nd Lieutenant Alexander R. Mackenzie, A Company

2nd Lieutenant James D. Bookless, B Company
2nd Lieutenant Thomas Chalmers, D Company

15 April 1915 (Replacement Officers from 2/4th Cameron Highlanders)

2nd Lieutenant Henry J. Scott, D Company
2nd Lieutenant William G.M. Dobie
2nd Lieutenant H. Donald Ross, A Company
2nd Lieutenant Angus Urquhart, D Company

18 April 1915 (Draft of Replacements from 2/4th Cameron Highlanders)

2569	Sergeant William Guthrie
2634	Lance Corporal Charles Angus
2545	Lance Corporal Duncan A. Clark
2455	Lance Corporal Alexander Milligan
2550	Lance Corporal John Macdonald
2875	Lance Corporal Duncan Mackenzie
2872	Lance Corporal James Mackenzie
3095	Lance Corporal Alexander MacLean
2876	Lance Corporal Duncan MacLean
2726	Private Hugh Allan
2688	Private Robert Arnott
2896	Private Abraham Blair
2880	Private John W. Briskham
2835	Private James Campbell
2595	Private James Carmichael
2939	Private James Carruthers
2660	Private Bernard Chrystal
2722	Private James Collins
2603	Private James Crichton
2259	Private James Crumlin
2964	Private John Cullen
2464	Private Edward Dalton
2727	Private Ian J. Donald
2774	Private Horace Dukes
2588	Private James Dunlop
2600	Private Robert Eglinton
2593	Private Robert Erwin
2646	Private James F. Forbes

2270	Private William Forbes
2517	Private Charles Fraser
2870	Private Evan Fraser
2944	Private Hugh Fraser
2589	Private Peter Fraser
2881	Private William D. Fraser
2921	Private Robert Gibson
2863	Private John Goodall
2578	Private Peter H. Gouldie
2871	Private George Hammond
2954	Private Henry Hendry
2717	Private Lowden M. Hillcoat
2909	Private John Martin
2741	Private Archibald D. Mathieson
2910	Private Allan Morrison
2360	Private John Morrison
2601	Private Thomas Miller
2793	Private Andrew C. Muir
2740	Private Gilmour McCulloch
2263	Private John McDermid
1374	Private Angus Macdonald
2544	Private Alexander Macdonald
2573	Private George Macdonald
2567	Private James Macdonald
2891	Private James Macdonald
2879	Private William Macdonald
2543	Private William Macdonald
2638	Private Alexander MacGregor
2672	Private A.G. McGregor
2806	Private Harold McGregor
2641	Private James McGregor
2815	Private William McGuire
3094	Private Duncan A. MacDonald
3098	Private John MacDonald
3029	Private Evan MacDougall
2948	Private Alexander Mackay
763	Private Alexander Mackenzie
2846	Private Duncan Mackenzie
2477	Private John Mackenzie
2575	Private Murdo Mackenzie
2955	Private Roderick Mackenzie

2422 Private William Mackie
3073 Private Harry Marello
465 Private John Maclennan
2814 Private Donald MacLeod
2658 Private Patrick MacMorrow
2719 Private Alexander MacNeill
2453 Private John Nelson
2957 Private D. Nicholson
2893 Private James Nugent
3093 Private Angus B.M. Nicholson
2580 Private James Prior
2865 Private Robert Palmer
2951 Private James Robertson
2264 Private Alexander Ross
2265 Private David Ross
2516 Private George Ross
2633 Private James Saunders
2632 Private William Saunders
2591 Private William Scott
2856 Private Angus Stewart
2822 Private John Stoddart
2579 Private Jeffrey Summers
2817 Private Thomas Sibbald
1668 Private James G. Smith
2250 Private Robert Turner
2575 Private William Turnbull
2602 Private James Walker
2616 Private Hugh Wordie
2998 Private Charles Willis
2488 Private William J. Young

1 May 1915 (4th Cameron Highlanders men attached to the Headquarters of 152nd Brigade, 51st Highland Division)

1518 CQMS Arnold Brownson
1051 Private James F. Dunbar
896 Private William Johnstone
1565 Private Alexander Kennedy
1086 Private Neil MacKinnon
129 Private Alexander Mackintosh
1134 Private Andrew Scott

9 May 1915 (Draft of Replacements from 2/4th Cameron Highlanders)

2627	Sergeant Robert J Bryant
835	Corporal Farquhar Nicholson
2372	Lance Corporal Lachlan Black
1187	Lance Corporal Kenneth Logan
1220	Lance Corporal James McGregor
1324	Lance Corporal William McGregor
871	Lance Corporal Alexander Stewart
3064	Private Alexander Bain
2273	Private Alexander Campbell
3067	Private Andrew M. Crombie
2444	Private Donald Cattanach
1173	Private Donald Fraser
2442	Private John Fyfe
1229	Private Alexander Finlayson
2759	Private William J. Matthews
1829	Private Alexander Munro
3051	Private John Munro
1685	Private Kenneth MacDonald
1688	Private Angus MacKenzie
2238	Private Simon MacKenzie
1093	Private Kenneth MacKenzie
1569	Private Peter MacKinnon
1908	Private Alick MacLennan
1188	Private Neil MacLeod
1227	Private John MacPherson
1467	Private James MacPherson
2379	Private John MacQueen
1570	Private John Nicholson
1404	Private James Stewart
1562	Private John Urquhart

8 June 1915 (Officer Promoted from the Ranks)

2nd Lieutenant Donald M. Finlayson, C Company (formerly 1412, Private in A Company)

14 July 1915 (Replacement Officers from 2/4th Cameron Highlanders)

Lieutenant Neil McArthur, D Company
Lieutenant James A. Symon

Lieutenant William E. Cattanach
Lieutenant George C. MacMillan, D Company
Lieutenant Charles C. Douglas, D Company
2nd Lieutenant Archibald A. MacDonald, B Company
2nd Lieutenant Donald John Maciver, A Company
2nd Lieutenant Donald Morrison, C Company
2nd Lieutenant Charles S. Powell
2nd Lieutenant William S. Valentine, C Company
2nd Lieutenant James R. Park, B Company

21 July 1915 (Replacement Officer from 2/4th Cameron Highlanders)

2nd Lieutenant A.W. Hughes, A Company

3 August 1915 (Draft of Replacements from 3/4th Cameron Highlanders)

492	Corporal John Beaton*
3412	Corporal John Jardine
137	Corporal Richard MacLean
1779	Lance Corporal David Mair*
1503	Lance Corporal Hugh S.F. Munro*
3255	Private William G. Anderson
1741	Private Norman Beaton*
3241	Private William Borkwood
3249	Private John Bown
3407	Private Alexander Boyes
3270	Private Reginald Bridge
1348	Private William Cowie*
3291	Private George Dungworth
3284	Private Harold Dutton
1455	Private Adam R. Fraser*
3267	Private Leslie Fraser
3279	Private Alfred Farniss
3259	Private William Higgins
454	Private John Hossack*
3260	Private Samuel Lomas
3394	Private Francis J. Lowe
2135	Private Ernest G. Major*
1939	Private John M. Matheson*
2426	Private Thomas Morgan

3235 Private Albert Mutton
1680 Private Ewen MacAskill*
3285 Private Roderick MacDonald
1197 Private William J. MacDonald*
829 Private Robert J. McGregor*
162 Private Colin Macinnes*
1599 Private Donald W. Macinnes*
2987 Private John Macintyre
197 Private John Mackenzie*
2421 Private Donald MacLean*
2876 Private Duncan MacLean
2557 Private James MacLennan*
972 Private William MacLeod*
1767 Private William MacPherson*
3283 Private Thomas C. Nicholson
3316 Private William Nolan
3278 Private James H. Paterson
3245 Private William Paterson
2233 Private James Phillip*
2377 Private George C. Robertson*
3247 Private Robert L. Robertson
3069 Private P. Stuart
3269 Private Frederick Stocks
3277 Private William C. Tyrrell
3268 Private Nelson Whittaker

Those men marked with an asterisk had previously served with the battalion.

7 September 1915 (Draft of Replacements from 3/4th Cameron Highlanders)

2267 Sergeant Robert K. Davidson
3251 Sergeant Lawrence Kitson
1851 Sergeant Bertram W. Tawse
192 Corporal James Beaton
1196 Corporal William G. Fraser
320 Corporal John MacEachen
1167 Corporal Beveridge A. Matthewson
3242 Corporal Donald Polwarth
1205 Corporal Alexander Robertson
2864 Corporal William Ross

448	Lance Corporal David G. Grant
2088	Private Charles N. Anderson
3266	Private Walter S. Andrews
3421	Private Ernest Atkinson
3452	Private Edgar Austin
3231	Private Albert Bagshaw
3476	Private Duncan Bain
3482	Private Samuel Bankhead
3320	Private James T. Barker
3263	Private Harry Barlow
3436	Private Frederick W. Barrier
3230	Private Joseph Baxendall
1717	Private William Baxter
2896	Private Abraham Blair
3276	Private Albert Bolton
3402	Private Joseph Boothby
3406	Private Robert Boothby
3224	Private Arthur Bowman
3369	Private Robert Brannan
3318	Private Archibald Butler
3297	Private Anthony Button
3382	Private John Byth
3352	Private John Cameron
3480	Private William Cameron
3449	Private Samuel Christy
3483	Private William H. Clegg
3265	Private William G. Cockerill
3366	Private Benjamin Coldwell
3435	Private James Connor
2259	Private James Crumlin
3323	Private John Cumming
3334	Private Alexander Dunn
3264	Private James Dunnigan
3306	Private Charles Dyce
3401	Private James Elliot
3112	Private William W. Evans
3455	Private John Ferrin
3461	Private James Fields
1691	Private David Forbes
2180	Private John A. Forbes
2547	Private Robert Forbes
1233	Private Alick Fraser

3324	Private Alexander Fraser
3453	Private John Garland
3393	Private Walter Garton
2578	Private Peter H. Gouldie
3361	Private Alexander Garden
1910	Private A. Gray
3354	Private Joseph Hamil
3467	Private Thomas J. Housell
3395	Private William A. Harding
3340	Private Douglas Hardwick
3471	Private Harry Hartley
3303	Private William Haslam
3363	Private John W. Hawley
3262	Private Edward Heaton
3371	Private Ernest Hill
3385	Private Victor Hodgson
3261	Private Frederick Holmes
3416	Private Peter Horne
3309	Private Alexander Hunt
3448	Private Robert Hunter
3204	Private William Jefferson
3236	Private Charles Jones
2109	Private Arthur J. Kelleher
1383	Private Donald Kennedy
1891	Private Thomas Kennedy
3332	Private Frederick Lobb
3248	Private Joseph E. Marshall
3321	Private Albert E. Magee
2175	Private Alexander Menzies
3282	Private Edwin Middlecote
3431	Private William Moore
2096	Private Frederick Mott
1915	Private Donald J. Munro
1897	Private Thomas McCallum
1757	Private John MacDonald
1092	Private John MacDougall
3322	Private John A. Mackenzie
3328	Private Alexander J. MacLean
1188	Private Neil MacLeod
1560	Private Roderick MacNeil
516	Private Ewan D. MacPherson
1494	Private Peter MacQueen

3454	Private James O'Hara
3434	Private Thomas Paulson
3479	Private Joseph A. Power
3281	Private Clifford Rogers
2059	Private Wilfred A. Rogers
3319	Private Charles V. Ross
3288	Private William Ross
3275	Private A. Shaw
3238	Private John L. Sheard
1754	Private Thomas Sinclair
2555	Private Duncan Smith
3237	Private Samuel Stead
3105	Private John Watson
3442	Private A. Whyte
3223	Private Stanley J. Youell

21 September 1915 (Draft of Replacements from 3/4th Cameron Highlanders)

3343	Lance Corporal Donald MacDonald
3377	Lance Corporal Allan MacPherson
3337	Lance Corporal George W. Radcliffe
3466	Private Albert W. Bainbridge
3367	Private William G. Boot
3600	Private John Burgoyne
3565	Private Archibald Cameron
3462	Private James Chevers
3687	Private Ernest Cole
3460	Private James Craven
3438	Private David S. Cruden
3478	Private Robert Davis
1572	Private John Dunbar
3451	Private Patrick J. Fearon
3414	Private Albert Fuller
3289	Private Albert A. Gibson
2122	Private Robert Green
3298	Private Arthur Hill
2214	Private Leonard Higgins
3338	Private Francis W. Holt
3412	Private P.W. Jordan
3549	Private William Jones
3314	Private Tom Kendall

3667 Private Albert H. Lambert
3390 Private Herbert Lazenby
3725 Private George Little
3357 Private Albert F.G. Macartney
3424 Private James Mason
3463 Private John Metcalfe
3299 Private Cyril V. Montague
3293 Private Arthur Mosey
3339 Private John C.P. Musson
3378 Private James McCulloch
1274 Private John Mackintosh
1733 Private Joseph MacKenzie
3353 Private Angus MacMaster
3351 Private Duncan McPhee
3458 Private John W. Nadin
3469 Private William O'Neill
1768 Private James Rennie
2192 Private Albin F.L. Rous
3410 Private Harry Saxby
3311 Private William Scales
3256 Private Robert Simpson
3380 Private Albert Stenton
3326 Private James Stephen
3300 Private George H. Thomas
2451 Private William Tweedie
3240 Private William O. Winder

5 October 1915 (Replacement Officer from 2/4th Cameron Highlanders)

Lieutenant John Clift, A Company

24 October 1915 (Draft of Replacement Officers from 2/4th Cameron Highlanders)

Captain Alexander H. MacBean, C Company
Lieutenant Alfred W.H. Cooper, D Company
Lieutenant George M.W. Johnson, A Company
Lieutenant Alistair Birnie, C Company
Lieutenant Alfred G. Calder, A Company
2nd Lieutenant Hugo F. Henderson, A Company
2nd Lieutenant James Smith, B Company

2nd Lieutenant Benjamin J. Bartholomew, D Company
2nd Lieutenant Archie J. Macrae, D Company
2nd Lieuteanant Archibald R. Mackenzie, D Company

27 October 1915 (Draft of Replacements from 3/4th Cameron Highlanders)

3336	Lance Corporal William Dix
3253	Lance Corporal Richard L. Thompson
3418	Private Walter Blackburn
3490	Private J. Campbell
3800	Private Robert Corrigan
3605	Private Robert Crombie
3500	Private George B. Crowther
3375	Private Matthew Etherington
3497	Private John Fraser
3492	Private Edward Hall
3504	Private John W. Kevitt
3400	Private Frederick McCurdy
3495	Private Alexander MacDonald
3511	Private E.J. MacDonald
3578	Private Alexander Mackenzie
3359	Private Hugh Munro
3404	Private J. Murray
3503	Private Ellis Nadin
3348	Private William Nisbet
3475	Private John T. Parkin
3502	Private George Petty
3379	Private Peter Pirie
3583	Private Michael Stewart
3417	Private Robert M. Walton
3433	Private Robert Wilson

29 October 1915 (Officer Promoted from the Ranks)

2nd Lieutenant David Melville, C Company (formerly 1690, Private in A Company)

6 November 1915 (Draft of Replacements from the 3/4th Cameron Highlanders)

3335	Lance Corporal Thomas Percival
3472	Private John W. Carnall

3308 Private Harold Dryhurst
3420 Private Joseph Leeming
3422 Private William Pennells
3239 Private Benjamin Bradley
3477 Private Frederick Collins
3292 Private Frederick Farnley
3456 Private James Minty
3459 Private John Waite
3387 Private Sidney B. Tomlinson
3464 Private Herbert Davies
3427 Private H. Kerr
3355 Private George Palfreyman
3465 Private John A. Wrightson
3304 Lance Sergeant Arthur R. Mason
3658 Lance Corporal Angus M. Cattanach
3561 Lance Corporal John MacDonald
3551 Lance Corporal William Matthew
3553 Private Sydney Ainsworth
3576 Private John Alexander
3524 Private George C. Ball
3594 Private George Blackburn
3575 Private Alexander Brownlee
3601 Private John Cameron
3531 Private John J.B. Clarke
3528 Private Harry B. Collinson
3616 Private Stanley M. Downs
3515 Private James W. Freeman
3555 Private George W. French
3637 Private Frank Franklin
3521 Private Herbert Hanson
3513 Private William Hartley
3570 Private Matthew Heptinstall
3560 Private John W. Hough
3595 Private Arthur Jowitt
3573 Private James Kelly
3571 Private Frederick Longstaff
3602 Private John Lorimer
3592 Private Donald J. Macaskill
3593 Private James Mackintosh
3516 Private John W. McIver
3625 Private Ewen MacPherson

3584	Private Reginald H. Mathers
3556	Private William May
3559	Private Horace Maycock
3626	Private Frederick Medcalf
3572	Private Christopher Moody
3597	Private Thomas Murray
2522	Private Alick Davidson
3643	Private Louis H. Nelsey
3603	Private John Niven
3541	Private Walter Prime
3580	Private William Ramsay
3554	Private Walter Raynes
3566	Private George Reid
3590	Private Donald Robertson
3624	Private Roger Rose
3596	Private William Sharp
3612	Private John Shaw
2585	Private George Telfer
3557	Private Victor Thompson
3547	Private John Tulloch
3629	Private Walter Turton
3530	Private Alexander Webster
3517	Private Charles W. Wright

20 November 1915 (Officer Returning from Sick Leave)

Captain Archibald M. Fletcher, D Company

21 November 1915 (Replacement Officer from 3/4th Cameron Highlanders)

2nd Lieutenant Illtyd MacKintosh, B Company

30 December 1915 (Officer Returning from Wounds)

Captain Angus Ross, C Company (wounded at Neuve Chapelle, March 1915)

20 January 1916 (Replacement Officers from 3/4th Cameron Highlanders)

2nd Lieutenant Charles F. MacGillivray, C Company
2nd Lieutenant Charles H.S. Hunter, D Company
2nd Lieutenant Harry A. Mackintosh, B Company

2nd Lieutenant Harold M. White, C Company
2nd Lieutenant James MacDonald, B Company

19 February 1916 (Officer Promoted from the Ranks)

2nd Lieutenant Donald MacDonald (formerly Lance Corporal 826, A Company)

24 February 1916 (Draft of Replacements from 3/4th Cameron Highlanders)

1398	Private Patrick Dailly
1431	Private Donald Grant
1471	Private Donald MacPherson
1612	Private Donald MacLeay
1712	Private Robert Lipp
1924	Private Daniel Stanger
1951	Private Duncan MacDonald
2468	Private Stuart Forsyth
2488	Private W.G. Young
2500	Private Thomas Davies
2545	Private Duncan A. Clark
2557	Private James MacLennan
2573	Private Donald MacDonald
2589	Private Peter Fraser
2591	Private William Scott
2638	Private Alexander McGregor
2875	Private Duncan Mackenzie
2881	Private W.D. Fraser
3237	Private Samuel Stead
3246	Private Harold Taylor
3342	Private Donald MacLeod
3346	Private John Girvan
3370	Private J.T. Brown
3405	Private George Dunkerley
3426	Private H. McKevitt
3439	Private J. Petrie
3443	Private Thomas Dand
3454	Private James O'Hara
3470	Private Arnold E. Wilson
3523	Private Fred Graham
3526	Private T. Kirkbride

3544	Private Ewart Downs
3577	Private George James
3582	Private Alexander Smith
3598	Private Walter Greaves
3599	Private W. Allan
3604	Private J. MacKintosh
3607	Private Richard Burton
3609	Private Horace Wilson
3613	Private William Wood
3627	Private Charles Dickens
3635	Private Harry Simpson
3636	Private Bernard Drabble
3638	Private Oliver Brownlow
3639	Private John G. Fraser
3642	Private H. Wasridge
3645	Private Alfred Bellhouse
3647	Private R. Chisholm
3649	Private Fred Spink
3653	Private John Jeffreys
3654	Private Mark Alderson
3656	Private Isaac Steinberg
3662	Private Frank Martin
3663	Private John Beanland
3668	Private John Hardaker
3670	Private Donald MacDonald
3680	Private Percy McManus
3681	Private John Easy
3686	Private Albert Griffiths
3692	Private William H. Wood
3693	Private W. Smith
3694	Private Walter H. Ward
3701	Private Albert A. Barber
3703	Private D. Carson
3704	Private Reginald C. Whinnett
3716	Private C. Knowling
3720	Private P. Crawford
3724	Private J.H. Butler
3735	Private Horace Marshall
3739	Private R. Turner
3746	Private S. Moorhouse
3753	Private Harold Adelson

3760	Private William Pryce
3663	Private Harry Hemingway
3775	Private Frank Ludbrook
3800	Private Robert Corrigan
3805	Private Bert Harrison
3814	Private John Call
3818	Private Hugh Fraser
4089	Private Donald McKenzie
4082	Private Alexander Garden

7 March 1916 (Officer Returning from Wounds)

2nd Lieutenant Archibald A. MacDonald, B Company

7 March 1916 (Draft of Replacements from 3/4th Cameron Highlanders)

172	Sergeant Finlay Kemp
742	Private Donald MacKenzie
1375	Private Hugh MacPherson
1414	Private Murdo McDermid
2580	Private James Prior
3110	Private William J. Dunbar
3280	Private H. Robinson
3281	Private J. McGowan
3290	Private J. Senior
3313	Private Maurice Thomson
3325	Private Alexander Long
3329	Private D. MacDonald
3330	Private R. MacDonald
3489	Private William R. Knight
3494	Private Ernest V. Talbot
3501	Private William H. Sawdon
3505	Private Arthur Plackett
3535	Private Joseph Suckley
3543	Private William Lee
3564	Private William Grant
3569	Private Frederick Tingle
3591	Private Thomas D Mackenzie
3608	Private J. Carr
3623	Private Harold Coe
3641	Private Victor Sanderson

3652	Private Joseph Knight
3660	Private John W. Fowler
3661	Private Harry B. Braithwaite
3664	Private J. Stewart
3669	Private William H. Brookes
3676	Private George Hewson
3677	Private Richard Denby
3684	Private Harold Wood
3690	Private H. Scholey
3691	Private John T. Thompson
3700	Private William Rollinson
3702	Private George Ferguson
3705	Private Leonard Summerscales
3722	Private Seth Ellwood
3723	Private Herbert Cawthra
3736	Private William Hyder
3757	Private A. Hargreaves
3769	Private Alfred Watson
3770	Private John W. Asquith
3776	Private Alexander McIver
3786	Private John Taylor
3790	Private Arthur Muscroft
3791	Private Ewan Fraser
3792	Private Angus J. MacCuish
3794	Private James Gordon
3802	Private James S. Mackintosh
3804	Private Peter Fraser
3810	Private John Macintyre
3812	Private Harold B. Airton
3815	Private John Donald
3816	Private Harry B. Clough
3825	Private Charles A. Foster
3826	Private William Gabriel
3829	Private Johnstone McCormack
3839	Private J. Rennie
3845	Private Harold Miller
3847	Private Joseph Kitson
3851	Private George M. Broughton
3853	Private George Mercer
3854	Private David Hewitt
3859	Private Hugh MacLean

3875	Private John Buchanan
3877	Private John W. McGowan
3795	Private Kenneth Mackenzie
3880	Private Francis MacDonald
3886	Private F. Mackenzie
3887	Private C.A. Barber
3893	Private William Jowitt
3900	Private William Sim
3902	Private Maurice Walmsley
3903	Private David Moulson
3923	Private Roderick MacCuish
3929	Private Thomas L. Howell
3963	Private Donald F. Marsh
3976	Private Matthew Hilton
3977	Private Alexander Skinner
3978	Private Peter MacDougall
3979	Private Duncan Mackay
3989	Private John Gledhill
3990	Private D.J. Carpenter
3991	Private Thomas W Webb
3994	Private William C. Iredale
3995	Private James H. Sykes
4001	Private Norman Kaye
4008	Private Raymond Lister
4018	Private John E. Dawson
4029	Private Frederick Barry
4030	Private Ralph Avery
4031	Private John Codman
4088	Private Charles Sanderson
4135	Private Ralph Sugden
4137	Private J. Bromilow
4198	Private Thomas Barker
4614	Private A. Smedley

Appendix 5

Roll of Honour

Roll of Honour of the 4th Battalion, Cameron Highlanders from mobilisation in August 1914 to the end of the battalion in March 1916.

1718 Alexander, James John (Private)
Born on 22 March 1894 at 9a Grant Street, Nairn to Donald Alexander and Christina MacIntosh. Lived at the Hermitage, Nairn and worked as a Chauffeur. He served in B Company. He travelled to France on 19 February 1915. Killed at the Battle of Loos on 28 September 1915, aged 21. Commemorated on the Loos Memorial.

1928 Allan, Private Duncan (Private)
Born on 7 September 1890 at 59 Cumberland Street, Edinburgh to Robert Allan and Grace McPhee. Lived in Fort William. He served in C Company. He travelled to France on 19 February 1915. Killed at the Battle of Festubert on 18 May 1915, aged 24. He was shot in the advance on the Southern Breastwork Trench. Body was found by Canadian soldiers and buried where he fell. Commemorated on the Le Touret Memorial.

1849 Allan, William Bethune (Acting Lance Corporal)
Born on 31 January 1890 at Rockburn, Southside Road, Inverness to Alexander Allan and Isabella Bethune. Lived at Seafield, Inverness and worked

as an apprentice dentist in Inverness. He served in A Company's Grenade Platoon. He travelled to France on 19 February 1915. Killed at the Battle of Loos on 27 September 1915, aged 25. Shot through the chest when the enemy attacked Stone Alley Trench after taking command of the platoon when all officers and NCOs were hit. Buried by his comrades in Stone Alley and commemorated on the Loos Memorial.

2041 Anderson, George Gordon (Corporal)

Born in 1876 in London to John Anderson and Jessie Ellis. He served in the Boer War. He married and lived at Lulworth, Lyme Regis Road, Banstead, Surrey. He enlisted in London *c.*7 September 1914. He served in A Company. He travelled to France on 19 February 1915. Killed at the Battle of Festubert on 18 May 1915, aged 39. Commemorated on the Le Touret Memorial.

1126 Anderson, John James (Private)

Born on 29 March 1891 at Fernieflatt, Colinton, Midlothian to John Anderson and Jane Meikle. He was adopted by Mrs Donald, Temperance Hotel, Auldearn. He worked as a gardener in Auldearn. Contracted measles while at Bedford and died at the 1st Scottish General Hospital in Aberdeen on 20 February 1916, aged 24. Buried in Auldearn Parish Churchyard.

2511 Baker, James (Private)

Born on 11 January 1894 at Sunderland, Parish of Kilchoman, Islay to John Baker and Mary McKenzie. He served in D Company. He travelled to France on 19 February 1915 and died on 18 May 1915, aged 21. Commemorated on the Le Touret Memorial.

1344 Beaton, Donald (Private)

Born on 22 April 1894 at Bailgowan, Kilmuir, Isle of Skye, the illegitimate son of Marion Beaton. Died of measles in Bedford on 28 December 1914, aged 20. Buried at Kilmuir Churchyard in Skye.

192 Beaton, James (Corporal)

Born on 26 July 1893 at Bonville Terrace, Portree, Isle of Skye to Alexander Beaton and Catherine Lawrie. He served in D Company. He travelled to France on 19 February 1915. He was wounded at the Battle of Festubert on 18 May 1915 and evacuated to England. He returned to the front on 7 September 1915 and was killed in action on 25 September 1915, aged 22. Commemorated on the Loos Memorial.

1047 Beattie, William (Lance Corporal)
Born on 13 March 1894 at 33 Reid Street, Glasgow to Robert Beattie and Elizabeth F Bruce. Lived in Tweedale Place, Fort William. He served in C Company. He travelled to France on 19 February 1915 and died at the Battle of Festubert on 18 May 1915, aged 21. Commemorated on the Le Touret Memorial.

2065 Belk, Eric Herbert (Private)
Born in London, son or grandson of Minna Seymour Belk. He served in A Company. He travelled to France on 19 February 1915 and died at the Battle of Loos on 28 September 1915. Commemorated on the Loos Memorial.

2194 Berg, Douglas (Private)
Born in 1894 in London to John and Elizabeth Berg. Lived at 11 Chardmore Road, Stoke Newington, London. He served in D Company. He travelled to France on 19 February 1915 and died at the Battle of Festubert on 18 May 1915, aged 21. Commemorated on the Le Touret Memorial.

2211 Bevan, Lawrence Percy (Private)
Born in 1889 at London to John Percy Bevan. He served in D Company. He travelled to France on 19 February 1915 and was wounded at the Battle of Festubert on 17 May 1915. He died at Choques on 19 May 1915, aged 26. Buried at Choques Military Cemetery.

2896 Blair, Abraham (Private)
Born on 9 January 1895 at 12 Ritchie Street, Glasgow to Francis Blair and Mary Cranston. He served in D Company. He travelled to France on 18 April 1915 and died at the Battle of Loos on 25 September 1915, aged 20. Commemorated on the Loos Memorial.

2138 Bowles, Geoffrey (Private)
Born in 1892 in London to John William Bowles. Lived at 70 Elmhurst Road, Forest Gate, Essex. He served in D Company. He travelled to France on 19 February 1915 and died at the Battle of Festubert on 17 May 1915, aged 23. Commemorated on the Le Touret Memorial.

2013 Brister, John Edmund (Lance Corporal)
Born in 1887 in London to John and Emily Brister. Lived at 41 Second Avenue, Chelsea. He served in A Company. He travelled to France on 19 February 1915 and died at the Battle of Festubert on 18 May 1915, aged 28. Commemorated on the Le Touret Memorial.

2115 Brown, John Allinson (Private)
Born in 1890 in Bishop Auckland, County Durham to Simpson and Mary A Brown. He served in C Company. He travelled to France on 19 February 1915 and died at the Battle of Festubert on 18 May 1915, aged 25. Commemorated on the Le Touret Memorial.

1994 Brown, Peter Dalziel (Private)
Born on 26 October 1887 at 6 Struan Villas, Kilmarnock to Peter Brown and Christina Dalziel. He served in C Company. He travelled to France on 19 February 1915 and died of an accident on 4 May 1915, aged 27. Buried at Le Grand Hasard Military Cemetery, Morbecque.

2048 Buckby, Henry Fisher (Private)
Born in 1888 in London to George W and Elizabeth Buckby. He served in B Company with his brother Charles. Lived at 1 Cliftonville Road, Margate. He travelled to France on 19 February 1915 and died at the Battle of Festubert on 18 May 1915, aged 27. Commemorated on the Le Touret Memorial.

3297 Button, Anthony (Private)
Born in 1892 in Deepcar, Stocksbridge, Yorkshire to Timothy and Jessie Button. Lived at 53 Haywood Park, Deepcar. He travelled to France on 7 September 1915 and died at the Battle of Loos on 26 September 1915, aged 23. Commemorated on the Loos Memorial.

1652 Campbell, William (Bugler)
Born on 9 June 1898 at Culcabock, Inverness to Donald Campbell and Mary Anne MacLennan. Parents emigrated to South Africa. He travelled to France on 19 February 1915 and died after being shot in the head on 8 March 1915, aged 16. Buried at Rue de Bacquerot Cemetery No.1, Laventie.

1761 Carmichael, Hugh (Private)
Born on 1 June 1890 at Duart, Torosay, Isle of Mull to Hugh Carmichael and Julia Macintyre. He enlisted at Fort William. He travelled to France on 19 February 1915 and was wounded in action on 12 March 1915 at the Battle of Neuve Chapelle. He returned to duty and was killed at the Battle of Festubert on 18 May 1915, aged 24. Commemorated on the Le Touret Memorial.

2595 Carmichael, James (Private)
Born on 7 April 1888 at 10 Cavendish Street, Glasgow to James Carmichael and Eliza Jane Fisher. He served in D Company. He travelled to France on

18 April 1915 and died at the Battle of Festubert on 18 May 1915, aged 27. Commemorated on the Le Touret Memorial.

2939 Carruthers, James (Private)

Born on 12 October 1892 at 148 Blackburn Street, Govan, Glasgow to Donald Carruthers and Isabella McLean. He served in D Company. He travelled to France on 18 April 1915 and died at the Battle of Festubert on 18 May 1915, aged 22. Commemorated on the Le Touret Memorial.

1760 Cameron, Alexander (Private)

Born on 28 November 1889 at Ballachulish, Glencoe to Hugh Cameron and Clementina Cameron. Lived at New Pier, Fort William. He served in C Company. He travelled to France on 19 February 1915 and died at the Battle of Festubert on 18 May 1915, aged 25. Commemorated on the Le Touret Memorial.

1740 Cameron, Donald (Private)

Born on 23 December 1890 at Hazelbank, Tomatin, Moy to Donald Cameron and Lillias Fraser. He served in C Company. He travelled to France on 19 February 1915 and was wounded in action on at Neuve Chapelle on and died of his wounds on at No.13 Stationary Hospital in Boulogne on 21 March 1915, aged 24. Buried at Boulogne Eastern Cemetery.

1916 Cameron, Duncan (Private)

Born on 29 May 1890 at Boleskine Glebe, Boleskine to John Cameron and Annie MacGillivray. He served in B Company. He travelled to France on 19 February 1915 and was killed during the Battle of Festubert on 17 May 1915, aged 24. Commemorated on the Le Touret Memorial.

1156 Cameron, John Alexander (Private)

Born on 18 June 1895 at Fort William to John Cameron and Catherine McPherson. He served in C Company. He travelled to France on 19 February 1915 and was wounded during the Battle of Festubert, 18 May 1915. Died on 20 May 1915, aged 19 at No.1 Casualty Clearing Station. Buried at Chocques Military Cemetery.

260 Cattanach, Donald Alexander (Sergeant)

Born on 10 June 1879 at Newtonmore to Alexander Cattanach and Catherine Campbell. He worked as a mas in Newtonmore. He married to Jessie Wotherspoon. Died of tuberculosis on 9 August 1914 at East End, Newtonmore, aged 35. Buried at Banchor Burial Ground, Newtonmore.

2444 Cattanach, Donald, (Private)
Born on 27 July 1892 at Newtonmore to John Cattanach and Christina Ferguson. He served in C Company. He travelled to France on 9 May 1915 and died at the Battle of Festubert on 18 May 1915, aged 22. Commemorated on the Le Touret Memorial.

1847 Charles, John (Private)
Born on 4 June 1893 at 1 Willowside Place, Aberdeen to George Charles and Jane Simpson. He served in A Company. He travelled to France on 19 February 1915 and was killed by enemy shelling at the Battle of Aubers Ridge, 8 May 1915, aged 21. Buried at Royal Irish Rifles Graveyard, Laventie.

1895 Charker, Arthur (Private)
Born on 10 July 1890 at Lochluichart, Contin to Henry John Charker and Isabella Smith. He served in C Company. Lived at 120 Academy Street, Inverness. Killed in a drunken fight by Private John Fraser (No.1888) on 9 October 1914 at 6 Albert Terrace, Union Street, Bedford on, aged 24. Fraser was charged initially with wounding but it was changed to murder after Charker died. Fraser pled guilty to a reduced sentence of manslaughter and was sentenced to 15 months hard labour despite witnesses at the trial and inquest saying that it seemed to be an accident. Buried at Bedford on Cemetery, Bedford.

2069 Chase, Edwin Henry (Private)
Born in 1892 in London to George and Eliza Chase. He served in A Company. He travelled to France on 19 February 1915. Killed at the Battle of Neuve Chapelle on 13 March 1915, aged 22. Commemorated on Le Touret Memorial.

1120 Cheyne, John Thomas (Private)
Born on 10 August 1890 at Stronhill, Lhanbryde to Charles Cheyne and Elizabeth Hood. Lived at Milbuis, Elgin and enlisted at Kingussie. He served in C Company. He travelled to France on 19 February 1915. Killed at the Battle of Festubert on 18 May 1915, aged 24. Employed in the battalion Pipe Band. Commemorated on the Le Touret Memorial.

39 Chisholm, Robert Darling (Sergeant)
Born on 10 December 1875 at 17 Bell Place, Edinburgh to David Chisholm and Jane Darling. Before the war employed in the Highland Book Shop, High Street, Inverness. He served in A Company. He travelled to France on

19 February 1915 and was promoted Machine Gun Sergeant. Killed instantly on 28 September 1915, aged 39 at the Battle of Loos when the trench he was manning came under heavy German artillery fire and he took a direct hit. Commemorated on the Loos Memorial.

2182 Clark, Alexander Harry (Private)

Born in 1890 in London. Adopted son of Edith Nash, 39 Ravenslea Road, Wandsworth Common, London. He served in D Company. He travelled to France on 19 February 1915. Killed at the Battle of Festubert on 17 May 1915, aged 25. Commemorated on the Le Touret Memorial.

2202 Coates, Arthur Frederick (Private)

Served in D Company. He travelled to France on 19 February 1915. Killed at the Battle of Festubert on 17 May 1915. Commemorated on the Le Touret Memorial.

3265 Cockerill, William G (Private)

Born in 1888 in Northallerton, Yorkshire. He married to Belle Cockerill of Waterloo Yard, Northallerton. He served in D Company. He travelled to France on 7 September 1915 and was wounded at the Battle of Loos on 25 September 1915, aged 27. Died on 29 September 1915 at Wimereaux. Buried at Wimereaux Communal Cemetery.

2098 Collins, Arthur James (Private)

Born in 1891 in London to George D and Mary M Collins. Lived at 157 Mount Pleasant Lane, Upper Clapton, London. He served in C Company. He travelled to France on 19 February 1915. Killed at the Battle of Festubert on 18 May 1915, aged 24. Commemorated on the Le Touret Memorial.

2162 Cooley, John Roger (Sergeant)

Born in London. He travelled to France on 19 February 1915 and was killed on 16 June 1915 at the Battle of Givenchy on when a shell came through the parapet in a support trench behind Piccadilly Trench killing 10 men and wounding many more. Commemorated on the Le Touret Memorial.

1416 Corner, Albert Just (Private)

Born on 27 July 1895 at Brookside, Drummond Road, Inverness to William Corner and Hedwig Dorothea Just. His mother was German. He served in A Company. He travelled to France on 19 February 1915 and was killed at the Battle of Neuve Chapelle on 12 March 1915, aged 19. He was seen to fall during the battalion advance on Pietre but his colleagues could not find him later that day and assumed he had been picked up by a field ambulance. Commemorated on the Le Touret Memorial.

657 Curley, William (Private)

Born on 4 July 1891 at Milton of Muide, Kingussie to Alexander Curley and Marjory MacDonald. Brother John also served with the battalion. He served in C Company. He travelled to France on 19 February 1915. Killed at the Battle of Festubert on 18 May 1915, aged 23. Commemorated on the Le Touret Memorial.

2464 Dalton, Edward (Private)

Born on 17 June 1896 at 14 Clark Street, Kinning Park, Glasgow to Edward Dalton and Mary Anne Gillespie. He served in A Company. He travelled to France on 18 April 1915. Killed at the Battle of Festubert on 17 May 1915, aged 18. Commemorated on the Le Touret Memorial.

1890 Davidson, James Donald (Private)

Born on 10 November 1889 at the Waverley Hotel, Inverness to Donald Davidson and Emily Umpleby. He was educated at Inverness Royal Academy. He worked as a barman for his father who owned the Waverley Hotel and in the Inverness Branch of the National Bank. Keen golfer and hockey and tennis player. He served in A Company. He travelled to France on 19 February 1915 and was killed at the Battle of Festubert on 18 May 1915, aged 25. Previously served with the Lovat Scouts and volunteered for the 4th Camerons on the outbreak of war along with all his friends. He was hit by a shell beside his best friend Lance Corporal Donald Melven, who also died. Commemorated on Le Touret Memorial.

2707 Donald, Ian James (Private)

Born on 21 March 1895 at Inchmore, Kirkhill to John Donald and Mary Fraser. Lived at Inchmore Schoolhouse. He worked as an accountant in the Rosehearty Branch of the Union Bank. He served in B Company. He travelled to France on 18 April 1915 and died at the Battle of Festubert on 17 May 1915, aged 20. Buried at Guards Cemetery, Windy Corner, Cuinchy.

3003 Dott, Alexander (Private)

Born on 12 September 1894 at Spey Street, Kingussie to John Dott and Helen Cumming. His brother William also served with the 4th Camerons. He served in C Company. He travelled to France on 19 February 1915 and died at the Battle of Festubert on 18 May 1915, aged 20. Commemorated on the Le Touret Memorial.

1883 Dow, Alistair (Lance Corporal)
Born on 22 June 1892 at Church of Scotland Manse, Strathfillan, Perthshire to Reverend John Dow and Jessie S Harvey. Lived at Foyers. He served in B Company. He travelled to France on 19 February 1915 and was wounded at Neuve Chapelle on 12 March 1915. He returned to duty and was killed during the Battle of Givenchy on 16 June 1915, aged 22. Commemorated on the Le Touret Memorial.

1000 Duff, John Barbour (Corporal)
Born on 14 May 1892 at Grigorhill, Auldearn to Finlay Duff and Isabella Barbour. Lived at Woodfield Cottage, Auldearn. He worked as a mechanic with Knowles and Cumming in Nairn before the war. He served in B Company. He travelled to France on 19 February 1915 and was wounded at the Battle of Givenchy on 16 June 1915. Died of gunshot wounds at No.1 Canadian General Hospital, Étaples on 20 June 1915, aged 23. Buried at Étaples Military Cemetery.

2744 Dukes, Horace Harold (Private)
Born in 1896 at Watford, Hertfordshire to Job and Mary Anne Dukes. Lived at 23 Shaftesbury Road, Watford. He served in D Company. He travelled to France on 19 February 1915 and was wounded at the Battle of Festubert on 18 May 1915, aged 19. Died later the same day at No.6 Field Ambulance. Buried at Bethune Town Cemetery.

3306 Dyce, Charles (Private)
Born on 14 March 1894 at Little Cantray, Croy to Charles Dyce and Johan Mackenzie. He served in D Company. He travelled to France on 7 September 1915 and was wounded on 25 September 1915. Evacuated and died on the same day, aged 21. Buried at Fouquieres Churchyard Extension.

2086 Edwards, Ralph (Private)
Born in 1889 at Woodford, Essex to Samuel J and Harriet A Edwards. Lived at 8 Eatington Road, Leyton, London. He served in A Company. He travelled to France on 19 February 1915 and was killed in action on 9 March 1915, aged 25. Buried at Rue du Bacquerot Cemetery No.1, Laventie.

2176 Ernest or Pratten, George William (Private)
Born in 1896 at Woodford, Essex to Henry and Isobel Pratten. He enlisted under the name George Ernest. He travelled to France on 19 February 1915 and was killed in action on 28 September 1915, aged 19. Commemorated on the Loos Memorial.

3112 Evans, William Wilson (Private)

Born on 11 July 1891 at 51 Reid Street, Bridgeton, Glasgow to Henry Evans and Sarah Wilson. He served in A Company. He travelled to France on 7 September 1915 and was killed in action on 28 September 1915, aged 24. Commemorated on the Loos Memorial.

1371 Ferguson, Ronald (Private)

Born on 13 March 1896 at Tarbert, Harris to Roderick Ferguson and Ella Macinnes. He served in D Company. He travelled to France on 19 February 1915 and was killed at the Battle of Festubert on 18 May 1915, aged 19. Commemorated on the Le Touret Memorial.

1484 Fitzgerald, James (Private)

Born on 15 May 1895 at 134 Garngad Road, Glasgow to Ellen Fitzgerald. He served in D Company. He travelled to France on 19 February 1915 and was wounded at Neuve Chapelle on 12 March 1915. He returned to duty and was wounded again at Festubert on 17 May 1915. Evacuated and died of spinal meningitis at Monsall Fever Hospital, Manchester on 31 May 1915, aged 20. Buried at Moston St Joseph's Roman Catholic Churchyard, Manchester.

1384 Fleming, William (Private)

Born on 16 June 1896 at Cloichard Cottage, Pitlochry, Perthshire to Peter Fleming and Jane Cramond. Lived at 28 Middle Street, Fort William. He served in C Company. He travelled to France on 19 February 1915 and was wounded on 17 May 1915. Evacuated and succumbed to his wounds on 6 June 1915 at the Meerut General Hospital in Rouen, aged 18. He died of a wound to the right lung and spinal meningitis. Buried at St Sever Cemetery, Rouen.

2367 Forbes, George (Private)

Born in 1895 in Edinburgh. He enlisted in Edinburgh. He served in D Company. He travelled to France on 19 February 1915 and was killed at the Battle of Festubert on 18 May 1915, aged 20. Commemorated on the Le Touret Memorial.

2270 Forbes, William (Private)

Born on 11 November 1896 at Bahill, Rafford to Hugh Forbes and Anne Mitchell. He served in D Company. He travelled to France on 18 April 1915 and died of typhoid on 4 July 1915, aged 18. Buried at Le Treport Military Cemetery.

1819 Fraser, Alexander (Lance Corporal)
Born on 9 February 1885 at 5 Reay Street, Inverness to Alexander Fraser and Catherine Young. Lived at 44 Denny Street, Inverness. Before the war he worked as a postman with his father in Inverness. He served in B Company. He travelled to France on 19 February 1915 and was killed at the Battle of Neuve Chapelle on 10 March 1915, aged 30. Commemorated on the Le Touret Memorial.

1336 Fraser, Colin (Private)
Born on 30 August 1895 at Abbey Cottage, Fort Augustus to Hugh Fraser and Williamina Fraser. Lived at The Schoolhouse, Tomcharrich, Fort William. He served in C Company. He travelled to France on 19 February 1915 and was killed on 8 March 1915, aged 19, in C Lines trenches in front of Neuve Chapelle village when a shell hit and exploded a bomb store in the British trench. Buried at Rue du Bacquerot Cemetery No.1, Laventie.

1394 Fraser, Duncan (Corporal)
Born on 26 September 1895 at Forsinard, Strathy, Sutherland to John Fraser and Elizabeth Macduff. Lived at Glen Banvie, Beaufort Gardens, Beauly. He enlisted at Beauly on 3 February 1913 and went to France on 19 February 1915. He served in D Company. He was wounded at the Battle of Loos on 4 October 1915 and was evacuated to Britain where he died of typhoid fever on 20 November 1915, aged 20. Buried at Kilmorack Cemetery, Beauly.

1142 Fraser, Harry (Private)
Born on 1 November 1893 at the village of Kirkhill to John Fraser and Catherine Corbett. He served in D Company. He travelled to France on 19 February 1915 and was killed at the Battle of Festubert on 18 May 1915, aged 21. Commemorated on the Le Touret Memorial.

1797 Fraser, Hugh (Private)
Born on 5 August 1886 at Farraline, Fort Augustus, Boleskine to Thomas Fraser and Eliza McKenzie. He travelled to France on 19 February 1915 and died at the Battle of Festubert on 18 May 1915, aged 28. Commemorated on the Le Touret Memorial.

1766 Fraser, John (Private)
Born in 1880 at Inverness to Donald and Mary Fraser. He served in B Company. He travelled to France on 19 February 1915 and was killed at the Battle of Festubert on 17 May 1915, aged 35. Commemorated on the Le Touret Memorial.

717 Fraser, Thomas (Private)
Born on 11 April 1890 at Cammault, Kiltarlity to Hugh Fraser and Catherine Fraser. He served in D Company. He travelled to France on 19 February 1915 and was wounded in action on at the Battle of Neuve Chapelle on 13 March 1915. Evacuated to Britain and died at Norwich on 20 March 1915, aged 24. Buried at Tomnacross Cemetery.

2434 Fraser, William (Private)
Born in 1897 at Invergordon to Mr and Mrs H. Fraser, Poyntzfield, Invergordon. He served in C Company. He travelled to France on 19 February 1915 and died of scarlet fever at Number 10 Stationary Hospital, St Omer on 28 February 1915, aged 18. Buried at Longuenesse St Omer Souvenir Cemetery.

2437 Fraser, William (Private)
Born on 14 December 1898 at Fornighty, Ardclach to James Fraser and Mary MacDonald. Before the war he worked as a farm servant. He served as a Private in the 2/4th Camerons and died of pneumonia at Blair Atholl on 22 August 1915, aged 16. Buried at Auldearn Churchyard.

2030 Fyfe, Albert Sidney (Private)
Born in 1886 at 13 Stanley Villas, Tottenham, London to William W. Fyfe and Sophia Jamieson Fyfe. He served in A Company. He travelled to France on 19 February 1915 and was killed in action during the Battle of Loos on 25 September 1915, aged 29. Commemorated on the Loos Memorial.

1195 Gallacher, Thomas (Private)
Born in 1892 in Glasgow. He enlisted at Beauly. He served in D Company. He travelled to France on 19 February 1915. He was wounded at the Battle of Aubers Ridge on 9 May 1915. Died of wounds at No.14 Stationary Hospital, Wimereaux on 11 May 1915, aged 22. Buried at Wimereaux Communal Cemetery.

1669 Geddes, James (Private)
Born in Brora. He enlisted at Culloden and served in B Company. Died of measles on 13 December 1914 at Bedford. Buried at Bedford on Cemetery.

2921 Gibson, Robert (Private)
Born on 21 June 1885 at 34 Castle Street, Inverness to Peter Gibson and Isabella Kennedy. He served in B Company, employed as an officer's servant. He travelled to France on 18 April 1915 and was wounded in action

during the Battle of Loos on 27 September 1915. Evacuated and died on 29 September 1915, aged 30. Buried at Lillers Communal Cemetery.

1260 Gollan, Alexander (Private)

Born on 5 March 1896 at Stromeferry, Lochalsh to Donald Gollan and Christina Mackay. He worked as a fireman on the railways. He served in B Company. He travelled to France on 19 February 1915 and was killed at the Battle of Neuve Chapelle on 10 March 1915, aged 19. Commemorated on Le Touret Memorial.

2188 Gooch, Frederick Harvey (Private)

Born in London. He served in D Company. He travelled to France on 19 February 1915 and was killed at the Battle of Loos on 28 September 1915. Commemorated on the Loos Memorial.

1711 Gordon, John (Corporal)

Born on 26 February 1891 at 5 King Street, Inverness to Peter Gordon and Isabella Cameron, Lived at Craigellachie, Milburn Road, Inverness. He served in A Company. He travelled to France on 19 February 1915 and was killed at the Battle of Festubert on 18 May 1915, aged 24. Commemorated on the Loos Memorial.

411 Graham, Peter (Lance Corporal)

Born in 1890 in Snizort, Isle of Skye to Donald Graham and Helen Campbell. He served with the 2/4th Cameron Highlanders. Died of tuberculosis at Stobhill Hospital, Glasgow on 18 June 1916, aged 26. Buried at Uig Cemetery, Snizort.

448 Grant, David George (Lance Corporal)

Born on 17 October 1890 at Auchnaba, Lochgilphead to George Grant and Jessie Bryce. He served in C Company and the Machine Gun Section. He travelled to France on 19 February 1915 and was promoted Lance Corporal 29 March 1915. He was wounded in action at the Battle of Givenchy on 16 June 1915. He returned to France on 7 September 1915 and was wounded at the Battle of Loos on 28 September 1915. Evacuated and died of wounds on 7 October 1915, aged 24. Buried at Le Treport Military Cemetery.

1796 Grant, Donald (Lance Corporal)

Born on 18 June 1887 at Old Schoolhouse, Invergarry to John Grant and Margaret MacDonald. Before the war he worked as a forester at Fersit. He served in C Company. He travelled to France on 19 February 1915 and was killed in action on 12 March 1915 at the Battle of Neuve Chapelle, aged 27. A shell exploded in C Company's trenches wounding 2 officers and 6 NCOs and killing Lance Corporal Grant. Commemorated on the Le Touret Memorial.

1535 Grant, James (Private)

Born on 14 March 1893 at Delnies Cottage, Nairn to James Grant and Annie McGregor. Before the war he worked as a farm labourer at Easter Delnies. He served in C Company. He travelled to France on 19 February 1915 and was wounded at the Battle of Festubert on 17 May 1915. Evacuated and died on 23 May 1915, aged 22. Buried at Chocques Military Cemetery. His brother William had died two weeks earlier with the 2nd Seaforth Highlanders.

1564 Grant, John (Private)

Born on 20 October 1891 at Fasach, Duirinish, Isle of Skye to Ewen Grant and Mary Anne Beaton. He served in D Company. He travelled to France on 19 February 1915 and was killed at the Battle of Festubert on 18 May 1915, aged 23. Commemorated on the Le Touret Memorial.

2034 Hammerton, Leslie (Private)

Born in 1896 at London to Ernest and Clara Hammerton. He served in A Company. He travelled to France on 19 February 1915 and served as a machine gunner. Killed in action at the Battle of Loos on 28 September 1915, aged 19. Commemorated on the Loos Memorial.

2871 Hammond, George William (Private)

Born in 1896 in St Ives to William and Charlotte Hammond. He enlisted in Inverness. He served in A Company. He travelled to France on 18 April 1915. Killed at the Battle of Givenchy on 16 June 1915, aged 19. Commemorated on the Le Touret Memorial.

2131 Hands, Sidney Ernest (Private)

Born in 1892 in Faversham, Kent. He served in D Company. He travelled to France on 19 February 1915 and was killed at the Battle of Festubert on 18 May 1915, aged 23. Commemorated on the Le Touret Memorial.

2091 Henderson, Thomas (Private)

Born in 1892 at Balham, Surrey to Thomas and Matilda Henderson. Lived at 72 Alderbrook Road, Balham, London. He served in A Company. He travelled to France on 19 February 1915 and was killed at the Battle of Neuve Chapelle on 10 March 1915, aged 22. Commemorated on the Le Touret Memorial.

2954 Hendry, Henry (Private)

Born in 1896 in Glasgow. He served in D Company. He travelled to France on 18 April 1915 and was killed at the Battle of Festubert on 17 May 1915, aged 19. Commemorated on the Le Touret Memorial.

1657 Hendry, John (Private)

Born on 30 December 1892 at Phones, Kingussie to John Hendry and Anne Stronach. He served with the 2/4th Cameron Highlanders. Died of measles at Bedford on 1 January 1915, aged 22. Buried at Kingussie Churchyard.

2186 Hislop, Walter Richard (Private)

Born in 1891 in London to Thomas and Emily Hislop. He served in D Company. He travelled to France on 19 February 1915 and was killed at the Battle of Festubert on 17 May 1915, aged 24. Commemorated on the Le Touret Memorial.

3385 Hodgson, Victor (Private)

Born in 1896 in Hull to John and Harriet Hodgson. Lived at 20 Wycliffe Grove, Hull. He served in B Company. He travelled to France on 7 September 1915 and was killed in action on 28 September 1915 at the Battle of Loos, aged 19. Commemorated on the Loos Memorial.

2355 Hoggan, Matthew (Private)

Born on 23 July 1892 at Broadrig, Airdrie to James Hoggan and Catherine Penman. He served in B Company. He travelled to France on 19 February 1915 and was killed (shot in the stomach) in action on 17 May 1915 at the Battle of Festubert, aged 22. Commemorated on the Le Touret Memorial.

454 Hossack, John (Lance Corporal)

Born on 4 September 1887 at Newton of Budget, Cawdor to John Hossack and Eliza Fraser. He served in B Company. He travelled to France on 19 February 1915 and was wounded on 17 April 1915 in E Lines Trenches. He returned to France on 6 August 1915 and died on 25 September 1915 at the Battle of Loos, aged 28. Commemorated on the Loos Memorial.

272 Johnston, Alexander (Sergeant)

Born on 22 March 1879 at 9 Albert Place, Inverness to James Johnston and Mary MacLean. Before the war he was a farmer with his father at Rait, Nairn. He served in B Company. He travelled to France on 19 February 1915 and was struck on the forehead by a piece of shrapnel on the morning of

10 March 1915. He fell unconscious instantly and died the following morning, aged 35. Buried at Rue du Bacquerot Cemetery No.1, Laventie.

1507 Kennedy, Louis (Private)

Born on 29 September 1895 at Drumochter, Laggan to Donald Kennedy and Margaret Smith. He served in C Company. He travelled to France on 19 February 1915. Died as a result of getting into difficulty while swimming in a canal at Robecq on 23 May 1915, aged 19. Buried at Robecq Communal Cemetery.

2164 King, William (Private)

Served in C Company. He travelled to France on 19 February 1915 and was killed in action on 12 March 1915 at the Battle of Neuve Chapelle. Commemorated on the Le Touret Memorial.

2080 Lambert, Francis William (Lance Corporal)

Born in 1885 at London to George and Ella Lambert of Chingford, Essex. He served in A Company. He travelled to France on 19 February 1915 and was wounded in action on at the Battle of Loos on 28 September 1915. He died of his wounds on 9 October 1915, aged 30. Buried in Cambrin Churchyard Extension.

1593 Lamont, Malcolm (Private)

Born on 12 December 1897 at Achtercairn Schoolhouse, Gairloch to Malcolm Lamont and Nellie Maclennan. Lived at Woodbine Cottage, Auldearn. He served in B Company. He travelled to France on 19 February 1915 and worked as a signaller. Killed in action by a shell blast in a support trench behind Piccadilly at the Battle of Givenchy on 16 June 1915, aged 17. Commemorated on the Le Touret Memorial.

2002 Law, Robert McLaren (Private)

Born on 15 June 1891 at 6 Bowmont Terrace, Strathburgo, Glasgow to Robert Law and Helen Duncan. He served in C Company. He travelled to France on 19 February 1915 and was killed at the Battle of Festubert on 18 May 1915, aged 23. Commemorated on the Le Touret Memorial.

2448 Little, James (Private)

Born in 1896 at Glasgow to William and Sarah Little. He served in D Company. He travelled to France on 19 February 1915 and was killed at the Battle of Festubert on 18 May 1915, aged 19. Commemorated on the Le Touret Memorial.

2216 Locke, Harry (Acting Lance Corporal)

Born in 1890 at London to William and Alice Locke of Cheam, Surrey. He served in D Company. He travelled to France on 19 February 1915 and was killed at the Battle of Givenchy on 16 June 1915, aged 25. Commemorated on the Le Touret Memorial.

2364 Lowe, Francis (Private)

Born in 1884 in Edinburgh. He served in D Company. He travelled to France on 19 February 1915 and was wounded on 8 May 1915 at the Battle of Aubers Ridge. Evacuated and died on his way to a Casualty Clearing Station, aged 30. Buried at Merville Communal Cemetery.

1957 MacAdam, John (Private)

Born on 21 August 1897 at 37 Stanhope Street, Glasgow to Hamilton MacAdam and Annie Skinner. He served in B Company. He travelled to France on 19 February 1915 and was wounded in action on at the Battle of Festubert on 17 May 1915. Evacuated and died of his wounds on 21 May 1915, aged 17. Commemorated on the Le Touret Memorial.

2158 McAfee, Archibald David (Sergeant)

Born in 1882 in Belfast to Mrs E.M. McAfee. Lived in Barnet. He served in D Company. He travelled to France on 19 February 1915. Killed at the Battle of Festubert on 17 May 1915. Commemorated on the Le Touret Memorial.

2561 MacAulay, Alexander (Private)

Born on 20 September 1897 at Grinsay, North Uist to Ewen MacAulay and Mary MacKenzie. Before the war he worked as a fisherman. He served with the 2/4th Cameron Highlanders. Contracted measles and pneumonia and died on 18 February 1915 at the Kindergarten Hospital, Academy Street, Inverness, aged 17. Buried at Carinish Old Churchyard.

718 McBain, Alexander (Lance Corporal)

Served in D Company. Contracted measles while in Bedford and died on 9 January 1915. His body was repatriated and he was buried in Tomnacross Cemetery.

1597 MacBean, Alexander (Private)

Born on 15 October 1896 at Milehead Cottage, Alvie to Duncan MacBean and Jane Macdonald. He served in C Company. He travelled to France on 19 February 1915 and was wounded at the Battle of Loos on 26 September 1915. Evacuated and died of his wounds in Bethune on 6 October 1915, aged 18. Buried in Bethune Town Cemetery.

1995 McDermott, Charles Edward (Private)

Born in London. He served in C Company. He travelled to France on 19 February 1915 and was wounded in action on 10 March 1915. Evacuated and died of his wounds on 20 March 1915. Buried in Boulogne Eastern Cemetery.

1660 McDonald, Angus (Private)

Served in the 2/4th Cameron Highlanders. While at Bedford he contracted measles and pneumonia and died on 2 January 1915. Buried at Bedford on Cemetery.

1556 MacDonald, Donald McLeod (Lance Sergeant)

Born on 10 December 1888 at Kilmuir, Duirinish, Isle of Skye to John MacDonald and Anne MacLeod. He served in D Company. He travelled to France on 19 February 1915 and was wounded in action on at the Battle of Festubert on 17 May 1915. Died at Westminster Hospital, Le Touquet as a result of septicaemia following the amputation of his left leg at the thigh on 31 May 1915, aged 26. Buried at Le Touquet Paris Plage Cemetery.

1926 MacDonald, Duncan Kennedy (Private)

Born on 22 August 1894 at 20 Cornwall Street, Glasgow to Alexander MacDonald and Isabella Kennedy. Before the war he worked as a barman in Inverness. He served in B Company. He travelled to France on 19 February 1915 and was killed in action on 12 March 1915 at the Battle of Neuve Chapelle, aged 20. Buried at Royal Irish Rifles Graveyard, Laventie.

1772 MacDonald, Duncan (Lance Corporal)

Born on 31 August 1879 at Plainfeld Cottage, Inverness to Baillie Robert MacDonald and Margaret Fraser. He was educated at the High School and Inverness Royal Academy before becoming an apprentice with his father's carpenters firm Fraser and Macdonald. He served in A Company as a stretcher bearer. He travelled to France on 19 February 1915 and was killed in action on 29 September 1915 at the Battle of Loos, aged 36. Captain McErlich wrote to his father that he had been shot in the head by a sniper in the trench while carrying a wounded man. Commemorated on the Loos Memorial.

772 MacDonald, Henry Alexander Watson (Acting Corporal)
Born on 17 October 1890 at Fort William to Angus MacDonald and Zipporah Shaw. He served in C Company. He travelled to France on 19 February 1915 and was wounded in action on at the Battle of Festubert on 17 May 1915. Evacuated and died of his wounds on 23 May at No.13 Stationary Hospital in Boulogne, aged 24. Buried at Boulogne Eastern Cemetery.

1215 MacDonald, James Aitchison (Acting Sergeant)
Born on 5 May 1887 at Station Cottages, Kingussie to James MacDonald and Margaret Campbell. Lived at Dellifour, Kingussie. He served in C Company with his brother John (below). He travelled to France on 19 February 1915 and was killed at the Battle of Festubert on 17 May 1915, aged 28. Commemorated on the Le Touret Memorial.

513 MacDonald, John Campbell (Private)
Born on 3 September 1888 at Station Cottages, Kingussie to James MacDonald and Margaret Campbell. Lived at Dellifour, Kingussie. He served in C Company with his brother James (above). He travelled to France on 19 February 1915 and was killed at the Battle of Festubert on 17 May 1915, aged 26. Commemorated on the Le Touret Memorial.

827 MacDonald, John (Corporal)
Born on 29 November 1892 at Harpool, Strath, Isle of Skye to Christopher MacDonald and Catherine MacDonald. Before the war he was a student of divinity. He served in A Company. He travelled to France on 19 February 1915 and was killed at the Battle of Neuve Chapelle on 10 March 1915, aged 22. Commemorated on the Le Touret Memorial.

1317 MacDonald, Kenneth Stewart (Corporal)
Born on 25 January 1884 at 3 Glebe Street, Inverness to Donald Macdonald and Annie Stewart. He served in A Company. He travelled to France on 19 February 1915 and was killed at the Battle of Festubert on 17 May 1915, aged 31. Commemorated on the Le Touret Memorial.

505 MacDonald, Peter (Sergeant)
Born on 29 January 1884 at Lagganlia, Alvie to Donald MacDonald and Liza Campbell. He served in C Company. He travelled to France on 19 February 1915 and promoted Sergeant after the Battle of Neuve Chapelle. Killed in action at the Battle of Festubert on 18 May 1915, aged 31. Commemorated on the Le Touret Memorial.

1115 MacDonald, Ronald Roderick (Sergeant)

Born on 13 July 1883 at 7 Queen Street, Inverness to Alexander MacDonald and Jessie McDonald. Before the war he worked as a grocer's assistant. He served in B Company and was the Sergeant in charge of the Machine Gun Section. He was the first casualty caused by enemy fire in the battalion's first tour in the trenches, dying on 1 March 1915, aged 31. The Machine Gun Section had just returned to billets when a German shell burst through the roof and exploded, killing Sergeant MacDonald and wounding six others. Buried at Rue du Bacquerot Cemetery No.1, Laventie.

1216 MacDonald, William (Lance Corporal)

Born on 20 June 1894 at Wentworth Street, Portree, Isle of Skye to Archibald MacDonald and Kate Robertson. He served in D Company. He travelled to France on 19 February 1915 and was killed at the Battle of Festubert on 18 May 1915, aged 20. Commemorated on the Le Touret Memorial.

1197 MacDonald, William (Private)

Born on 14 April 1895 at High Street, Kingussie to Jonathan MacDonald and Jane MacKenzie. He served in C Company. He travelled to France on 19 February 1915 and was evacuated sick on 1 April. He returned to France on 6 August 1915 and was wounded in action on 30 September 1915. Evacuated and died of wounds on 5 October 1915, aged 20. Buried at Chocques Military Cemetery.

1828 MacDonald, William (Private)

Served in the old F Company. Contracted measles and died in Bedford on 28 October 1914. Buried at Cromdale Parish Churchyard.

1209 MacDougall, John (Private)

Born on 23 June 1894 at Wood Park, Portree, Isle of Skye to Alexander MacDougall and Ellen Macdonald. He served in D Company. He travelled to France on 19 February 1915 and was killed at the Battle of Festubert on 18 May 1915, aged 20. Commemorated on the Le Touret Memorial.

1239 MacFarlane, John (Private)

Born on 19 February 1895 at Portree Green, Portree, Isle of Skye to Thomas MacFarlane and Euphemia MacLean. Lived at 4 Beaumont Crescent, Portree. He served in D Company. He travelled to France on 19 February 1915 and was killed at the Battle of Festubert on 18 May 1915, aged 20. Commemorated on the Le Touret Memorial.

1490 MacGillivray, William (Private)
Born on 9 October 1883 at High Street, Kingussie to William MacGillivray and Helen Stewart. Lived at Riverdale, Kingussie. He served in C Company. He travelled to France on 19 February 1915 and was killed at the Battle of Festubert on 18 May 1915, aged 31. Commemorated on the Le Touret Memorial.

1220 MacGregor, James (Lance Corporal)
Born in 1894 at Glasgow to Catherine MacCorquhidale. He served in D Company. He travelled to France on 9 May 1915 and was killed at the Battle of Neuve Chapelle on 17 May 1915, aged 21. Commemorated on the Le Touret Memorial.

1324 MacGregor, William (Lance Corporal)
Born on 27 August 1896 at Knockard, Cawdor to Alexander MacGregor and Anne Macdonald. Before the war he worked on his father's farm at Whinhill, Cawdor. He served in B Company. He travelled to France on 9 May 1915 and was killed at the Battle of Loos on 28 September 1915, aged 19. Commemorated on the Loos Memorial.

1689 MacInnes, Neil (Private)
Served in the 2/4th Cameron Highlanders. Contracted measles and pneumonia at Bedford and died there on 6 January 1915. Buried at Sleat Parish Churchyard, Skye.

1061 MacIntosh, William (Private)
Born in 1893 at Kingussie. He served in C Company. He travelled to France on 19 February 1915 and was wounded in action on at the Battle of Neuve Chapelle on 13 March 1915. Evacuated and died of his wounds on 16 March 1915. Buried at Boulogne Eastern Cemetery.

1836 MacKintosh, William (Private)
Born in 1895 at Inverness. He served in B Company. He travelled to France on 19 February 1915 and was killed at the Battle of Festubert on 18 May 1915, aged 20. Commemorated on the Le Touret Memorial.

913 Macintyre, Alexander Matheson (Lance Corporal)
Born on 15 September 1893 at Fort William to Malcolm MacIntyre and Dora Matheson. He served in C Company. He travelled to France on 19 February 1915 and died of wounds received at the Battle of Festubert on 18 May 1915, aged 21. Commemorated on Le Touret Memorial.

1401 MacIntyre, Duncan (Private)
Born on 4 April 1896 at Balnacraig Dunain, Inverness to Alexander MacIntyre and Dora Calder. He served in B Company. He travelled to France on 19 February 1915 and was killed in action on when a shell exploded in his dugout at Vermelles on 22 September 1915, aged 19. Buried at Fouquieres Churchyard Extension.

2502 MacIntyre, James (Private)
Born on 13 August 1897 at Kinning Park, Glasgow to James MacIntyre and Elizabeth Johnston. He served in B Company. He travelled to France on 19 February 1915 and was wounded in action on at the Battle of Neuve Chapelle on 10 March 1915. He returned to duty and killed in action on 17 May 1915, aged 17. Commemorated on the Le Touret Memorial.

93 MacIntyre, William Ambrose (CSM)
Born on 25 April 1883 at Breadalbane Street, Tobermory, Islay to Malcolm MacIntyre and Dora Matheson. He served in C Company. He travelled to France on 19 February 1915 and was shot in the leg on 8 March 1915. Evacuated and died on 25 March 1915 at No.11 General Hospital, Boulogne, aged 31. Buried at Boulogne.

2948 Mackay, Alexander (Private)
Born on 18 February 1880 at Allarburn, Kiltarlity to Donald Mackay and Mary Chisholm. He served in A Company. He travelled to France on 18 April 1915 and was killed at the Battle of Festubert on 17 May 1915, aged 35. Commemorated on the Le Touret Memorial.

602 Mackay, Duncan (Lance Corporal)
Born on 1 March 1892 at 34 Crown Street, Inverness to John Mackay and Annie MacGillivray. He served in A Company. He travelled to France on 19 February 1915 and was killed at the Battle of Neuve Chapelle on 12 March 1915, aged 23. Commemorated on the Le Touret Memorial.

2878 Mackenzie, Alexander (Lance Corporal)
Born on 11 February 1891 at Cull, Glendessary, Kilmallie to John Mackenzie and Margaret Stuart. Lived at Corpach, Invergarry. He served in the 2/4th Cameron Highlanders. Contracted measles and scarlet fever and died at the Northern Infirmary in Inverness on 1 February 1915, aged 23. Buried at Kilchuimen Burial Ground.

1670 Mackenzie, Angus (Private)

Born on 24 August 1897 at Mid of Tore, Glenurquhart to Thomas Mackenzie and Christina Macdonald. He served in the 2/4th Cameron Highlanders. Contracted measles and pneumonia and died at Bedford on 6 January 1915, aged 17. Buried at Drumnadrochit Burial Ground.

1154 Mackenzie, George Forrest (Lance Corporal)

Born on 1 February 1893 at 5 Southside Place, Inverness to Murdo G. Mackenzie and Jenny MacDonald. Lived at Creggan Cottage, Southside Place, Inverness. He served in A Company. He travelled to France on 19 February 1915 and was killed at the Battle of Festubert on 17 May 1915, aged 22. Buried at Guard Cemetery, Windy Corner, Cuinchy.

2695 Mackenzie, Donald (Lance Corporal)

Born in 1889 in Lochaber to Joan Mackenzie, afterwards Ramage. Before the war he lived in Auldearn and worked as a gardener. He served in the 2/4th Cameron Highlanders. Contracted cerebro-spinal meningitis and died at the Citadel Hospital, Inverness on 24 April 1915, aged 25. Buried in Auldearn Parish Churchyard with full military honours. The *Nairnshire Telegraph* reported the 'it was felt that this young soldier had given his life to his country as truly as if he had fallen on the battlefield'.

1380 Mackenzie, Donald (Lance Corporal)

Born on 18 June 1894 at Fort William to Donald Mackenzie and Jessie Smith. Lived at 32 Middle Street, Fort William. He served in C Company. He travelled to France on 19 February 1915 and was killed at the Battle of Festubert on 18 May 1915, aged 20. Commemorated on the Le Touret Memorial.

1852 Mackenzie, Duncan (Private)

Born on 29 March 1872 at Dunkeld Street, Aberfeldy to William MacKenzie and Jessie MacLean. Before the war he worked as a cabinetmaker in Nairn. He enlisted at Inverness. He served in B Company. He travelled to France on 19 February 1915 and was killed at the Battle of Aubers Ridge on 8 May 1915, aged 43. Buried in Rue du Bois Military Cemetery, Fleurbaix.

2477 Mackenzie, John (Private)

Born in Stornoway. He served in D Company. He travelled to France on 18 April 1915 and was killed in action at the Battle of Festubert on 18 May 1915. Commemorated on the Le Touret Memorial.

1710 Mackenzie, John (Private)

Born on 1 December 1891 at King Street, Kingussie to Hugh Mackenzie and Jessie Ann Macintosh. He served in A Company. He travelled to France on 19 February 1915 and was wounded on 10 March 1915. Evacuated and died of his wounds on 16 March 1915, aged 23. Buried at Le Touquet Paris Plage Cemetery.

2872 Mackenzie, James Donald (Private)

Born on 14 January 1892 at Culaird, Dores to Alexander MacKenzie and Margaret Mackintosh. Lived at Dochgarroch, Inverness. He served in B Company. He travelled to France on 18 April 1915 and was killed at the Battle of Festubert on 18 May 1915, aged 23. Commemorated on the Le Touret Memorial.

1972 Mackenzie, Roderick John (Private)

Born on 30 November 1892 at 44 Shore Street, Inverness to Donald Mackenzie and Flora MacKinnon. He served in B Company as a Headquarters Orderly. He travelled to France on 19 February 1915 and was killed in trenches at Le Plantin on 26 November 1915, aged 22. Buried at Browns Road Military Cemetery, Festubert.

2955 Mackenzie, Roderick (Private)

Born on 17 September 1880 at Shore Street, Ullapool, Lochbroom to Murdoch Mackenzie and Catherine Mackenzie. He travelled to France on 18 April 1915 and was wounded on 22 September 1915 by German shelling of his dugout. Died the following day, aged 35. Buried at Fouquieres Churchyard Extension.

1770 MacKerlich, Christopher Macrae (Private)

Born on 14 December 1885 at 17 Church Street, Inverness to Christina MacKerlich. He enlisted at Kingussie. He served in C Company. He travelled to France on 19 February 1915 and was killed at the Battle of Festubert on 18 May 1915, aged 29. Commemorated on the Le Touret Memorial.

2422 Mackie, William (Private)

Born in 1896 in Glasgow to George Mackie of 30 Kilberry Street, Glasgow. He served in B Company. He travelled to France on 18 April 1915 and was killed at the Battle of Festubert on 18 May 1915, aged 19. Commemorated on the Le Touret Memorial.

1361 MacKinnon, Donald (Private)
Born on 7 May 1884 at Taransay, Harris, Western Isles to Malcolm MacKinnon and Mary Morrison. He served in the 2/4th Cameron Highlanders. Contracted measles and pneumonia at Bedford and died on 20 December 1914, aged 30. Buried at Bedford on Cemetery.

1291 MacKinnon, Donald (Lance Corporal)
Born on 25 March 1881 at Breakish, Strath, Isle of Skye to Neil MacKinnon and Catherine Finlayson. He served with the 2/4th Cameron Highlanders. Contracted measles and pneumonia at Bedford and died on 6 January 1915, aged 33. Buried at Kilchrist Churchyard, Skye.

1111 MacKinnon, Donald (Private)
Born in 1892 at Harris, Western Isles. He served in C Company. He travelled to France on 19 February 1915 and was killed at the Battle of Festubert on 18 May 1915, aged 23. Buried at Guards Cemetery, Windy Corner, Cuinchy.

2350 MacKinnon, Ian (Private)
Born on 18 November 1892 at 16 Elgoll, Brim of Strath, Isle of Skye to Lachlan MacKinnon and Janet McInnes. He served in A Company as an officer's servant to Lieutenant William Mackay. He travelled to France on 19 February 1915 and was killed at the Battle of Festubert on 18 May 1915, aged 22. Commemorated on the Le Touret Memorial.

1526 MacKinnon, John (Private)
Born on 2 November 1886 at 16 Elgoll, Strath, Isle of Skye to Neil MacKinnon and Christy MacGillivray. He served in the old H Company. Contracted measles and died in Bedford on 19 January 1915, aged 28. Buried at Kilmarie Cemetery, Skye.

1568 MacKinnon, Peter John (Private)
Born on 15 June 1892 at Struan, Bracadale, Isle of Skye to Duncan MacKinnon and Jessie Stewart. He served in the old H Company. Contracted measles and died in Bedford on 21 December 1914, aged 22. Buried at Bedford on Cemetery.

1938 MacKintosh, Alexander (Lance Corporal)
Born on 9 July 1881 at Balnapick, Inch, Kingussie to John MacKintosh and Mary MacGrigor. He served in C Company. He travelled to France on 19 February 1915 and was wounded in action in trenches at Richebourg on

17 July 1915. He died of his wounds on 20 July 1915, aged 34. Buried at Lillers Communal Cemetery.

1451 MacKintosh, Alexander (Private)
Born on 29 October 1895 at Caggan, Alvie to Neil MacKintosh and Jane Fraser MacKintosh. He served in C Company. He travelled to France on 19 February 1915 and was killed at the Battle of Festubert on 18 May 1915, aged 19. Commemorated on the Le Touret Memorial.

691 MacKintosh, Duncan (Sergeant)
Born on 3 March 1875 at Druminlochan, Alvie to James Mackintosh and Margaret Mackintosh. He served in C Company and as the battalion signal sergeant. He travelled to France on 19 February 1915 and was shot through the heart on 1 October 1915, aged 40. Commemorated on the Loos Memorial.

1802 Mackintosh, Henry Davidson (Lance Corporal)
Born on 7 April 1884 at Dunachtan Mill, Alvie to Alexander Mackintosh and Margaret Grant. He served in C Company. He travelled to France on 19 February 1915 and was killed in action on 27 September 1915, aged 31. Commemorated on the Loos Memorial.

226 Mackintosh, John (Private)
Born on 11 December 1889 at Inch, Kingussie to Angus MacKintosh and Annie MacPherson. He served in the old F Company. Contracted measles at Bedford and died on 4 January 1915, aged 25. Buried in Kingussie Churchyard.

2445 MacKintosh, John (Private)
Born on 20 May 1879 at Mid Urchany, Nairn to David Mackintosh and Margaret MacBean. He served in D Company. He travelled to France on 19 February 1915 and was killed at the Battle of Festubert on 18 May 1915, aged 35. Commemorated on the Le Touret Memorial.

776 MacLachlan, Angus (Lance Corporal)
Born on 15 December 1888 at Blackwood, Laggan to Allan MacLachlan and Isabella Ross. Lived at Torcroy, Kingussie. He served in C Company. He travelled to France on 19 February 1915 and was killed at the Battle of Festubert on 18 May 1915, aged 26. He was one of four brothers serving with the 4th Camerons. Commemorated on the Le Touret Memorial.

1707 MacLean, Alexander Fraser (Private)
Born on 3 April 1893 at 112 Church Street, Inverness to Ewen MacLean and Alexandrina Fraser. He served in A Company as a stretcher bearer. He travelled to France on 19 February 1915 and was killed at the Battle of Festubert on 18 May 1915, aged 22. Commemorated on the Le Touret Memorial.

1583 MacLean, Alexander James (Private)
Born on 18 September 1896 at 28 Hill Terrace, Inverness to Roderick MacLean and Isabella MacDonald. He served in A Company as a bomber. He travelled to France on 19 February 1915 and was killed at the Battle of Loos on 26 September 1915, aged 19. Commemorated on the Loos Memorial.

1280 MacLean, Charles (Lance Corporal)
Born on 2 April 1896 at Broadford, Strath, Isle of Skye to Charles MacLean and Barbara Coull. He served in A Company. He travelled to France on 19 February 1915 and was killed at the Battle of Loos on 27 September 1915, aged 19. Commemorated on the Loos Memorial.

1675 MacLean, Donald (Private)
From North Uist. He served in the old H Company. Contracted measles at Bedford and died on 6 January 1915. Buried at Bedford on Cemetery.

1558 MacLean, Donald McDairmid (Private)
Born on 2 January 1887 at Griep, Duirinish, Isle of Skye to Neil MacLean and Mary MacLean. Lived at 9 Roag, Dunvegan, Skye. He served in D Company. He travelled to France on 19 February 1915 and was killed at the Battle of Festubert on 1 May 1915, aged 28. Commemorated on the Le Touret Memorial.

2535 MacLean, John (Private)
Born on 23 February 1884 at Clachan, Raasay to John MacLean and Margaret MacLeod. He enlisted at Bedford. He served in A Company. He travelled to France on 19 February 1915 and was killed in action in trenches in E Lines in the Neuve Chapelle sector on 16 April 1915, aged 31. Commemorated on the Le Touret Memorial.

1632 MacLean, John (Private)
Born on 14 July 1895 at Milton of Kilravock, Croy to John MacLean and Harriet Mackenzie. He worked as a farm servant before the war. He served in B Company. He travelled to France on 19 February 1915 and was killed in

action on 28 September 1915 at the Battle of Loos, aged 20. Commemorated on the Loos Memorial.

1619 MacLean, Roderick (Private)

Born on 26 August 1897 at Aberchalder, Fort Augustus to Hector MacLean and Mary McBean. Contracted measles at Bedford and died on 10 January 1915, aged 17. Buried at Kilchuimen Cemetery.

1823 MacLeman, William (Private)

Born on 1 February 1894 at 8 Shoe Lane, Inverness to John MacLeman and Margaret Innes. He served in B Company. He travelled to France on 19 February 1915 and was killed in action by German shelling in trenches at Vermelles on 22 September 1915, aged 21. Buried at Vermelles Military Cemetery.

1888 MacLennan, Alexander (Private)

Born in 1896 at Cromarty to Alexandrina MacLennan. He served in D Company. He travelled to France on 19 February 1915 and was wounded in action on 14 April 1915. Evacuated and died of his wounds on 23 April 1915, aged 19. Buried in Merville Communal Cemetery.

2553 MacLennan, Duncan (Private)

Born on 29 January 1884 at Conon Bridge to Norman MacLennan and Mary Mackenzie. Lived at 35 High Street, Ardersier. He served in D Company. He travelled to France on 19 February 1915 and was wounded in action on at the Battle of Aubers Ridge on 9 May 1915. Evacuated and died of his wounds on 11 May 1915, aged 31. Buried at Pont du Hem Military Cemetery, La Gorgue.

465 MacLennan, John (Private)

Born in 1892 at Inverness. He served in B Company. He travelled to France on 18 April 1915 and was killed at the Battle of Festubert on 18 May 1915, aged 22. Commemorated on the Le Touret Memorial.

1705 MacLennan, Murdo (Private)

Born on 28 November 1897 at Isle Fladda, Raasay to Norman MacLennan and Mary Grahame. He served with the 2/4th Cameron Highlanders. Contracted measles while in Bedford and died on 29 December 1914, aged 17. Buried at Raasay New Cemetery.

555 MacLeod, Donald (Lance Sergeant)

Born on 17 June 1890 at Drumfearn, Sleat, Isle of Skye to Donald MacLeod and Mary MacKinnon. He served in D Company. He travelled to France on 19 February 1915 and was killed at the Battle of Festubert on 18 May 1915, aged 24. Commemorated on the Le Touret Memorial.

833 MacLeod, Donald (Sergeant)

Born on 16 August 1891 at Glen Druid, Inverness to William MacLeod and Elizabeth Smith. He was educated at Daviot Public School where he gained the Clark Bequest Bursary which took him to Kingussie School for four years. He then passed the Arts Course at Glasgow University and was studying for a Masters of Arts with a view of a career in the church when he volunteered for overseas service. He served in C Company. He travelled to France on 19 February 1915 and was killed at the Battle of Neuve Chapelle on 14 March 1915, aged 24. Commemorated on the Le Touret Memorial.

1297 MacLeod, John (Sergeant)

Born on 27 December 1886 at Breakish, Strath, Isle of Skye to Angus MacLeod and Rebecca MacKinnon. Before the war he worked as an inspector of the poor. He served in A Company. He travelled to France on 19 February 1915 and was killed at the Battle of Neuve Chapelle on 10 March 1915, aged 28. Commemorated on the Le Touret Memorial.

967 MacLeod, Malcolm (Corporal)

Born on 23 December 1892 at Arnish, Raasay to Alexander MacLeod and Julia MacKinnon. Contracted measles at Bedford and died there on 27 January 1915, aged 22. Buried at Raasay New Cemetery.

1598 MacLeod, Norman (Private)

Born on 15 September 1895 at Renigidil, Harris to Kenneth MacLeod and Effy MacLeod. He served in the old H Company. Contracted measles at Bedford and died there on 1 January 1915. Buried at Bedford on Cemetery.

972 McLeod, William (Private)

Born on 12 June 1891 at Balmeanoch, Raasay to Donald MacLeod and Marion Macintosh. He served in A Company. He travelled to France on 19 February 1915 and was evacuated sick on 3 May 1915. He returned to France on 6 August 1915 and was killed in action on 25 September 1915, aged 24. Commemorated on the Loos Memorial.

943 McNeil, John (Lance Corporal)
Born on 15 October 1893 at 8 Caledonian Street, Nairn to John McNeil and Margaret Foley. Before the war he worked as a barman at the Imperial Hotel, Inverness. He served in B Company. He travelled to France on 19 February 1915 and was shot through the lung and killed on 12 March 1915, aged 21. Buried at Rue du Bacquerot Cemetery No.1, Laventie.

1406 McPhee, Duncan (Private)
Born on 9 May 1895 at Fort William to John McPhee and Flora McDougall. He served in C Company. He travelled to France on 19 February 1915 and was wounded at the Battle of Festubert on 17 May 1915. Evacuated and died of his wounds on 19 May 1915, aged 20. Buried in Bethune Town Cemetery.

1467 MacPherson, John (Private)
Born on 12 August 1893 at Catlodge, Laggan to John MacPherson and Jessie MacGillivray. He served in C Company. He travelled to France on 9 May 1915 and was wounded in action on 17 May 1915. Evacuated and died of his wounds on 27 May 1915, aged 21. Buried at Chocques Military Cemetery.

2556 MacPherson, William Thomas Butler (Private)
Born on 7 July 1886 at the Gillons Hotel, Church Street, Inverness to John MacPherson and Emma Miles. He served in C Company. He travelled to France on 19 February 1915 and died of syncope on 7 June 1915, aged 28. Buried at Chocques Military Cemetery.

1659 Macrae, Gilbert (Private)
Born on 13 May 1896 at Laggan Farm, Laggan to Alexander Macrae and Flora Macdonald. Contracted measles and died at Bedford on 24 February 1915, aged 18. Buried at Laggan Churchyard.

1736 MacRae, Hugh (Private)
Born on 18 September 1891 at 3 Ross's Close, Inverness to Grigor Macrae and Alexandrina Macrae. His father was noted by the *Highland News* to be the 'Hero of Majuba Hill' and the family was known as the 'Fighting MacRaes'. He served in B Company. He travelled to France on 19 February 1915 and was killed at the Battle of Festubert on 17 May 1915, aged 23. Commemorated on the Le Touret Memorial.

1495 Macrae, John (Private)
Born on 14 March 1896 at Oskaig, Raasay to Malcolm Macrae and Eliza Urquhart. He served in A Company as a Grenadier. He travelled to France

on 19 February 1915 and died of wounds received at the Battle of Loos on 1 October 1915, aged 19. Buried at Bethune Town Cemetery.

2036 Marshall, Alfred Edgar George (Lance Corporal)
Born in 1892 in Grays, Essex to Samuel and Eliza Marshall. He served as a Grenadier in A Company. He travelled to France on 19 February 1915 and died as the result of an accident on 2 February 1916, aged 23. Buried at Viller Bocage Communal Cemetery.

1512 Mellis, William (Private)
Born on 19 November 1883 at 10 Murdoch's Wynd, Elgin to John Mellis and Catherine Ross. Before the war he worked as a nightwatchman at the railway station. He served in C Company. He travelled to France on 19 February 1915 and was killed at the Battle of Neuve Chapelle on 10 March 1915, aged 31. Commemorated on the Le Touret Memorial.

2165 Melven, Donald Clark (Lance Corporal)
Born on 25 November 1878 at Hay Lodge, Nairn to Joseph Melven and Jane Clark. Before the war he worked for his father's bookseller and stationers in Inverness. He served in A Company. He travelled to France on 19 February 1915 and was killed in action by an enemy shell on the night of 17/18 May 1915 at the Battle of Festubert, aged 36. Commemorated on the Le Touret Memorial.

2141 Miller, Duncan McMartin (Private)
Born in 1892 in Edinburgh. He served in A Company. He travelled to France on 19 February 1915 and was wounded in action on 8 March 1915. Evacuated and died of his wounds on 20 October 1915, aged 23. Buried at Comely Bank Cemetery, Edinburgh.

2552 Miller, James G.
Born on 29 October 1895 at 3 Strathmore Road, Hamilton to Alfred Miller and Christina Gillon. He served in A Company. He travelled to France on 19 February 1915 and was killed in action on 12 March 1915, aged 19. Commemorated on the Le Touret Memorial.

1631 Moir, Alexander (Private)
Born on 21 January 1894 at Mains of Clunas, Cawdor to John Moir and Jessie Clark. Before the war he worked as a woodcutter. He served in B Company. He travelled to France on 19 February 1915 and was wounded at the Battle of Neuve Chapelle on 10 March 1915. Evacuated and returned to duty shortly

after. He was wounded at the Battle of Loos on 26 September 1915 and died of his wounds on 29 September 1915, aged 21. Buried at Fouquieres Churchyard Extension.

1485 Moran, John (Private)

Born in 1890 at Glasgow. He served in C Company. He travelled to France on 19 February and was killed at the Battle of Festubert on 17 May 1915, aged 25. Commemorated on the Le Touret Memorial.

2910 Morrison, Allan (Private)

Born on 28 September 1895 at 56 Surrey Street, Glasgow to John Morrison and Mary Rankin. He served in D Company. He travelled to France on 18 April 1915 and was killed at the Battle of Festubert on 18 May 1915, aged 19. Commemorate on the Le Touret Memorial.

1250 Munro, Donald (Private)

Born on 10 September 1896 at 27 Telford Street, Inverness to Donald Munro and Isabella Downie. He served in B Company. Before the war he worked as a painter. He travelled to France on 19 February 1915 and was wounded in action on 16 May 1915 on the way to the front line during the Battle of Festubert. Evacuated and died on the same day, aged 18. Buried at Lillers Communal Cemetery.

1503 Munro, Hugh Simon Fraser (Lance Corporal)

Born on 23 November 1889 at Percival Street, Inverness to James Munro and Catherine Fraser. He served in B Company. He travelled to France on 19 February 1915 and evacuated sick on 25 March 1915. He returned to France on 6 August 1915 and was killed in action on 25 September 1915, aged 25. Buried in Vermelles Military Cemetery.

1781 Munro, James Scott (Private)

Born on 9 March 1886 at Delnies, Nairn to Finlay Munro and Margaret Scott. Before the war he worked in the grocery department of Mr Urquhart's Stores in Nairn. He served in B Company. He travelled to France on 19 February 1915 and was shot in the head while doing sentry duty during the Battle of Givenchy on 16 June 1915, aged 29. Commemorated on the Le Touret Memorial.

1810 Munro, Ranald Campbell (Private)

Born on 9 June 1884 at 25 Bridge Street, Banff to James Munro and Lizzy Mearns. He served as a cook in A Company. He travelled to France on

19 February 1915 and was killed at the Battle of Loos on 25 September 1915, aged 31. Commemorated on the Loos Memorial.

795 Nicholson, John (Private)
Born on 22 January 1890 at Banfield, Portree to Alexander Nicholson and Isabella Morrison. He served in D Company. He travelled to France on 19 February 1915 and was killed at the Battle of Festubert on 18 May 1915, aged 25. Commemorated on the Le Touret Memorial.

1654 Nicholson, Peter (Private)
Born on 19 January 1897 at Orchard Cottage, Raasay to Neil Nicholson and Helen MacDougall. He served with the 2/4th Cameron Highlanders. Contracted measles and pneumonia and died on 16 January 1915, aged 17. Buried in Raasay New Cemetery.

3283 Nicholson, Thomas Crichton (Private)
Enlisted at Bradford. He served in C Company. He travelled to France on 6 August 1915 and was killed in action on 25 September 1915 at the Battle of Loos. Commemorated on the Loos Memorial.

1294 Nicolson, Donald (Private)
Born on 16 April 1894 at Elgoll, Strath, Skye to John Nicolson and Mary MacLean. He served in A Company as a Grenadier. He travelled to France on 19 February 1915 and was wounded on 17 September 1915. Evacuated and died on the following day, aged 21. Buried at Chocques Military Cemetery.

200094 Nicolson, Norman (Private)
Born on 3 June 1882 at Torrin, Strath, Isle of Skye to Archibald Nicolson and Mary Fraser. Contracted measles in Bedford and died there on 28 December 1914, aged 32. Buried at Bedford Town Cemetery.

2558 Nicolson, James Charles (Private)
Born on 29 September 1898 at Gardie, Bressay, Shetland Isles to Samuel Nicolson and Jessie Sinclair. He served in the 2/4th Cameron Highlanders. Contracted measles while at Bedford and died on 31 January 1915 at the Kindergarden Hospital, Academy Street, Inverness, aged 16. Buried at Bressay Cemetery, Shetland.

645 Paterson, Donald (Corporal)
Born on 20 December 1891 at Yewbank Villa, Beauly, Kilmorack to John Paterson and Mary MacLennan. He served in D Company with his brother, 2nd Lieutenant (previously CQMS) Alistair F. Paterson. He travelled to

France on 19 February 1915 and was killed in action on 17 May 1915, aged 23. Commemorated on the Le Touret Memorial.

3278 Paterson, James Harvey (Private)
Born in 1895 at Carlisle to George and Janet Paterson. Lived at 56 Bowman Street, Carlisle. He served in D Company. He travelled to France on 6 August 1915 and was wounded at the Battle of Loos. Evacuated and died of his wounds on 28 September 1915, aged 20. Buried at Bethune Town Cemetery.

1178 Paterson, William (Acting Corporal)
Born on 18 September 1886 at Charleton, Collessie to William Paterson and Euphemia Muckersie. He served in C Company. He travelled to France on 19 February 1915 and was killed at the Battle of Givenchy on 16 June 1915, aged 28. Commemorated on the Le Touret Memorial.

2159 Penn, James Robert (Private)
Born in Essex. He served in D Company. He travelled to France on 19 February 1915 and was killed at the Battle of Neuve Chapelle on 12 March 1915. Commemorated on Le Touret Memorial.

2481 Ramsay, Alexander Farquharson (Private)
Born on 31 March 1880 at 462 New Keppochhill Road, Glasgow to Henry Ramsay and Mary Farquharson. He served in B Company. He travelled to France on 19 February 1915 and was killed at the Battle of Festubert on 17 May 1915, aged 35. Commemorated on the Le Touret Memorial.

1417 Reid, Harold Wilson (Private)
Born on 5 February 1895 at Drummond Villa, Inverness to John Wilson Reid and Jessie Newton. He served in A Company as a signaller. He travelled to France on 19 February 1915 and was killed at the Battle of Givenchy on 16 June 1915, aged 20. Commemorated on the Le Touret Memorial.

1993 Robertson, Frederick Andrew (Private)
Born in London. He served in C Company. He travelled to France on 19 February 1915 and was killed at the Battle of Neuve Chapelle on 12 March 1915. Commemorated on the Le Touret Memorial.

1498 Robertson, Kenneth MacKinnon (Private)
Born on 7 June 1896 at Waterloo, Strath, Isle of Skye to Charles Robertson and Margaret McInnes. Contracted measles at Bedford and died there on 2 February 1915, aged 18. Buried at Kilchrist Churchyard.

1450 Robertson, James Bruce (Acting Corporal)
Born on 3 January 1897 at 2 Court House Lane, Nairn to Alexander Robertson and Annabella Bruce. Before the war he worked as an apprentice draper with James Sinclair of Nairn. He served in B Company. He travelled to France on 19 February 1915 and was killed at the Battle of Festubert on 18 May 1915, aged 18. Commemorated on the Le Touret Memorial.

2351 Robertson, John C (Private)
Born in 1895 in Kent to William Robertson J.P., later of Herne Bay. He served in D Company. He travelled to France on 19 February 1915 and was killed at the Battle of Festubert on 18 May 1915, aged 20. Commemorated on the Le Touret Memorial.

979 Robertson, Peter John McLeod (Private)
Born on 14 September 1894 at Knappoch, Kingussie, the illegitimate son of Jessie Robertson. He served in C Company. He travelled to France on 19 February 1915 and was killed at the Battle of Festubert on 18 May 1915, aged 20. Commemorated on the Le Touret Memorial.

1306 Rose, Lewis (Private)
Born on 5 May 1896 at Tomatin, Moy to William Rose and Elsie MacBean. He served in C Company. He travelled to France on 19 February 1915 and was killed at the Battle of Festubert on 18 May 1915, aged 19. Commemorated on the Le Touret Memorial.

2265 Ross, David (Private)
Born on 12 October 1894 at Ashton of Raigmore, Inverness to William Ross and Marion Beaton. Before the war he worked as a farm servant at Blinkbonny, Brodie. He served in B Company. He travelled to France on 18 April 1915 and died of wounds received in the field on 7 May 1915, aged 20. Buried at Merville Communal Cemetery. It was reported in the *Inverness Courier* that his wounds had been self-inflicted, a fact refuted by a 4th Camerons officer who wrote to the paper saying Private Ross had died 'a hero's death'.

1584 Ross, Duncan (Private)
Born on 7 November 1893 at Fanellan, Kiltarlity to John Ross and Jessie MacLean. He served in D Company. He travelled to France on 19 February 1915 and was killed at the Battle of Festubert on 18 May 1915, aged 21. Commemorated on the Le Touret Memorial.

402 Ross, William (CSM)

Born on 12 September 1869 at Portree to William Ross and Mary MacCowan. Before the war he worked as a shoemaker in Portree. He served in D Company. Known as the 'father of the battalion'. He travelled to France on 19 February 1915 and was killed at the Battle of Festubert on 17 May 1915, aged 45. When CSM Ross charged into the Southern Breastwork Trench four Germans surrendered. One subsequently fired on CSM Ross and killed him instantly. D Company soldiers then killed all the Germans in the trench. Commemorated on the Le Touret Memorial.

2282 Sim, William (Private)

Born on 17 August 1892 at Station House, Carrbridge, Duthil to William Sim and Jessie Bruce. He served in C Company. He travelled to France on 19 February 1915 and was killed at the Battle of Festubert on 17 May 1915, aged 22. Commemorated on the Le Touret Memorial.

2064 Simons, Alexander (Private)

Born in 1893 at London to Thomas and Margaret Simons of 47 Cricklade Avenue, Streatham Hill, London. He served in A Company. He travelled to France on 19 February 1915 and was killed at the Battle of Loos on 27 September 1915, aged 22. Commemorated on the Loos Memorial.

175 Sinclair, Charles (Acting Corporal)

Born on 27 February 1893 at Grey Street, Portree to David Sinclair and Maggie Macdonald. He served in D Company. He travelled to France on 19 February 1915 and was killed at the Battle of Festubert on 17 May 1915, aged 22. Commemorated on the Le Touret Memorial.

1997 Smith, Alexander (Private)

Born in 1895 in London to James and Hannah Smith of 200 Grove Green Road, Leytonstone, London. He served in C Company. He travelled to France on 19 February 1915 and was wounded in action at the Battle of Neuve Chapelle on 12 March 1915. Evacuated and died of his wounds on 16 March 1915, aged 19. Buried at Merville Communal Cemetery.

1032 Smith, Archibald MacGillivray (Private)

Born on 1 August 1892 at Inis nan Caorach, Cawdor to John Smith and Catherine MacGillivray. He served in B Company. He travelled to France on 19 February 1915 and was killed at the Battle of Loos, aged 23 on 28 September 1915 while seconded to the 2nd Highland Company, Royal Field Artillery (as of 15 July 1915). Commemorated on the Loos Memorial.

1727 Smith, Duncan Stephen (Private)
Born on 13 September 1895 at Balloan of Geddes, Cawdor to Alexander Smith and Elizabeth Davidson. He served in B Company. Before the war he worked as a farm servant with his father at Raitloan, Nairn. He travelled to France on 19 February 1915 and was killed at the Battle of Festubert on 17 May 1915, aged 19. Commemorated on the Le Touret Memorial.

2163 Smith, Frederick (Private)
Born in Sussex and enlised in London. He served in C Company. He travelled to France on 19 February 1915 and was wounded at the Battle of Aubers Ridge on 9 May 1915. Evacuated and died of his wounds the same day. Buried at Estaires Communal Cemetery.

3405 Smith, John (Private)
Born in 1894 in Hull to Frank Joseph Schmeig and Antonia Bosse. He served in the 3/4th Cameron Highlanders. Died of spinal injuries caused by a bathing accident in Inverness on 12 August 1915, aged 21. He appears to have changed his name from Schmeig to Smith on enlistment to hide evidence of his German roots.

4043 Smithson, Albert Arthur (Private)
Born in 1891 in Yorkshire to Joseph and Annie Smithson. He served in the 3/4th Cameron Highlanders and died at Ripon 7 January 1916, aged 25. Buried at Batley Cemetery, Yorkshire.

2116 Spurr, Douglas Bateman (Private)
Born in 1895 at Hitchin, Hertfordshire to George and Ethel Spurr. He served in C Company. He travelled to France on 19 February 1915 and was killed at the Battle of Neuve Chapelle on 10 March 1915, aged 19. Commemorated on the Le Touret Memorial.

2200 Stacey, William Marks (Acting Lance Corporal)
Born in 1892 in London to William and Mary Stacey, later of Teignmouth, Devon. He served in D Company. He travelled to France on 19 February 1915 and was killed at the Battle of Givenchy on 16 June 1915, aged 23. Commemorated on the Le Touret Memorial.

2458 Stark, Thomas Wilson (Private)
Born on 11 October 1893 at Albert Place, Uddingston to Thomas Wilson Stark and Margaret Marshall. He served in B Company. He travelled to France

on 19 February 1915 and was killed at the Battle of Festubert on 17 May 1915, aged 21. Commemorated on the Le Touret Memorial.

1175 Stephen, John (Private)
Born on 25 October 1895 at Craigmill, Dallas to James Stephen and Jane Cumming. Before the war he worked as a farm servant at Earlsmill, Brodie. He served in B Company. He travelled to France on 19 February 1915 and was wounded at the Battle of Neuve Chapelle. Evacuated and died of his wounds on 21 March 1915 at St Thomas's Hospital, London, aged 19. Buried at Brompton Cemetery, London.

1887 Stewart, David (Private)
Born on 21 August 1891 at 18 Market Street, Montrose to David Stewart and Elizabeth Crombie. He served in D Company. He travelled to France on 19 February 1915 and was killed at the Battle of Festubert on 18 May 1915, aged 23. Commemorated on the Le Touret Memorial.

1200 Stewart, Donald (Private)
Born on 29 May 1895 at East End, Kingussie to John Shand Stewart and Sarah Macdonald. He served in C Company. He travelled to France on 19 February 1915 and was wounded at the Battle of Loos. Evacuated and died of his wounds on 28 September 1915, aged 20. Buried at Nouex Les Mines Communal Cemetery.

1078 Stoddart, Adam (Private)
Born on 5 November 1895 at Loch Ness Cottage, Fort Augustus to James Stoddart and Margaret Finlayson. He served in A Company. He travelled to France on 19 February 1915 and was killed at the Battle of Neuve Chapelle on 10 March 1915, aged 19. Commemorated on the Le Touret Memorial.

2204 Stoddart, Thomas (Private)
Born in 1892 in London to Mr and Mrs R Stewart Stoddart of Kingshaw, Kingswood, Surrey. He served in D Company. He travelled to France on 19 February 1915 and was killed at the Battle of Givenchy on 16 June 1915, aged 23. Commemorated on the Le Touret Memorial.

1511 Stott, James (CSM)
Born in 1873 at Montrose to George Stott and Isabella Grant. He married and lived at Coreen, Spey Street, Kingussie. He enlisted at Dalwhinnie. He travelled to France on 19 February 1915 and was killed at the

Battle of Givenchy on 16 June 1915, aged 42. Commemorated on the Le Touret Memorial.

1977 Strachan, Duncan Lothian Martin (Private)
Born on 22 June 1893 at Floors, Cookney, Kincardine, to David Stewart and Elizabeth Reith. He served in D Company. He travelled to France on 19 February 1915 and was killed at the Battle of Festubert on 18 May 1915, aged 21. Commemorated on the Le Touret Memorial.

1971 Sutherland, Robert (Private)
Born in 1892 at Invergordon to Alexander and Anne Sutherland. His parents emigrated to Australia. He served in B Company. He travelled to France on 19 February 1915 and was wounded in action at the Battle of Neuve Chapelle. He returned to duty and was killed during the Battle of Loos on 28 September 1915, aged 23. Commemorated on the Loos Memorial.

1851 Tawse, Bertram Wilkie (Sergeant)
Born on 14 September 1884 at 19 Broomhill Place, Aberdeen to Peter Tawse and Marion Storey. He served in A Company. He travelled to France on 19 February 1915 and was wounded at the Battle of Givenchy on 16 June 1915. Evacuated and returned to France on 15 September 1915. Killed at the Battle of Loos on 26 September 1915, aged 31. Commemorated on the Loos Memorial.

1931 Tolmie, William (Private)
Born on 5 April 1892 at 73 High Street, Dingwall to William Tolmie and Davidina Black. He served in D Company. He travelled to France on 19 February 1915 and was killed at the Battle of Festubert on 18 May 1915, aged 23. Commemorated on the Le Touret Memorial.

1644 Tulloch, Hugh (Lance Corporal)
Born on 7 December 1893 at Tomhommie, Gollanfield to Charles Tulloch and Margaret Campbell. Before the war he worked as a farm labourer. He travelled to France on 19 February 1915 and was wounded at the Battle of Neuve Chapelle on 10 March 1915. Evacuated and rejoined for duty before being killed at the Battle of Givenchy on 16 June 1915, aged 21. Commemorated on the Le Touret Memorial.

2572 Turnbull, William (Lance Corporal)
Born on 26 February 1885 at Mill Road, Portree to Thomas Turnbull and Catherine MacLean. He served in D Company. He travelled to France on

18 April 1915 and was killed at the Battle of Festubert on 17 May 1915, aged 30. Commemorated on the Le Touret Memorial.

2546 Vass, James (Private)
Born on 12 February 1876 at Clyde Street, Invergordon and Isabella Mackay. He served in D Company. He travelled to France on 19 February 1915 and was killed at the Battle of Givenchy on 16 June 1915, aged 39. Commemorated on the Le Touret Memorial.

2000 Waterston, William James (Lance Corporal)
Born in 1890 in London to John and Annie Waterston. He served in C Company. He travelled to France on 19 February 1915 and was killed at the Battle of Festubert on 17 May 1915, aged 25. Commemorated on the Le Touret Memorial.

3105 Watson, John Simon Fraser (Private)
Born on 20 July 1888 at 35 Lower Kessock Street, Inverness, the illegitimate son of Robina Watson. He served in B Company. He travelled to France on 7 September 1915 and was wounded at the Battle of Loos on 25 September 1915. Evacuated and died of his wounds on 7 October 1915, aged 27. Buried at Valenciennes Communal Cemetery.

2523 Whiteford, Alexander B (Private)
Born on 2 October 1896 at Church Place, Old Mill Road, Uddingston to James Whiteford and Helen McGreadie. He served in D Company. He travelled to France on 19 February 1915 and was killed at the Battle of Festubert on 18 May 1915, aged 18. Commemorated on the Le Touret Memorial.

2222 Whittingham, William H (Private)
Born in London. He served in C Company. He travelled to France on 19 February 1915 and was killed at the Battle of Festubert on 17 May 1915. Commemorated on the Le Touret Memorial.

1965 Williamson, John (Private)
Born on 7 September 1893 at 3 Telford Terrace, Inverness to Donald Williamson and Alice Southwell. Before the war he worked for Macrae and Dick as a mechanical engineer. He served in B Company and with the Machine Gun Section. He was wounded in action by trench mortar fire and died on 9 May 1915, aged 21. Buried at Rue du Bois Military Cemetery, Fleaurbaix.

1989 Wilson, Thomas Robertson (Private)

Born on 14 January 1896 at 309 Rutherglen Road, Glasgow to David R. Wilson and Jeanie Robertson. Lived at 95 Windus Road, Stamford Hill, London. He served in A Company. He travelled to France on 19 February 1915 and was wounded in action on 6 March 1915 in the C Lines Trenches in front of Neuve Chapelle. Evacuated and died of his wounds on 7 March 1915, aged 19. Buried at Merville Communal Cemetery.

2234 Winstone, Charles (Private)

Born in 1895 in London. He served in D Company. He travelled to France on 19 February 1915 and was wounded at the Battle of Neuve Chapelle. He returned to duty and was killed in action on 18 May 1915 at the Battle of Festubert, aged 20. Commemorated on the Le Touret Memorial.

3223 Youell, Stanley John (Private)

Born in 1896 in London to John and Rosina Youell. He served in C Company. He travelled to France on 7 September 1915 and was wounded on 27 September 1915. Evacuated and died of his wounds on 14 October 1915, aged 19. Buried at Le Treport Military Cemetery.

Appendix 6

Officer Biographies

Allison, Thomas

Born on 30 April 1870 at Balgray, Irvine, Ayrshire to Robert Dunlop Allison, a farmer, and his wife Mary Faulds. He was educated at Glasgow University where he read law. He moved to Fort William in the early 1890s where he practised law for over 20 years, becoming factor for the Inverlochy, Inverlair, Arisaig and Ardgour estates. He was commissioned into the Inverness Volunteers as a 2nd Lieutenant on 4 March 1899 before being promoted full Lieutenant on 9 August 1902 and Captain on 5 April 1909. He mobilised with E (Lochaber) Company of the 4th Cameron Highlanders on 4 August 1914 before being appointed to command C Company in the restructuring before departing for France. He travelled to France on 19 February 1915 and was wounded on 12 March while in trenches to the south of the Moated Grange position. Corporal Alistair MacDougall describes this event in the *Inverness Courier* of 23 March as a shell burst burying the officers and non-commissioned officers of C Company. Allison returned to command C Company on 27 March and was killed at the Battle of Festubert on 17 May. While leading C Company in the charge on the Southern Breastwork Trench, Captain Allison was shot in the ankle. He rose to charge again and was shot in the head and died instantly. Captain Allison is commemorated on the Le Touret Memorial.

Baillie, Ian Henry

Born on 3 September 1870 at Househill, Nairn to Duncan James Baillie, Lieutenant-Colonel of Horse Guards, and his wife Ann Elizabeth Burnaby. He was educated at Wellington College from 1884–1888 and served as a Lieutenant with the 1st Lanark Rifle Volunteers before joining the 2/4th Cameron Highlanders in Inverness on 20 November 1914. He was responsible for the recruitment to that battalion in the early months of 1915, including giving speeches at local cinemas. Baillie travelled to France on 23 March and was appointed junior Captain of B Company. He was wounded in the leg on 17 May as he attempted to cross a canal to obtain reinforcements for the beleaguered battalion in the Southern Breastwork Trench. The water in the canal was polluted and he contracted gangrene and died of his wounds on 22 May at Rouen Military Hospital. Captain Baillie is buried at St Sever Cemetery, Rouen and commemorated on the family gravestone in Nairn Cemetery.

Bartholomew, Benjamin James

Born in 1897 in Beckenham, Kent to Milton and Georgina Bartholomew. He was commissioned into the 2/4th Cameron Highlanders as a 2nd Lieutenant on 2 July 1915, posted to the 1/4th Battalion on 19 October and attached to D Company. Bartholomew transferred to Number 1 Entrenching Battalion at Poperinghe on 28 March 1916 and joined the 1st Cameron Highlanders on 27 April. He was wounded in action on 20 June at Les Brebis and rejoined the battalion on 26 July before being killed on 18 November 1916 in trenches to the east of Eaucourt L'Abbeye. The 1st Camerons' war diary records that 'Enemy started a heavy barrage about 6am on the Support Company and inflicted several casualties'. 2nd Lieutenant Bartholomew is buried in Becourt Military Cemetery, Becordel-Becourt.

Beaton, Murdoch

Born on 8 December 1869 at Ardelve, Gairloch, Wester Ross to John Beaton, a fisherman, and his wife Helen MacLennan. He was educated at Raining's School, Inverness; the Old Grammar School, Aberdeen; and Aberdeen University. He was commissioned into the Inverness Volunteers on 17 January 1903 as a 2nd Lieutenant before being promoted full Lieutenant on 9 September and Captain on 26 February 1910. He was appointed to command A Company and travelled to France on 19 February 1915. He served with distinction through the Battles of Neuve Chapelle, Aubers Ridge and Festubert before being appointed Temporary Major and second in command of the battalion on 21 July. He was appointed Commanding Officer and Temporary Lieutenant-Colonel on 29 October and continued in this role until his return to England on 7 April 1916 because of illness. Lieutenant-Colonel Beaton was the commanding officer when the decision was made to disband the battalion in February 1916 and he fought hard for his men, securing the future of the battalion nucleus. Beaton was appointed Major (as opposed to temporary rank) on 4 December 1915 and after convalescing took command of a Company of the 3rd Cameron Highlanders at Invergordon, Birr and Ballyvonare. He was the only pre-war Territorial Force officer to have served from the outset of war until the disbandment of the battalion. He worked as a schoolteacher from 1902–1905 and as HM Inspector of Schools from 1905–1910. Beaton also worked as Secretary of the Highlands and Islands Medical Commission from 1910–1911, a Divisional Inspector of the Scottish Insurance Commission from 1911–1925, General Inspector of the Poor Board of Health from 1923–1928 and General Inspector of the Department of Health from 1928–1935. He married Barbara McKenzie Ross in Edinburgh in 1908 and they had two sons. He died on 3 February 1948 at 7 Strathairn Place, Edinburgh.

Birnie, Alastair

Born on 19 February 1895 at Balnafettack, Inverness to John Birnie, a distiller, and his wife Catherine Jane Stronach. It appears his original name was Alexander but it was changed just after his birth. He joined the Lovat Scouts in 1914. He was commissioned into the 2/4th Cameron Highlanders as a 2nd Lieutenant on 16 May 1915 before being posted to the 1/4th Camerons on 19 October. He served in C Company. Birnie transferred to Number 1 Entrenching Battalion at Poperinghe on 12 March 1916 and then to the 1st Cameron Highlanders on 27 April before being wounded in 1917. He was promoted to full Lieutenant on 1 July 1917 and attached to the 6th Camerons Highlanders. Lieutenant Birnie died on 20 February 1946.

Black, John Daniel McLeod

Born on 15 June 1873 at Gruids, Lairg to William Black, a labourer, and his wife Annie McLeod. He was educated at Edinburgh University. Before the war he was the headmaster of Culcabock School in Inverness and married Joanna Sutherland on 25 September 1901 at Edinburgh. He enlisted in the ranks of the Volunteer Regiment and was commissioned into the 4th Cameron Highlanders as a 2nd Lieutenant on 3 October 1914 and posted to A Company. He travelled to France on 19 February 1915 and was wounded in action on 7 April when a ricochet bullet struck the badge of his Glengarry and caused his injury. He suffered from dizziness and migraines and was sent back to England on 15 April. Black was promoted Temporary Lieutenant on 30 September and full Lieutenant on 1 June 1916 and later served with the 1st Camerons. 2nd Lieutenant Black died on 14 June 1938 at 25 Leys Drive, Inverness.

Bookless, James Donald

Born on 2 May 1894 at Woodbourne, Glenurquhart Road, Inverness to James Bookless, a commission agent and his wife Christina MacLeod. He was commissioned into the 2/4th Cameron Highlanders on 30 December 1914 and was posted to France on 23 March 1915. His medal index card gives his address as The Rigg, Abertarff Road, Inverness. Bookless served in B Company until being wounded at the Battle of Festubert on 16 May 1915. He was on his way to the trenches from the battalion's billets in Rue de L'Epinette with his platoon when a shell exploded above him, wounding him in the thigh. Several of his men were injured by the same shell. He was taken to hospital in Boulogne where he died on 24 May. Lieutenant Bookless was buried in Boulogne Eastern Cemetery.

Calder, Alfred George

Born on 17 July 1896 at 3 Westhall Gardens. Edinburgh to William Calder, a law clerk and his wife Margaret Ann Yeadon. He was commissioned in the 4th Cameron Highlanders on 6 May 1915 as a 2nd Lieutenant and promoted Temporary Lieutenant on 24 October. He travelled to France on 19 October and was posted to A Company. On 25 March 1916 Lieutenant Calder was appointed to the post of Assistant Adjutant before being transferred to Number 1 Entrenching Battalion on 28 March. Calder transferred to the 1st Cameron Highlanders on 27 April and joined that battalion in the field on 15 July. He was wounded in action at Bazentin Le Petit on 15 August.

Calder, William

Born in Edinburgh. He was commissioned into the 4th Cameron Highlanders at Bedford on 26 August 1914 from Edinburgh University Officer Training Corps. He travelled to France on 19 February 1915 and was attached to C Company. He was wounded on 12 March when a shell exploded in a C Company trench and shrapnel fragments peppered his whole body. After recovering from his wounds in England he was attached to the Command Depot in Randallstown before being promoted full Lieutenant on 1 June 1916. He was demobilised on 16 October 1917 with the rank of Captain.

Campbell, Charles

Born on 5 October 1879 at Broadford, Strath, Isle of Skye to Samuel Campbell, a general merchant, and his wife Marion McLean. He joined the ranks of the Volunteer Battalion 17 May 1907 and was promoted to Sergeant on 21 October 1907. He was commissioned from the ranks to 2nd Lieutenant on 9 April 1912. Before the war he worked as a merchant with his father in Broadford. He was mobilised as the only officer of the old D (Broadford) Company. He was promoted Temporary Lieutenant on 7 September 1914 at Bedford and attached to B Company. Campbell travelled to France on 19 February 1915 and was promoted full Lieutenant on 14 March. He served through the Battles of Neuve Chapelle, Aubers Ridge and Festubert before being promoted Temporary Captain on 18 June. Captain Campbell commanded B Company at the Battle of Loos and was evacuated to England sick on 16 February 1916. He was then posted to the 3rd Cameron Highlanders before being appointed to the Special Military Area at Kyle of Lochalsh in 1917. He was posted to the 13th (Home Service) Battalion, Royal Scots Fusiliers on 26 June 1918. Captain Campbell died in 1966 in Skye.

Campbell, John

Born on 31 October 1864 at Kingussie to John Campbell, an innkeeper and his wife Margaret Aitchison. John Campbell was the younger brother of Lieutenant-Colonel Ewan Campbell, commanding officer of the 4th Cameron Highlanders from 1913–1914 and uncle of Captain John Campbell, junior Captain of C Company. He was educated at Raining's School, Inverness. He enlisted in the Volunteer Battalion in 1875 as a boy bugler. Campbell was commissioned as a 2nd Lieutenant on 2 June 1897 and was promoted full Lieutenant on 29 November 1899 before serving in the Boer War in South Africa with the Cameron Highlanders Volunteer Service Company in 1900–1901. He was promoted Captain on 27 May 1905 and Major on 6 January 1912. He was mobilised to war as the officer commanding the old F Company and travelled to France on 19 February 1915, in command of D Company. Major Campbell was severely wounded at the Battle of Neuve Chapelle on 13 March and was evacuated to the UK on 19 March, where he spent several months in hospital. He was promoted to Temporary Lieutenant-Colonel on 7 September 1915 and appointed to command the 2/4th Cameron Highlanders from 25 September. After the 2/4th Camerons were broken up, Campbell was promoted full Colonel and given command of the 51st Battalion, Cheshire Regiment, based at the Curragh in Ireland. Colonel Campbell died at Kingussie in 1934.

Campbell, John

Born on 4 October 1882 at Spey Street, Kingussie to Ewan Campbell, a house carpenter and his wife Elsie Cameron. Before the war he worked as an assistant ironmonger and cabinet maker for his father in Kingussie. His father commanded the 4th Cameron Highlanders from 1913–1914 and his uncle John Campbell was wounded at the Battle of Neuve Chapelle. Campbell joined the Volunteer Battalion and saw rapid promotion to Sergeant before being commissioned as a 2nd Lieutenant on 18 March 1908. He was promoted full Lieutenant on 25 June 1910 and Captain at Bedford on 7 September 1914. He travelled to France on 19 February 1915 as junior Captain of C Company. Killed in action at the Battle of Festubert on the night of 17/18 May while covering the retreat of his men from the Southern Breastwork Trench. Dugald MacEachern described it in *The Sword of the North* as 'thus did the hero give his own life to save others, making his own body the shelter for his men from the storm of bullets.'

Carruthers, Cameron Roy

Born in 1890 in Thornton Heath in Surrey to the future Sir William Carruthers, a bank inspector, and Lady Margaret Carruthers. He joined the 4th Cameron Highlanders at London in early September 1914 and was commissioned 2nd Lieutenant on 30 September. He travelled to France on 19 February 1915 as part of D Company and was wounded at the Battle of Festubert on 17 May. After evacuation to England he was promoted Temporary Lieutenant on 26 May. He transferred to the 6th Cameron Highlanders and was killed in action on 31 July 1917, the first day of the Third Battle of Ypres. Carruthers is commemorated on the Ypres (Menin Gate) Memorial.

Cattanach, William Ernest

Born on 21 December 1882 at Newtonmore, Kingussie to Alexander Cattanach, a journeyman mason, and his wife Eliza MacIntosh. Before the war he worked as an architect in Inverness. He was commissioned into the 4th Cameron Highlanders as a 2nd Lieutenant on 28 March 1915 and promoted Temporary Lieutenant on 27 May 1915. He was posted to France on 14 July, three days after his brother Alexander was wounded with the same battalion. Cattanach was seconded to the 187th Tunnelling Company of the Royal Engineers from 4 September to 4 December. He transferred from C to D Company on 9 January 1916 and seems to have been seconded for duty with the 51st (Highland) Division from the break-up of the battalion in March 1916. He was seconded to the 4th Seaforth Highlanders on 1 September.

Chalmers, Thomas

Born on 6 July 1881 at Blackburn, Livingston, West Lothian to Thomas Chalmers, a blacksmith, and his wife Georgina Philips. Before the war he worked as a junior science master at Stewarts College, Edinburgh. He was commissioned as a 2nd Lieutenant on 3 January 1915, travelled to France on 23 March 1915 and was posted to D Company. He was wounded in the shoulder by shrapnel and evacuated to England. After a month of hospital treatment and convalescing at his home in West Lothian he joined up with the 2/4th Cameron Highlanders at Rip in Yorkshire. He was promoted Temporary Captain on 28 July. He married Bessie Brydon in Edinburgh in June 1916. Captain Chalmers died on 15 September 1944 at 11 Greenbank Drive, Edinburgh.

Clift M.C., John

Born on 23 August 1893 at St John's, Newfoundland, the second son of Mr J.A. Clift. He was educated at Bishop Field College, St John's and Fettes College, Edinburgh, where he spent five years. Before the war he worked in the Bank of Montreal in St John's for three years. He enlisted into the 1st Newfoundland Regiment on 7 September 1914 as a Private (No.503) and trained at Salisbury Plain; Fort George, Inverness; Edinburgh Castle; Stob's Camp; and Ayr. He was promoted Lance Corporal on 26 April 1915 and discharged to commission in the 4th Cameron Highlanders in May. He was promoted full Lieutenant in August 1915 and travelled to France on 5 October 1915 where he was attached to A Company. He transferred to the 1st Cameron Highlanders on 4 May 1916 and then to the 1st Newfoundland Regiment on 19 May. He was wounded in action at Gueudecourt on 12 October in an action which killed his brother Lieutenant Cecil Clift. He was promoted Captain on 26 October 1917 and awarded the Military Cross for Bravery on 16 September 1918. He returned to Newfoundland on 30 January 1919.

Cooper, Alfred William Howden

He was commissioned into the 4th Cameron Highlanders on 23 April 1915 and promoted Temporary Lieutenant on arrival in France on 24 October 1915. He was posted to D Company and given command of that Company on 6 March 1916. Cooper transferred to Number 1 Entrenching Battalion on 12 March and sent back to England sick on 25 March. He was attached to the Trench Mortar Battery on 25 April 1917.

Cram D.S.O., Peter MacFarlane

Born on 11 February 1879 at North Castle Street, Alloa to George Cram, a joiner, and his wife Ann MacFarlane. He was educated at the Burgh Board School, Alloa. He married Mary Helen Roberts in Alloa in 1901 and they lived at 8 Bath Street, Nairn, then Mountbury, Nairn. He worked as the Nairnshire County Road Surveyor. He was commissioned as a 2nd Lieutenant into the 4th Cameron Highlanders on 30 March 1909 and promoted full Lieutenant on 12 December 1911 before being promoted Temporary Captain in the 2/4th Cameron Highlanders on 29 October 1914 at Bedford. Cram travelled to France on 23 March 1915 and was attached to B Company before being promoted full Captain and given command of C Company on 18 May. He was wounded at the Battle of Loos on 28 September 1915 and evacuated to England two days later. After recuperating, Captain Cram served with the 3rd Cameron Highlanders until transferring to the 7th Cameron Highlanders as a Major on 14 August 1917. He served as second in command of the 6th Cameron Highlanders after they were amalgamated with the 7th Camerons on 11 June 1918. He took over command of the 6th Cameron Highlanders as an Acting Lieutenant-Colonel when the CO was gassed in July 1918, and served in this capacity for the duration of the war. Lieutenant-Colonel Cram was awarded the Distinguished Service Order for leadership in the field on 3 June 1919 and was Mentioned in Despatches on three occasions: 7 April 1918, 8 November 1918 and 16 March 1919. During the Second World War, Lieutenant-Colonel Cram commanded the Nairn Home Guard. He died in Inverness in 1963.

Dobie, William Gardiner Murchie

Born on 9 November 1893 at Craiglea, Maxwelltown, Dumfriesshire to Alexander Dobie, a solicitor, and his wife Mary Jane Murchie. Before the war he was a law student. He was commissioned into the 4th Cameron Highlanders as a 2nd Lieutenant and sent to France on 14 April 1915 and posted to D Company. He was seconded to the Army Cyclist Corps on 30 April before being sent back to England sick on 3 June. He married Jane Johnston in Edinburgh in 1916 while serving at Ripon with the 3/4th Cameron Highlanders. He later transferred to the Lovat Scouts in November 1916 and was invalided out in 1918. Lieutenant Dobie died in 1972 in Dumfries.

Douglas, Charles Cameron

Born on 14 June 1884 at 2 Woodburn Place, Edinburgh to James Douglas, a lather, and his wife Jessie Cameron. He was educated at George Watson's College, Edinburgh. Before the war he worked for an Edinburgh insurance firm before being employed in Major Murray's Estate Office in Polmaise, Stirlingshire. He then received an appointment as chief assistant on Lord Roseberry's estate of Mentmore, in Leighton Buzzard. He was commissioned into the 4th Cameron Highlanders as a 2nd Lieutenant on 18 March 1915. He travelled to France on 11 July and was posted to D Company. Douglas was promoted full Lieutenant on 1 October and seconded to 154 Brigade as

Grenade Officer on 14 January 1916. He died as the result of an accident on 25 May. Lieutenant Douglas is buried in Louez Military Cemetery, Duisans.

Duff D.S.O., Garden Beauchamp

Born on 6 December 1879 at Hatton Castle, Turriff to Garden Duff, a landed proprietor, and his wife Annie Urquhart. He served as Captain and Adjutant of the 4th Cameron Highlanders from 1 March 1913. He travelled to France on 19 February 1915 and served with distinction through all the five battles fought by the 4th Camerons in 1915; he was awarded the Distinguished Service Order for his leadership at the Battle of Festubert in May 1915. He was promoted Major on 1 September and left the battalion on 30 October to command the 8th Battalion, Black Watch. He was promoted Lieutenant-Colonel and commanded the 5th Cameron Highlanders before being wounded and losing his arm. He was Mentioned in Despatches on 1 January and 22 June 1916. Lieutenant-Colonel Duff married Doris Mildred Smith and died on 6 September 1952 at Hatton Castle, Turriff.

Finlayson, Donald McKenzie

Born on 31 July 1893 at Kimuir, Knockbain to John Finlayson and his wife Jane H. Calder. He joined the ranks of the 4th Cameron Highlanders in 1913 and went to France on 19 February 1915 as a Private in A Company. He was wounded on 17 May 1915 at the Battle of Festubert and was absent in hospital until 8 June. He was commissioned as a 2nd Lieutenant in the 4th Cameron Highlanders on 13 July and took up his position on 15 August. He was wounded on 11 November while on a working party in Annezin and was evacuated to England on 18 November. On recovering from his wound was transferred to the Royal Air Force.

Fletcher, Archibald McPhail

Born on 29 March 1876 at Landle, Morven to Archibald Fletcher, a factor, and his wife Jane Black. He was commissioned into the 4th Cameron Highlanders as a 2nd Lieutenant on 30 April 1913 and promoted Temporary Lieutenant on 7 September at Bedford. He travelled to France on 19 February 1915 and served with C Conpany. He was invalided to England sick on 1 April and while there was promoted Temporary Captain on 20 May. He returned to France on 20 November and was given command of D Company. He was appointed the Adjutant of the Machine Gun Base Depot in Camiers on 7 March 1916. He transferred to the 5th Cameron Highlanders in 1918 and served with them until the end of the war. On his return to Scotland he was one of the officers chosen to reconstitute the 4th Cameron Highlanders. Captain Fletcher died in 1962 at Dores, near Inverness.

Fraser, Alexander

Born on 6 May 1865 at Beauly, to Alexander Fraser, agent of the Commercial Bank, and his wife Elizabeth Spray. He joined the Volunteer Battalion in 1883 and transferred to the Royal Scots Volunteers in Edinburgh in 1887 before obtaining his commission as a 2nd Lieutenant in the Inverness Volunteers on 17 May 1890. He was educated at Inverness Royal Academy, Inverness College and Edinburgh University where he read law, after which he started his own law firm, Fraser and Ross, in Inverness. He married Isabella Menzies in 1893 in Inverness and they had two sons and seven daughters. He was promoted full Lieutenant on 20 December 1890, Captain on 9 August 1898, Major on 25 February 1905 and took over command of the battalion as a Lieutenant-Colonel on 24 February 1909. He retired to the Reserve of Officers on 23 August 1913. On the outbreak of war Lieutenant-Colonel Fraser was given command of the 2/4th Cameron Highlanders and took over command of the 1/4th Camerons on 10 November 1914 at Bedford. He travelled to France on 19 February 1915 and was present at the Battles of Neuve Chapelle and Festubert. He was killed at the Battle of Festubert when covering the retreat from the Southern Breastwork Trench on the night of 17/18 May. He was twice Mentioned in Despatches in May and October 1915. Lieutenant-Colonel Fraser is commemorated on the Le Touret Memorial.

Fraser, Frederick William

Born on 31 December 1874 at 1 View Place, Inverness to Archibald Thomas Frederick Fraser, a clothier, and his wife Isabel Leith. Before joining the battalion, Fraser held the rank of Captain in the (Highland) Royal Garrison Artillery Volunteers and was in command of the position battery. He was commissioned as a Lieutenant into the 4th Cameron Highlanders on 20 January 1912 and promoted Captain on 7 September 1914. He travelled to France on 19 February 1915 as officer commanding B Company. He served through the Battle of Neuve Chapelle, Aubers Ridge, Festubert and Givenchy before being invalided to England sick on 28 July 1915. He was given an appointment on the Staff of the Reserve Highland Division on 3 September. Captain Fraser married Rosa Mackintosh in Edinburgh in 1916 and died on 27 August 1942 at Lower Ardnagask, Beauly.

Fraser, Hector

Born on 10 June 1869 at Lochside, Fort William to Donald Fraser, Sheriff Clerk Depute, and his wife Jean Grieve. Before the war he worked as the Sheriff Clerk of Fort William, a position he held for 43 years. He was commissioned into the Inverness Volunteers as a 2nd Lieutenant on 4 March 1899 and promoted full Lieutenant on 12 September 1900,

Captain on 4 May 1902 and Major on 5 May 1909. He travelled to France on 19 February 1915 as second in command of the battalion. He took over command of the 4th Camerons on 18 May after the death of Lieutenant-Colonel Alexander Fraser at the Battle of Festubert. He was slightly wounded in action at the Battle of Givenchy on 16 June but remained at duty, commanding the battalion until being invalided to England sick on 28 October. He was promoted Lieutenant-Colonel on 4 December and given command of a reserve battalion of the Argyll and Sutherland Highlanders and later the 2/6th Essex Regiment. Lieutenant-Colonel Fraser married Mary McGregor in 1901 in Dunblane and died on 21 October 1953 at Blythe, Douglas Road, Melrose.

Henderson, Hugh Fraser

Born on 12 June 1877 at Partick, Glasgow to John Henderson, a marine engineer, and his wife Elizabeth Fraser. He married Jane Russell Fleming. He travelled to France on 19 October 1915 and was posted to A Company. He was dismissed for drunkenness by General Court Martial on 26 April 1916. He re-enlisted or was conscripted into the 2nd Royal Irish Rifles as a Private, reaching the rank of Sergeant, and served with them until being killed in action on 15 October 1918. Lieutenant Henderson is buried in Dadizeele New British Cemetery.

Hughes, A.W.

Commissioned into the 4th Cameron Highlanders as a 2nd Lieutenant on 7 April 1915, Hughes travelled to France on 18 July and served with A Company. He was promoted Temporary Lieutenant on 1 October. He was seconded to 154 Brigade as Machine Gun Officer on 14 January 1916.

Hunter, Charles Haddon Spurgeon

Born on 21 July 1894 in Victoria County, Ontario, Canada. His next of kin was Mr John Hunter of Dunsford, Ontario. He joined the 7th (1st British Columbia) Canadian Infantry Battalion on 18 September 1914 and travelled to France with the rest of the 1st Canadian Division on 22 February 1915. He served at the Second Battle of Ypres, the Battle of Festubert and the Battle of Givenchy with the Canadians before obtaining a commission as a 2nd Lieutenant in the 4th Cameron Highlanders on 10 October. He joined the 4th Camerons on 21 January 1916 and was attached to D Company. He was posted to Number 1 Entrenching Battalion at Poperinghe on 28 March and then to the 1st Cameron Highlanders on 27 April, joining them on 15 July and being posted to A Company. He was wounded on the night of 16/17 November 1917 northwest of Passchendaele.

Johnson, George Macness Whiteaway
Born in August 1893 in St John's, Newfoundland to the Honorable Mr Justice Johnson of the Supreme Court of Newfoundland. He was educated at Bishop Field College and Charterhouse School before studying medicine at Edinburgh University, where he was in his third year. He joined the 9th Royal Scots but never saw service overseas as he got his commission in the 4th Cameron Highlanders on 24 April 1915 as a 2nd Lieutenant. He travelled to France on 18 October and was attached to A Company. He was posted to Number 1 Entrenching Battalion in Poperinghe on 12 March 1916 and to the 1st Cameron Highlanders on 27 April. He was seconded to the 1st Newfoundland Regiment as a Lieutenant on 19 May before seeing service with the 108th Infantry and the 1/6th Devon Regiment as a Captain. After the war stayed on as a soldier and saw service in northwest Persia.

Kelly, Frederick James
Born on 9 April 1879 at 15 Ardconnel Terrace West, Inverness to John Kelly, a hatter, and his wife Robina Fraser. He served as a non-commissioned officer in the Inverness Volunteers and the 4th Cameron Highlanders before receiving a commission as a 2nd Lieutenant on 7 September 1914 at Bedford. He travelled to France on 19 February 1915 with B Company. He was taken ill after the Battle of Neuve Chapelle and was invalided home on 23 March. Afterwards he served with the Command Depot and was promoted full Lieutenant on 24 May. Lieutenant Kelly died in 1965 in Inverness.

Kidd, Herbert Dickie
Born in 1888 in Rangoon, Burma to William Kidd, Presbyterian Minister, and his wife Mina Kidd. He joined the 4th Cameron Highlanders on 7 September 1914 at London as a Private and was commissioned as a 2nd Lieutenant on 25 February 1915. He travelled to France on 19 February and was attached to C Company on 6 March. He was posted wounded and missing at the Battle of Festubert on 17/18 May. Lieutenant Kidd is commemorated on the Le Touret Memorial.

Laughton M.C., Francis Eugene
Born on 29 July 1887 in London to Sir John K. Laughton, Professor of Modern History at Kings College, London. He was educated at Kings College School, London University. He was commissioned into the 4th Cameron Highlanders as a 2nd Lieutenant on 9 August 1914. He travelled to France on 19 February 1915 attached to A Company. He was appointed Brigade Bombing Officer in April and was wounded in action on at the Battle of Givenchy. He was promoted full Lieutenant on 3 September 1915, awarded

the Military Cross on 14 January 1916. and made Captain on 1 June. He returned to France on 18 September with the 1st Cameron Highlanders and was wounded in action on 16 November. He was posted to the 2nd Cameron Highlanders on 6 October 1917 and served in Serbia, Greek Macedonia, Bulgaria, European Turkey and the Islands of the Aegean Sea until 23 December 1918. After the war he was British Military Representative at Nakhichevan, Caucasia. He was Mentioned in Despatches on 1 January 1916 and 20 May 1920. He was promoted Lieutenant-Colonel commanding the reconstituted 4th Cameron Highlanders on 11 December 1920 and Colonel on 11 December 1924. He retired from the 4th Cameron Highlanders on 10 December 1927 but commanded the 2nd Inverness Home Guard during the Second World War. He worked for the British Aluminium Company at Fort William and Foyers. He married Edwynna Stevenson and they had two sons and a daughter. Colonel Laughton died on 27 March 1955 at Crolinnhe, Fort William.

Law, Harold Burgin

Born on 22 August 1894 at 46 Belmont Gardens, Hillhead, Glasgow to Herbert Burgin Law, a steel manufacturer, and his wife Mary Eleanor Nicholson Taylor. He was commissioned into the 4th Cameron Highlanders on 11 March 1914 and promoted full Lieutenant at Bedford on 7 September. He travelled to France on 19 February 1915 and posted to B Company but attached to the Machine Gun Section as Machine Gun Officer. He was wounded at the Battle of Loos on 28 September when an enemy shell landed in B Company's Headquarters, killing 1 officer and 8 men and wounding 2 officers and 6 men. He was evacuated to England and returned to France on 5 May 1916 before being attached to the 1st Cameron Highlanders as a Captain on 8 May. He later served with the 2nd Cameron Highlanders and ended the war as a Major in the Machine Gun Corps. After the war Captain Law stayed with the Cameron Highlanders. He married firstly, Esme Goodman and secondly Winifred Robina Cumming in 1932 in Edinburgh. Captain Law died on 30 August 1951 at 19 Saughtonhall Avenue, Edinburgh. He died from coal gas poisoning which may or may not have been suicide.

Lindsay, Robert

Lindsay served as a surgeon in the Boer War in South Africa from 1900–1902 seeing service in Cape Colony and St Helena, March to May 1900; Operations in Orange River Colony, May 1900 to February 1901; Operations in the Transvaal, March to June 1901; Operations in Orange River Colony, July 1901 to March 1902 and in Griqualand in the Cape Colony from March to May 1902. He joined the Inverness Volunteers as a Lieutenant on 10 October 1905 before resigning his commission in 1907. He was attached to the Territorial Force of the RAMC on 1 April 1908. He travelled to France as Battalion Medical Officer on 19 February 1915 and transferred to Number 11 General Hospital in Camiers on 4 August.

Lockie, John

Born in 1857 in Colnbrook, Langley, Buckinghamshire to Joseph Lockie, a restaurant owner, and his wife Mary Skates. He enlisted in the 2nd East Yorkshire Regiment on 15 May 1874 and transferred to the 1/79th Cameron Highlanders as Lance Sergeant No.949 on 1 August 1884. Lockie served with the 1st Cameron Highlanders until 31 July 1887 before taking up a position as Instructor of the Inverness Volunteer Battalion. He was promoted Colour Sergeant on 15 May 1898 and transferred to the Lovat Scouts on 1 February 1900. He was appointed Sergeant Major of the Volunteer Battalion on 16 February 1903 and was discharged from active service on 3 October 1906. He was promoted Quartermaster Lieutenant on 1 November 1906, Quartermaster Captain on 11 October 1907 and Quartermaster Major on 14 April 1909. He served in India from 1875–1881, Egypt from 1884–1885 and South Africa from 1900–1901. Awarded the Afghan Medal 1879–1880; the Khedives Star; The Egypt Medal with clasps Nile 1884 and 1885; the Queen's South Africa Medal with clasps for Cape Colony, Transvaal, Orange Free State and South Africa 1901; the Long Service and Good Conduct Medal; King George V Coronation Medal 1911, Meritorious Service Medal of 1930; the 1914–15 Star; the British War Medal; the Victory Medal and was Mentioned in Despatches on 30 November 1915 and 16 March 1919 and awarded the OBE on 3 June 1919. He married Mary Campbell, sister of Lieutenant-Colonel Ewan Campbell and Major John Campbell on 1 July 1891 at Edinburgh. He travelled to France on 19 February 1915 and served as Quartermaster until being posted to the Machine Gun Corps Base Depot on 7 March 1916. Major Lockie died on 22 May 1941 at 1 Fairfield Road, Inverness.

Marr, D.M.

A Captain in the Royal Army Medical Corps, Marr was seconded to the 4th Cameron Highlanders from 1–6 December 1915. Later Mentioned in Despatches in May 1917.

Melville M.C., David

Born on 9 July 1896 at 3 Southside Place, Inverness to William Melville, a shoemaker, and his wife Jane Hutchison Lynn. He enlisted into the 4th Cameron Highlanders in July 1914 as Private no.1690 and attached to

A Company. He was commissioned as a 2nd Lieutenant on 24 October 1915 and made Acting Adjutant on 28 March 1916. He remained with the 4th Camerons' battalion nucleus until transferring to Number 10 Entrenching Battalion in March 1917. He transferred to the 5th Cameron Highlanders in 1917 and was awarded the Military Cross for bravery in the field in August 1918. Lieutenant Melville was killed in action on 26 October 1918.

Morrison, Donald

Commissioned as a 2nd Lieutenant into the 4th Cameron Highlanders on 15 April 1915. Morrison travelled to France on 14 July and attached to A Company. He was wounded in action at the Battle of Loos on 26 September and evacuated to England on 30 September. He was promoted Lieutenant on 8 September 1916 and later served with the 6th and 7th Cameron Highlanders.

Morison, Hector McDonald

Born in 1882 in Croydon, Surrey to Hector Morison, an accountant, and his wife Josephine Ashton, both from Scotland. Before the war he worked as an Articled Clerk for a Chartered Accountants. He joined the 4th Cameron Highlanders on 7 September 1914 at London as a Private No.2196. He travelled to France on 19 February 1915 and was commissioned on 25 February before being attached to C Company on 6 March. He was promoted Temporary Lieutenant on 21 July and Temporary Captain on 1 October. Given command of B Company on 9 January 1916 and was invalided home to England sick on 22 February. Later appointed to the Indian Army Reserve of Officers.

McArthur, Neil

Born on 20 March 1886 at Castleton, Lochgilphead, Argyll to John McArthur, a ploughman, and his wife Catherine MacIntyre. He was educated at Lochgilphead School and Glasgow University where he qualified as a solicitor in 1911. He was commissioned into the 4th Cameron Highlanders on 30 December 1914 as a 2nd Lieutenant and promoted Temporary Lieutenant on 27 May 1915. He travelled to France on 14 July and was attached to D Company, being promoted Temporary Captain on 1 October. He was appointed Adjutant of the battalion on 30 October and relinquished this position on 29 February 1916. He transferred to be Acting Adjutant and Quartermaster of Number 2 Training Camp, Étaples on 1 March. He was Mentioned in Despatches on 13 November 1916 and later served in the Royal Air Force in 1918. After the war, Captain McArthur was instrumental in resuscitating the battalion and was in command of the Uist Company. He was Lieutenant-Colonel in command of the battalion from 1927–1933. He became a partner in the law firm of Messrs Stewart, Rule and Co, a Director of Deltenne (Ceylon) Tea Estates Ltd, the North of Scotland Heritable Investment Co. and was made Deputy Lieutenant of Inverness-shire in 1954 and Honorary Sheriff Substitute of Inverness, Moray, Nairn, Ross and Cromarty. Lieutenant-Colonel Neil McArthur died in Inverness in 1973.

MacBean, Alexander Hamilton

Born in 1878 in Wolverhampton, Staffordshire, the grandson of Thomas Hamilton MacBean, Quartermaster in the Scots Greys and Roseanna Taylor. He was educated in Wolverhampton Grammar School and studied law at university. He was commissioned as a 2nd Lieutenant in the 2nd South Staffordshire Volunteer Battalion on 8 November 1899 and promoted Lieutenant on 21 November 1900 and Captain on 30 April 1904. He transferred to the 4th Cameron Highlanders on 6 May 1915 and travelled to France on 18 October, attached to C Company. He took over command of the battalion from 29 February 1916 to 3 July while at Étaples. He transferred to the 1st Cameron Highlanders on 5 July and was wounded on 11 July at Contalmaison. He returned to duty on 17 July and commanded B Company during the Battle of Pozieres Ridge in August. He was gassed at Mametz Wood on 31 August. After recovering he was posted to the 5th Cameron Highlanders in 1918.

MacDonald, Archibald Alexander

Born in 1891 to Thomas MacDonald, Her Majesty's British Consulate in Shanghai, China and Mary MacDonald. Before the war he also worked for the British Overseas Service in China and lived at 123 Szechnen Road, Shanghai. He was commissioned into the 4th Cameron Highlanders on 6 May 1915 and travelled to France on 11 July where he was attached to B Company. He was wounded in action at the Battle of Loos on 25 September and evacuated to England on 3 October. He returned to France on 6 March 1916 and was posted to Number 1 Entrenching Battalion on 12 March. On 17 April, while on a digging party with the Entrenching Battalion, he was shot and died of his wound some hours later. Lieutenant MacDonald is buried at Bailleul Communal Cemtery Extension (Nord).

MacDonald M.C. M.M., Donald

Enlisted into the 4th Cameron Highlanders as Private No.826 in 1910, MacDonald travelled to France on 19 February 1915 as a Lance Corporal in A Company. He was shot in the head while employed as a Bomber during the Battle of Loos and was evacuated to England; he was awarded the Military

Medal for Bravery in the Field. He returned to the front on 30 October 1915 and was commissioned as a 2nd Lieutenant on 6 February 1916 and posted to A Company. He was one of three officers to remain with the 4th Cameron Highlanders battalion nucleus at Étaples before being posted to the Guard Company for Ammunition Dumps with 50 of the 4th Cameron Nucleus men on 31 December. He was posted to the 6th Cameron Highlanders in June 1917 and awarded the Military Cross for bravery in the field. Lieutenant MacDonald died on 21 October 1955.

McDonald, James

Enlisted into the 4th Cameron Highlanders as Private No.506 in 1908, McDonald travelled to France on 19 February 1915 as a Sergeant in B Company. He served as Orderly Room Sergeant and with the Adjutant General's Office and forwarded material printed in the *79th News* about the battalion. He was commissioned as a 2nd Lieutenant on 1 November 1915 and joined the 4th Camerons as such on 29 January 1916 attached to B Company. He was appointed Battalion Quartermaster on 9 March and relinquished the position on 24 March. He was posted to the 1st Cameron Highlanders direct from the battalion nucleus on 4 May and was wounded in action by enemy shelling in front of Contalmaison on 10 July. Lieutenant McDonald was marked unfit for further service by a General Medical Board on 2 September 1916.

MacDonald, Ronald

Born on 31 July 1866 at Glenisladale, Snizort, Skye to Peter MacDonald, a farmer, and his wife Flora Matheson. He worked as a solicitor and was senior partner of the firm of MacDonald & Fraser in Portree. He was commissioned as a 2nd Lieutenant in the 4th Cameron Highlanders on 17 May 1899 and promoted Lieutenant on 9 August 1902 and Captain on 31 August 1909. Mobilised on 4 August 1914 as the officer commanding the old D Company and was prevented from accompanying the battalion to France as he had suffered an accident. He joined the Battalion at Sailly on 25 March 1915 and took command of D Company. While leading the attack on the Southern Breastwork Trench at the Battle of Festubert he was shot through the neck shortly after leaving the British trenches. He was sent to the south of France to recuperate and while there was promoted Major on 8 January 1916. Major MacDonald died as a result of his wounds on 10 June at Marseille and is buried at Mazargues War Cemetery in Marseilles.

McErlich, Roderick

Born 22 August 1869 at Meoble, Arisaig, Argyll, to Alexander McErlich and Mary Finlayson. Worked before the war as an estate factor. Enlisted in the Inverness Volunteers and went to France as Sergeant No.1378 in A Company, 4th Cameron Highlanders. Commissioned as a Temporary Lieutenant in the 4th Camerons on 25 February 1915 and took up his new role on 6 March. Served throughout the 4th Camerons battles and was promoted to the rank of Temporary Captain in July 1915, taking over command of A Company on 1 September. After the breakup of the battalion in March 1916, Captain McErlich stayed with the battalion nucleus in Étaples before being transferred to the 1st Cameron Highlanders on 7 May 1916. He transferred back to the 4th Camerons nucleus as officer commanding on 6 July 1916 and was finally transferred to the 11th Cameron Highlanders in June 1918. Captain McErlich was a member of the Gaelic Society of Inverness and died in Lewis Hospital, Stornoway on 22 January 1948.

MacGillivray, Charles Findlay

Born on 24 February 1885 at Ballachroan, Kingussie to John MacGillivray, a farmer and his wife, Elspet McArthur. He joined the 3/4th Cameron Highlander as a 2nd Lieutenant on 4 June 1915 and posted to the 1/4th Camerons on 21 January 1916 and attached to D Company. He was posted to Number 1 Entrenching Battalion on 28 March 1916 and to the 1st Cameron Highlanders on 27 April. He joined up with the 1st Camerons on 12 June with 65 other ranks from the 4th Camerons serving with No.1 Entrenching Battalion. Evacuated to hospital in September and then attached to the Records Office in Hamilton, processing soldiers released for discharge and to pension. He was promoted to Lieutenant on 1 July 1917 and Captain on 21 September 1920. After the war, he joined the reconstituted 4th Camerons. He married Frances Balfour Ritchie in Perth in 1926. Captain MacGillivray died on 11 January 1958 at Ashton, Kingussie.

Maciver, Donald John

Born on 14 May 1891 at 8 Callanich, Uig, Carloway, Isle of Lewis to Angus Maciver, a shoemaker, and his wife Christina MacLean. He was educated at the Nicholson Institute in Stornoway and Edinburgh University. He was commissioned into the 4th Cameron Highlanders on 7 April 1915 from the Edinburgh University Contingent of the Officers Training Corps and travelled to France on 11 July and attached to A Company. He was seconded for duty with the 7th Division Trench Mortar Battery from 1–11 September 1915. He was wounded in action at the Battle of Loos on 29 September when he was hit in the thigh by an explosive bullet. He was evacuated and died of his wounds on 14 October. Lieutenant Maciver is buried at Le Treport Military Cemetery.

Mackay, Ian

Born on 30 May 1883 at Craigmonie, Inverness to William Mackay, a solicitor, and his wife Margaret Elizabeth Mackay. He was educated at Inverness College, Edinburgh Academy and Edinburgh University where he read law. He was commissioned into the 4th Cameron Highlanders as a 2nd Lieutenant on 20 December 1909 and promoted Lieutenant on 31 March 1913. In private life he worked for his father's law firm Innes & Mackay and was Secretary of the Inverness Unionist Association. He travelled to France on 19 February 1915 attached to A Company and also serving as Assistant Adjutant. He was promoted Temporary Captain in command of D Company on 20 May 1915 and promoted Temporary Major on 1 October and made second in command of the battalion. He served in this capacity until invalided to England sick on 20 January 1916. On his recovery he served with the 3rd Cameron Highlanders at Ripon until posted to the 6th Cameron Highlanders on 4 August 1917. Major Mackay was killed in action on during the Battle of Arras on 28 March 1918 while commanding a Company of the 6th Cameron Highlanders. For his part in the battle he was posthumously recommended for the Victoria Cross. Major Mackay was the author of not only many extraordinarily detailed and interesting letters describing his time at the front in 1915, but also the *Diary of the 4th Battalion, The Queen's Own Cameron Highlanders During the European War* published by the *Northern Chronicle* in 1916. Major Mackay is commemorated on the Arras Memorial.

Mackay, William

Born on 12 June 1886 at Craigmonie, Inverness to William Mackay, a solicitor, and his wife Margaret Elizabeth Mackay. He was educated at Inverness College, Edinburgh Academy and Edinburgh University where he read law. He married Minna MacDonald in Edinburgh in 1915. He served as a Private in the Volunteer Battalion from 1906–1908. He was commissioned into the 4th Cameron Highlanders as a 2nd Lieutenant in October 1913 and promoted Lieutenant at Bedford on 7 September 1914. He travelled to France on 19 February 1915 attached to A Company as Signalling Officer. He was wounded in action in E Lines trenches on 16 April 1915 where he was shot in the thumb, chin and cheek. He was evacuated to England and promoted Temporary Captain on 30 September 1915 while serving with the 3/4th Cameron Highlanders at Ripon training recruits for action. In 1917 he was appointed Command Signal Officer of the Northern Command. In 1919, Captain Mackay carried the 4th Cameron Highlander King's Colour at the

Victory Parade in London. After the war he served with the 3rd Cameron Highlanders in Ireland and the 2nd Cameron Highlanders in Edinburgh before serving with the Inverness Home Guard from 1940–1945. During his time in the trenches he wrote letters back to his parents in Inverness telling of his experiences. He worked for his father's law firm Innes & Mackay in Inverness and clerk to the Lord Lieutenant of Inverness-shire, Honorary Secretary of the Inverness Unionist Society and member of the Gaelic Society of Inverness. Captain Mackay died in Inverness in 1976.

Mackenzie, Alexander

Commissioned into the 4th Cameron Highlanders as a 2nd Lieutenant on 20 November 1914, Mackenzie travelled to France on 23 March 1915 and was attached to C Company. He served through the battles of Aubers Ridge, Festubert and Givenchy before being invalided back to England sick on 15 July. He was promoted Lieutenant on 1 October and worked as the Railway Transport Officer of the Highland Division 3rd Line at Ripon. He worked in Argentina for a tramways company.

Mackenzie, Archibald R.

Commissioned into the 4th Cameron Highlanders as a 2nd Lieutenant on 18 August 1915, Mackenzie travelled to France on 24 October attached to B Company. He was injured on 11 November when he fell off a baggage wagon and he spent 29 November–7 December in hospital. He was posted to the 1st Cameron Highlanders direct from the 4th Camerons on 4 May 1915 and posted to D Company. He was wounded in action 16–17 November 1917, northwest of Passchendaele.

Mackenzie, David Ferguson

Born on 28 January 1869 at Dunvegan, Duirinish, Isle of Skye to John Tolmie Mackenzie, a postmaster and factor for the Dunvegan Estates, and his wife Henzell Ferguson. He was educated at George Watson's College, Edinburgh and Edinburgh University where he studied law. Mackenzie was a keen golfer and rugby player of some renown in the Highlands. He married Elizabeth Francis Russell in Edinburgh in 1901 and had several children. He was commissioned into the InvernessVolunteers as a 2nd Lieutenant on 2 February 1905 and was promoted full Lieutenant on 10 October 1906 and Captain on 26 August 1914 at Bedford. He travelled to France on 19 February 1915 as second in command of A Company. In April, Captain Mackenzie went back to Inverness to wrap up some business affairs after the death of his partner. He returned to France at the end of April and was killed in action on 17 May at the Battle of Festubert. In *The Sword of the*

North, Dugald MacEachern described Captain Mackenzie as being 'calm and quiet in demeanor, he had a saint's regard for duty and a lion's courage in action.' Captain Mackenzie was seen to fall in the attack on the Southern Breastwork Trench and refused all offers of assistance, saying the men should save themselves. His body was found some months later and buried on the battlefield by his comrades. Captain Mackenzie is commemorated on the Le Touret Memorial.

Mackenzie, Nigel Blair

Born on 17 April 1874 at Fort William to Nigel Banks Mackenzie, a writer and bank agent, and his wife Lillias Scott Mackenzie. He worked as a bank agent and was Provost of Fort William in 1927, commissioned into the 4th Cameron Highlanders on 5 May 1909 as a 2nd Lieutenant, promoted to full Lieutenant on 9 September 1912 and Captain on 7 September 1914 at Bedford. He travelled to France on 19 February 1915 as second in command of D Company. He was wounded in action at the Battle of Festubert on 17 May along with all the other D Company officers. He was evacuated to England and then posted to the 3/4th Cameron Highlanders as a staff captain before being promoted Temporary Major on 5 November. He married Kathleen Joanna Fay while at Bedford in a wedding which was attended by all the officers of the 4th Camerons. Major Mackenzie died on 11 October 1935 at Craigdarroch, Fort William.

Mackintosh, Harry Alexander

Enlisted into the 14th London Scottish Regiment as Private No.3335, Mackintosh travelled to France on 24 November 1914. He was commissioned as a 2nd Lieutenant in the 4th Cameron Highlanders on 18 August 1915 and joined them in France on 21 January 1916 attached to B Company. He was posted to the 1st Cameron Highlanders direct from the 4th Camerons on 4 May 1916 and attached to B Company.

Mackintosh, Illtyd

Enlisted into the Royal Engineers as Sapper No.951, Mackintosh travelled to France on 26 June 1915 before being discharged to a commission in the 4th Cameron Highlanders on 20 July. He joined up with the 4th Camerons on 9 November and was attached to C Company. He was invalided to England sick on 2 March 1916.

MacLaren, John Francis

Born on 24 May 1893 at 34 Caledonian Crescent, Edinburgh to Andrew MacLaren, a police constable, and his wife, Mary Campbell. Before the war he was an art student at Edinburgh University. He was commissioned into the 4th Cameron Highlanders on 26 August 1914 as a 2nd Lieutenant and travelled to France on 19 February 1915 attached to B Company. He was promoted Temporary Lieutenant on 20 May and Temporary Captain on 21 July. He was killed in action at the Battle of Loos on 28 September when a shell exploded in the doorway of B Company's Headquarters, killing nine men and wounding eight. Captain McLaren is commemorated on the Loos Memorial.

MacMillan, George C.

Enlisted into the 14th London Scottish Regiment as Private No.3017, MacMillan travelled to France on 24 November 1914. He was commissioned into the 4th Cameron Highlanders as a 2nd Lieutenant on 10 March 1915 and joined them on 11 July. He was posted to D Company and was wounded in action on 25 September and evacuated to England on 28 September. He returned to France on 19 September 1916 and returned to England after being accidentally injured on 8 January 1917. He relinquished his commission in 1917 on medical grounds.

MacPherson, James

Born on 7 September 1866 at Dunain, Inverness to Alexander MacPherson, a body servant, and his wife Elizabeth Barron. Before the war he worked as a farmer at Charlest in Inverness. He was promoted Captain in the 4th Cameron Highlanders on 10 November 1910 and travelled to France on 19 February 1915 in command of B Company. He became the first officer of the 4th Camerons to be killed in action in France when he died on 10 March 1915 at the Battle of Neuve Chapelle. Captain MacPherson is buried at Rue du Bacquerot Military Cemetery No.1 at Laventie.

MacPherson, John Donald

Born on 25 July 1883 at Newtonmore to James MacPherson, a carter, and his wife Ann Stewart. He was commissioned into the 4th Cameron Highlanders as a 2nd Lieutenant on 9 May 1912 and promoted full Lieutenant on 7 September 1914 at Bedford. He travelled to France on 19 February 1915 as Battalion Transport Officer. He was wounded in action on 1 April in E Lines Trenches but remained at duty. He was struck off sick when in England on leave on 29 January 1916 while holding the rank of Captain. Captain MacPherson married Mary K. Simpson in Edinburgh in 1922 and he died on 2 July 1960 at Peel Hospital in Galashiels.

Macrae, Archibald John

Born on 27 November 1892 at Gladstone House, Beauly to Roderick Macrae, a farmer and horse hirer, and his wife Margaret Mackenzie. He enlisted in the Lovat Scouts as Lance Corporal No.1997 and was commissioned into the 4th Cameron Highlanders on 15 July 1915. He travelled to France on 20 October and was attached to D Company. He transferred to Number 1 Entrenching Battalion at Poperinghe on 12 March 1916, then transferred to the 1st Cameron Highlanders on 27 April, joining them on 1 June. Lieutenant Macrae died on 5 October 1918 while attached to the 8th Seaforth Highlanders. He is buried in Houchin British Cemetery.

Nelson, Ian Theodore

Born on 11 July 1878 at St Leonards, Dalkeith Road, Edinburgh to Thomas Nelson, a publisher, and Jessie Kemp. He was commissioned into the 4th Cameron Highlanders in 1914 as a 2nd Lieutenant and travelled to France on 19 February 1915 attached to C Company. He was promoted Captain in late 1915 and transferred to B Company on 3 March 1916 and A Company on 7 March. He transferred to England on 7 April to join the Reserve of Officers. Captain Nelson was married to Vera Mandeville and died at Netherdale House, Marnoch on 14 April 1958.

Park, James Robert

Born on 24 May 1888 at 9 Claremont Place, Aberdeen to James Park, a master joiner, and his wife Isabella Robb. He enlisted into the 4th Cameron Highlanders as Private No.1893 in August 1914 and travelled to France on 19 February 1915. He was commissioned as a 2nd Lieutenant on 25 February but did not have time to take up his commission before being wounded at the Battle of Neuve Chapelle on 12 March. He returned to the front on 14 July and was again wounded in action on 28 September at the Battle of Loos when a shell exploded in B Company's Headquarters in Gun Trench. He was evacuated to England on 2 October.

Paterson, Alistair Finlay

Born on 4 February 1888 at Beauly to John Paterson, a master ironmonger, and his wife Mary McLennan. Before the war he was a noted shinty player and athlete. He enlisted into the 4th Cameron Highlanders in 1908 as Private No.302 before being promoted through the ranks to Company Quartermaster Sergeant in D Company. He travelled to France on 19 February 1915 and was commissioned as a 2nd Lieutenant on 25 February, attached to D Company. He was wounded in action at the Battle of Festubert on 17 May, early in the attack on the Southern Breastwork Trench, along with all the other

D Company officers. He was evacuated but died of his wounds on 5 June at Rouen. His brother Donald also served in D Company and was killed in action at Festubert. Lieutenant Paterson is buried at St Sever Cemetery in Rouen.

Powell, Charles Sydney

Born in 1894 in Camberwell, Surrey to Alfred E. and Elizabeth A. Powell. His brother Alfred Trevanian Powell served with the 3/4th Cameron Highlanders. He was commissioned into the 4th Cameron Highlanders as a 2nd Lieutenant in April 1915 and travelled to France on 14 July, attached to D Company. He was wounded in action on 21 August and evacuated on 24 August. He later joined the Royal Field Artillery.

Roemmele, Max Alexander

Born on 17 January 1892 at Lillieslea, Lenzie to Carl Hugo Roemmele, an iron merchant, and his wife Emilia Elizabeth Bost. He joined the 4th Cameron Highlanders as a Private No.2223 in September 1914. He travelled to France on 19 February 1915 attached to A Company and was commissioned on 25 February, joining B Company before the Battle of Festubert. He served with distinction throughout 1915 and was Mentioned in Despatches on 1 January 1916. He transferred to Number 1 Entrenching Battalion on 12 March and to the 1st Cameron Highlanders on 27 April, joining them in the field on 15 July and being posted to A Company.

Ross, Angus

Born on 6 July 1873 at Portree to William Ross, a shoemaker and leather merchant, and his wife Mary McLennan. Before the war he worked as the Inspector of the Poor in Portree. He married Annie Louisa Harley in Crieff in 1906. He enlisted in the Inverness Volunteers and was commissioned into the 4th Cameron Highlanders as a 2nd Lieutenant on 3 April 1912 and was promoted full Lieutenant on 26 August 1914. He travelled to France on 19 February 1915 attached to D Company. He was wounded in action at the Battle of Neuve Chapelle on 12 March and invalided to England. He rejoined the battalion on 29 December and was posted to C Company before being transferred to A Company on 3 March 1916 and back to C Company four days later. He transferred to Number 1 Entrenching Battalion on 12 March and to the 1st Cameron Highlanders. He served on the Somme and was then transferred to the Labour Corps before ending the war as a Lieutenant-Colonel in the Army of Reconstruction in Germany. Lieutenant-Colonel Angus Ross died of a brain tumour on 13 September 1920 at 21 Albyn Place, Aberdeen.

Ross M.C., O.B.E., Hugo Donald

Born in 1880 to Mr and Mrs Hugh R. Ross of Dibidale, Ross-shire. Before the war he worked in Siam and returned from there in January 1915 securing a commission in the 4th Cameron Highlanders as a 2nd Lieutenant on 17 February. He travelled to France on 17 April and attached to A Company. He was wounded in action at the Battle of Loos on 26 September and was evacuated to England. After recovering from his wounds he was placed in command of the 8th Battalion, The Rifle Brigade from March to August 1916. In January 1917 he was transferred to the 2nd Cameron Highlanders in Macedonia where he commanded B Company and was present at the recapture of Homondos. He was awarded the Military Cross in November 1917. From March to November 1918 he served as a Staff Captain with the 228th Brigade and then as Adjutant of the 2nd Cameron Highlanders from December 1918 to May 1919 at the end of the South Russian Campaign. Captain Ross carried the Regimental Colour of the 4th Cameron Highlanders at the Victory Parade in London in 1919. He became the first Adjutant of the reconstituted 4th Cameron Highlanders in 1920 and was later awarded the OBE. He married Dorothy Latimer and died on 2 October 1960 at Invergordon Hospital.

Scott, Henry James

Born on 6 October 1889 at St John's, Annan to Alexander Scott, a solicitor, and his wife Agnes Gillies. His birth certificate was named to Rachel Rosa Scott, his sister, which was a mistake by the Registrar and amended in the Register of Corrected Entries. He was educated at Stanley House, Bridge of Allan and George Watson's College in Edinburgh. He was commissioned as a 2nd Lieutenant on 30 December 1914 and travelled to France on 26 March 1915, attached to B Company. He was promoted Lieutenant on 21 July. He was wounded during the Battle of Loos on 25 September and died on 28 September at Number 2 Base Hospital in Rouen. Lieutenant Scott is buried at Annan Cemetery.

Shaw, William John

Born on 17 September 1879 at Oldtown, Dores to Alexander Shaw, a farmer, and his wife Elizabeth Boyd. Before the war he worked as the headmaster of Inverness Central School. He was educated at Errogie School in Ross-shire. He married Margaret Matheson in 1905 and had six children. He was commissioned into the 4th Cameron Highlanders on 9 May 1914 and promoted full Lieutenant on 7 September at Bedford. He travelled to France on 19 February, attached to B Company. He was wounded in action on 12 March at the Battle of Neuve Chapelle. He was evacuated to England and on recovering was posted to the

2/4th Cameron Highlanders and then to a position as an Instructor at the Officers Cadet School in 1916. Shaw was Mentioned in Despatches three times during the war. During the Second World War he became a Lieutenant-Colonel of Officer Cadets. Lieutenant Shaw died on 21 August 1953 at the Northern Infirmary, Inverness.

Smith, James

Commissioned into the 4th Cameron Highlanders as a 2nd Lieutenant on 19 June 1915, Smith travelled to France on 19 October attached to B Company. He transferred to Number 1 Entrenching Battalion on 12 March 1916 and to the 1st Cameron Highlanders on 27 April. He joined his new battalion on 20 May with a draft of 47 men of the 4th Cameron Highlanders from the Entrenching Battalion. He was wounded in action on 17 August at Bazentin Le Petit at the Battle of the Somme. He later transferred to the Royal Engineers.

Sutherland M.C., Andrew

Born on 12 May 1884 at Ballifeary, Inverness to James Sutherland, a bank teller, and his wife Catherine Munro. He enlisted into the Volunteer Battalion as a Private and was a noted shot, winning prizes for shooting at Bisley. He was home on leave from working in Argentina when the war broke out and he obtained his commission as a 2nd Lieutenant in the 4th Cameron Highlanders on 4 August 1914, the first day of the war. He travelled to France on 19 February 1915, attached to C Company. He became the first officer of the 4th Camerons to win the Military Cross. He was wounded in action at the Battle of Givenchy on 16 June but remained at his post. He was promoted Temporary Captain on 27 August, was seconded to the Highland Field Company of the Royal Engineers on 22 September and served with them at the Battle of Loos. He was later promoted Major with the Royal Engineers. After the war he became the Assistant Director of the Irrigation Department in the Sudan. On his retirement he returned to Inverness and served as a Squadron Leader in the RAF during the Second World War. Captain Sutherland died at 45 Culduthel Road, Inverness on 15 January 1955.

Symon D.S.O., O.B.E., James Alexander

Born on 14 May 1886 at Gateside, Strachan, Aberdeenshire to John Symon, a farmer, and his wife Margaret Cargill. He was educated at Robert Gordon College, Aberdeen and Aberdeen University. He was commissioned as a 2nd Lieutenant in the 4th Cameron Highlanders on 30 January 1915 and posted to the 2/4th Camerons where he was promoted Temporary Lieutenant on 27 May. He travelled to France on 14 July and was attached to A Company before being invalided to England sick on 25 September, being posted to the 3/4th Cameron Highlanders. He was posted to the 7th Cameron Highlanders on 22 September 1916 and was wounded in action on 27 January 1917. Present at the Battle of Arras, he was wounded on 8 April and again at the Third Battle of Ypres on 1 August. He was Mentioned in Despatches on 7 November and awarded the Distinguished Service Order on 8 January 1918 for his action at Third Ypres. His citation for that award stated that 'by his coolness and absolute disregard for personal danger he saved the situation, and afterwards, finding that we were suffering from the effect of snipers, went out himself and shot several of the enemy before he was finally wounded.' After the war he was appointed to the newly reconstituted 4th Camerons and was second in command from 1927–1933 and Lieutenant-Colonel commanding from 1933–1937. Before the war he was a farmer and later a lecturer on Agriculture at the South Eastern Agricultural College. He was also awarded the OBE. Lieutenant-Colonel Symon died in 1974 in Edinburgh.

Thompson, Joshua Clibborn

Born on 27 June 1874 at White Abbey, County Antrim, Northern Ireland to Elias Hughes Thompson, a linen merchant, and his wife Elizabeth Sim. He married Janet Davidson Torrence in 1917 in Edinburgh. Both were resident in Thurso. He studied at Corpus Christie College, Cambridge 1899–1902 and was ordained into the Church of England in Leeds in 1903. He moved to Fort Augustus around 1905. He enlisted into the 4th Cameron Highlanders on 23 August 1914 and travelled to France on 19 February 1915, attached to D Company. He was wounded in the attack on the Southern Breastwork Trench on 17 May at the Battle of Festubert. He was promoted full Lieutenant on 4 December and Captain on 10 June 1916 and was posted to the Special Military Area.

Urquhart, Angus

Born on 22 April 1893 at 15 Young Street, Inverness to George Urquhart, a master butcher, and his wife Jane Anne Calder. He was educated at Inverness Royal Academy. Before the war he worked as a seedsman for his uncle Farquhar Urquhart. He was commissioned as a 2nd Lieutenant in the 4th Cameron Highlanders on 20 December 1914 and attached to the 2/4th Battalion. He travelled to France on 15 April 1915 and was attached to D Company where he was promoted full Lieutenant on 21 July. He was killed in action at the Battle of Loos on 26 September 1915.

Valentine, William Stainer

Commissioned as a 2nd Lieutenant in the 4th Cameron Highlanders on 14 April 1915, Valentine travelled to France on 14 July and attached to

B Company. He was seconded to the Machine Gun Corps on 14 January 1916 and was wounded in June that year.

Wallace, Alexander Robert
Enlisted into the 4th Cameron Highlanders as Private No.2112 on 7 September 1914 at London, Wallace travelled to France on 19 February 1915, attached to C Company. He was commissioned as a 2nd Lieutenant in the 4th Cameron Highlanders on 25 February. He was wounded Battle of Neuve Chapelle on 10 March before he could take up his commission.

White, Harold Maxwell
Born on 2 June 1892 at 15 Goldenacre Terrace, Edinburgh to George F. White, a house furnisher, and his wife Kate Russell. He was commissioned into the 4th Cameron Highlanders as a 2nd Lieutenant on 7 September 1915 and travelled to France on 21 January 1916, attached to C Company. He transferred to the 1st Cameron Highlanders on 4 May and was wounded in action in a position to the southeast of the Butte de Warlencourt on 1 December. He married Mona Hume in 1920 in Edinburgh at which time he was a Cadet in the Royal Irish Constabulary. Lieutenant White died in Edinburgh in 1982.

Wood, J.H.
Wood was a Medical Officer with the Royal Army Medical Corps attached to the 4th Cameron Highlanders. He was wounded in action on 1 December 1915 and returned to duty on 6 December. On the break-up of the battalion he proceeded to the 9th Division as Medical Officer.

Appendix 7

Note on Service Numbers

As mentioned in Chapter 1, the first 4th Cameron Highlanders to leave Britain for France on 19 February 1915 were allotted unique service numbers in ascending order from their first date of service between 1 April 1908 and the start of the war. These one to four digit service numbers not only tell that the battalion was of the Territorial Force but also give an approximate date to the soldier's enlistment. On the day war was declared, 4 August 1914, the 4th Cameron Highlanders allocated the service number 1720 to Private John Macinnes.

In general, the men with service numbers before 1720 were pre-war Territorial Force soldiers with varying years of service. Those from 1720 to approximately 1975 were volunteers from all over Scotland who flocked to Inverness to enlist in the first month of the war. Once the battalion was based in Bedford, the men recruited in London were allocated service numbers between 1975 and 2222 and those recruited in the Highlands during that time were given service numbers up to 2500.

From August 1915 until the demise of the battalion in March 1916, large numbers of men, with service numbers from 3200 up to approximately 4000, were recruited from Yorkshire, where the 3/4th Camerons were based at Ripon, with a few men from Northern Ireland, where recruiting of Scots families had intensified, and from the local depots in the Highlands.

When the men were transferred to Number 1 Entrenching Battalion on 12 and 28 March 1916 they retained their original one to four digit 4th Cameron Highlanders number. The men who were sent in drafts to the 1st Camerons from May to August 1916 also retained their 4th Camerons number.
In February 1917, all Territorial Force soldiers were required to have a six digit number, the numbers being allocated to the old soldiers of the 4th Cameron Highlanders being between 200000 and approximately 201000. The soldiers receiving these new service numbers were either men who were retained by the battalion nucleus at Étaples or men who had been transferred to the 1st Cameron Highlanders but had been posted missing or presumed killed before February 1917 but had not been struck off strength.

The numbering system for soldiers transferring to the 5th, 6th and 7th Cameron Highlanders from August 1916 to February 1917 was completely different. As these units were service battalions, the men transferred to them were issued five digit numbers with an S/ prefix in the range S/40000 to S/43500. The following pattern broadly explains their allocation.

Date of Draft	Drafted to	Number
13 August 1916	7th Cameron Highlanders	S/43193-S/43226
13 August 1916	6th Cameron Highlanders	S/43277-S/43297*
15 August 1916	6th Cameron Highlanders	S/43252-S/43320**
19 August 1916	7th Cameron Highlanders	S/43248-S/43251
20 August 1916	7th Cameron Highlanders	S/43112-S/43247***
28 August 1916	7th Cameron Highlanders	S/40000-S/40039
30 August 1916	6th Cameron Highlanders	S/40040-S/40079
6 September 1916	6th Cameron Highlanders	S/40080-S/40109
8 September 1916	6th Cameron Highlanders	S/40410-S/40439
8 September 1916	1st Cameron Highlanders	S/40440-S/40459
9 September 1916	1st Cameron Highlanders	S/40110-S/40309
12 September 1916	1st Cameron Highlanders	S/40310-S/40409
15 September 1916	5th Cameron Highlanders	S/40460-S/40481
19 September 1916	6th Cameron Highlanders	S/40482-S/40721
7 October 1916	5th Cameron Highlanders	S/40682-S/40699
25 October 1916	5th Cameron Highlanders	S/40742-S/40841
30 October 1916	5th Cameron Highlanders	S/40842-S/40941
25 January 1917	5th Cameron Highlanders	S/41002-S/41020

* With 29 other men with four digit service numbers who were all killed or wounded before February 1917
** With 59 other men with four digit service numbers who were all killed or wounded before February 1917
*** Minus those from the 13 August draft to the 7th Cameron Highlanders

It must be noted that while these figures are broadly correct, there are a few anomalies, perhaps 100 out of the 2000 men who served, but largely the S/ service number does give a clear indication of the destination and date of transfer of a soldier. The men who made up these drafts came either from Number 1 Entrenching Battalion on at Poperinghe or from the numerous drafts which arrived from the 3/4th Cameron Highlanders during the summer of 1916. Within the drafts of men with S/ numbers they were arranged firstly alphabetically by surname and then allocated the number, meaning that there is little correlation between a man's old four digit 4th Cameron Highlanders number and his new number.

Notes

1 *Inverness Courier,* 24 March 1916, p.4.
2 *The Sword of the North: Highland Memories of the Great War,* by the Reverend Dugald MacEachern, p.178.
3 *1908 Regulations for the Territorial Force*, p.160–161.
4 *Historical Record of the Queen's Own Cameron Highlanders,* Vol.3, p.422.
5 From September 1914 the 4th Camerons were officially known as the 1/4th Battalion as second (2/4th) and third (3/4th) Battalions were raised in Inverness. For the purposes of this book where the 4th Cameron Highlanders are mentioned, the author means the 1/4th Battalion. The other units, and similar units in other Regiments, will be afforded the full double number if applicable.
6 *The Spirit of the Troops is Excellent*, Derek Bird, p.22.
7 Article '*With the Fourth Camerons*' in The Letters from Major Ian and Captain William MacKay, Craigmonie, Inverness, un-numbered pages between p.6–7.
8 *Inverness Courier,* 20 October 1914, p.5
9 *Historical Record of the Queen's Own Cameron Highlanders*, Vol.3, p.424.
10 Lieutenant-Colonel Fraser's will is held by the National Archives of Scotland under the reference number SC29/44/57 p.800–806.
11 Both these wills are held by the National Archives of Scotland under the reference numbers SC70/8/216/9/1-3 and SC70/8/172/23/1-3 respectively.

12 A list of the men killed before embarkation to France is given in the Appendix.
13 Bedfordhighlanders.blogspot.com
14 Of the men of the 4th Cameron Highlanders who were buried in Britain, 3 were buried in Auldearn, 1 in Kilmuir, 1 in Banchor, 8 in Bedford, 1 each in Moston St Joseph's Roman Catholic Church, Kilmorack, Kiltarlity, Uig, Carinish, Tomnacross, Cromdale, Sleat, Drumnadrochit, Kilmarie, Laggan, Comely Bank in Edinburgh, Bressay and Brompton, 2 in Kilchrist, Kilchuiman and Kingussie and 3 in the cemetery in the Hebridean Island of Raasay.
15 *79th News*, Issue of April 1915, p.89–90
16 Copy of Typed Order 49/15 by Lieutenant-Colonel Alexander Fraser in the letters from Major Ian and Captain William MacKay, Craigmonie, Inverness, unnumbered pages between p.6–7, dated 18 February 1915.
17 Cha Til MacCruimein, reproduced at net.lib.byu.edu/english/wwi/over/MacCrimmon.html.
18 Diary of Charles D. Bowdery, p.7, held by the Imperial War Museum (Ref: 3558 85/15/1).
19 Bowdery, p.8
20 Goodban, p.3
21 MacKay, p.8
22 Bowdery, p.11
23 *Historical Record of the Queen's Own Cameron Highlanders*, Vol.3 p.426
24 ibid.
25 Bowdery, p.13
26 *Highland News,* 13 March 1915, p.2
27 ibid, 20 March 1915, p.2
28 Hector MacDonald, taped interview with Peter Liddle, 1977, held by the Liddle Collection, Leeds University.
29 Lieutenant Charles Tennant, quoted in *The Battle of Neuve Chapelle*, Battleground Europe Series by Geoff Bridger, p.29.
30 Unnamed officer of the 2nd Middlesex Regiment quoted in *The Battle of Neuve Chapelle,* Battleground Europe Series by Geoff Bridger, p.30.
31 *Highland News,* 3 April 1915, p.3
32 1129 Cpl Alistair MacDougall was from Fort William, was commissioned and died on 30 April 1918 while seconded to the 2/14th London Regiment (London Scottish) and is buried in the Jerusalem War Cemetery in Israel.
33 *Scotsman* Digital Archive, *Scotsman*, 22 March 1915
34 Goodban, p.8
35 *Inverness Courier,* 23 March 1915 p.5

36 MacKay, p.15
37 The only officers of the 4th Camerons in Inverness at this time who were present at Neuve Chapelle were Lieutenant William Shaw and 2nd Lieutenant Fred Kelly, both of B Company.
38 *Inverness Courier,* 6 April 1915, p.5
39 *Scotsman* Digital Archive, 22 March 1915
40 Bowdery, p.20–21
41 MacKay, p.15
42 James MacBean was born in the Parish of Daviot in 1874 and farmed at Achnabeachan in that parish. The Strathnairn Heritage website (www.strathnairnheritage.org.uk/pics-and-stories-2) tells how James MacBean was a renowned sniper during the First World War. In the 1960s his medals and other war memorabilia were found in a field at Achnabeachan. Corporal MacBean died in Inverness in 1957.
43 MacKay, p.16
44 WO95/1659, War Diary of the 4th Cameron Highlanders
45 Bridger, p.84
46 War Diary of the 2nd Bedfordshire Regiment, 11 March 1915 www.bedfordregiment.org.uk/2ndbn/2ndbtn1915diary.html
47 Bridger, p.85
48 MacKay, additional pages between p.11–12 – photocopy of official order.
49 Lieutenant William MacKay and Captain David F Mackenzie, both of A Company.
50 Lieutenant Roderick McErlich
51 MacKay, p.13
52 ibid.
53 *Highland News,* 3 April 1915, p.3. A 'Jack Johnson' was a large calibre Howitzer shell.
54 *Inverness Courier,* 6 April 1915, p.5
55 *Historical Record of the Queen's Own Cameron Highlanders*, Vol.3, p.427 says Moulin du Pietre but this seems improbable. It is more likely to be the area round Pietre.
56 The War Diary of the 2nd Devons read 'Battalion received orders to lead Brigade in attack on line PIETRE-LA RUSSIE at 6.30pm. Battalion was collected as quickly as possible and proceeded via points 22-7-6-23-92 setting into position in dark on the enemy's side of our trench 87-92 with the 2nd Scottish Rifles in support.'
57 *Inverness Courier,* 13 April 1915, p.6
58 TNA Ref: WO95/1659
59 Bowdery, p.17
60 Goodban, p.10

61 *Inverness Courier,* 23 March 1915, p.5
62 Bowdery, p.18
63 Goodban, p.10
64 Mackay, p.14
65 TNA Ref: WO95/1659
66 *The Battle of Neuve Chapelle* by Geoff Bridger, p.96–98
67 Goodban, p.11
68 Bowdery, p.20–21
69 Mackay, p.16
70 Mackay, p.14
71 *Scotsman* Digital Archive, *Scotsman,* 22 March 1915
72 Bowdery, p.11
73 Goodban, p.6
74 *Inverness Courier,* 6 April 1915, p.5
75 Goodban, p.11
76 Bowdery, p.20–21
77 *Inverness Courier,* 2 April 1915, p.15
78 Bowdery, p.22
79 Goodban, p.11
80 Bowdery, p.23–24
81 *Inverness Courier,* 2 April 1915, p.5
82 Goodban, p.12
83 *Inverness Courier,* 20 April 1915, p.5
84 Bowdery, p.28
85 Mackay, p.24
86 Goodban, p.35
87 *Inverness Courier,* 6 April 1915 p.5
88 Mackay, p.25
89 *Inverness Courier*, 20 April 1915, p.5
90 ibid, 20 April 1915, p.5
91 Private Mackinnon was to be killed just one month later, during the Battle of Festubert.
92 Goodban, p.17
93 Bowdery, p.32
94 Goodban, p.19
95 *Inverness Courier,* 21 May 1915, p.4
96 ibid, 8 June 1915, p.5
97 *Aubers Ridge,* by Edward Hancock, p.24–25
98 Bowdery, p.34
99 Both the *Diary of the 4th Battalion, Queen's Own Cameron Highlanders,* written by Lieutenant Ian MacKay and published in 1916 by the *Northern*

Chronicle and the *Official Records of the Cameron Highlanders* state that 3 men were killed and 17 wounded and the battalion war diary, kept by Adjutant Captain Garden Duff states that 2 men were killed and 7 wounded. I have pieced together casualty figures from *Soldiers Died in the Great War, the 79th News* and the *Inverness Courier.*

100 *The Seventh Division 1914–1918,* by C.T. Atkinson, p.166
101 Atkinson, p.166
102 Atkinson, p.16–167
103 Goodban, p.20
104 Mackay, p.31
105 *Highland News,* 22 May 1915, p.5
106 Hancock, p.147
107 In *The Seventh Division 1914–1918* this position is marked as M9 on the trench map on p.181
108 Goodban, p.20–21
109 Mackay, p,31
110 Atkinson, p.172–173
111 Mackay, p.31
112 *Inverness Courier,* 28 May 1915, p.5
113 Hector MacDonald, taped interview with Peter Liddle, 1980, held by the Liddle Collection, Leeds University
114 Bowdery, p.38–39
115 *Inverness Courier,* 4 June 1915, p.4
116 2nd Bedford Regimental War Diary, www.bedfordregiment.org.uk/2ndbn/2ndbtn1915diary.html
117 2nd Lieutenant Alistair Paterson died of his wounds in Rouen on 5 June. His younger brother Lance Corporal Donald Paterson, also serving in D Company was killed on 17 May.
118 *Inverness Courier,* 4 June 1915, p.5
119 Mackay, p.33
120 David Ferguson Mackenzie is referred to in the Mackay letters usually just as D.F. In the text of those letters I have reproduced it exactly as Lieutenant Mackay wrote it.
121 Mackay, p.32
122 Mackay. p.32–33
123 *Inverness Courier*, 28 May 1915, p.5
124 Bowdery, p,38
125 *Inverness Courier,* 28 May1915, p.5
126 Hector Macdonald, taped interview with Peter Liddle, 1980, held by the Liddle Collection, Leeds University
127 Atkinson, p.178

128 TNA Ref: WO95/1659, *War Diary of the 2nd Battalion, Wiltshire Regiment*
129 Hector Macdonald, taped interview with Peter Liddle, 1980 held by the Liddle Collection at Leeds University
130 *Highland News,* 29 May 1915, p.2
131 *Inverness Courier,* 28 May 1915, p.5
132 ibid
133 Hector Macdonald, taped interview with Peter Liddle, 1980 held by the Liddle Collection, Leeds University
134 *Inverness Courier,* 28 May 1915, p.5
135 *Highland News,* 29 May 1915, p.2
136 *Inverness Courier,* 28 May 1915, p.5
137 Captain David Ferguson MacKenzie. See footnote 120.
138 Mackay, p.34
139 MacEachern, *Sword of the North – Highland Memories of the Great War,* p.185
140 Letter from Duncan Mackenzie to William Mackay, in the un-numbered pages of the Mackay papers.
141 *Inverness Courier,* 4 June 1915, p.6
142 This was in the Rue de l'Epinette. Even after the fact contemporary newspapers could not print exact locations for the battalions.
143 *Inverness Courier,* 4 June 1915, p.5
144 ibid
145 Mackay, p.34
146 *Inverness Courier,* 28 May 1915, p.4
147 ibid, p.5
148 Mackay, p.34–35
149 *Inverness Courier,* 8 June 1915, p.5
150 ibid, 28 May 1915, p.4
151 Mackay, p.35–36
152 *Inverness Courier,* 29 June 1915, p.5
153 ibid, 11 June 1915, p.5
154 *Diary of the 4th Battalion. The Queen's Own Cameron Highlanders During the European War*, by Lieutenant Ian Mackay, p.14–15
155 Mackay, p.35
156 *Inverness Courier,* 1 June 1915, p.5
157 ibid
158 ibid
159 Goodban, p.25
160 ibid
161 Mackay, p.37
162 Atkinson, Map 15, p.195
163 Mackay, p.37

164 Atkinson, p.189
165 ibid, p.189–190
166 Mackay, p.38
167 Goodban, p.26–27
168 Mackay, p.38–39
169 *Highland News,* 26 June 1915 p.3
170 Atkinson, p.184–192
171 ibid, p.192
172 Mackay, p.39
173 ibid
174 ibid
175 ibid, p.40
176 Goodban, p.27
177 Mackay, p.40
178 ibid
179 MacEachern, p.186–187
180 ibid, p.187
181 Letter from Private J.B. Mackenzie to his wife, dated 3 July 1915, held by the Imperial War Museum under the reference number 926 87/62/1
182 Goodban, p.27
183 ibid, p.28
184 ibid, p.29
185 ibid
186 ibid, p.30
187 ibid
188 ibid, p.31
189 ibid, p.33
190 ibid, p.34
191 The others being Private Alexander Cattanach (11th), Privates Goodban and William Watson (12th), Privates Duncan Clark and James Stewart (14th) and William MacDonald (18th). Lance Corporal William MacKintosh was wounded on 17 July died of his wounds on 20 July.
192 Mackay, p.41
193 *Inverness Courier,* 13 August p.4
194 Atkinson, p.199
195 *Inverness Courier,* 15 October 1915, p.4
196 *Loos 1915,* Nick Lloyd, p.99–100
197 *Loos – Hohenzollern,* by Andrew Rawson, p.21–30
198 Atkinson, p.202–203
199 Rawson, p.36
200 Atkinson, p.205

201 Mackay, p.43
202 Rawson, p.69–73
203 Atkinson, p.204–205
204 ibid, p.205
205 War Diary of the 1st South Staffordshire Regiment, TNA Ref: WO95/1664
206 Rawson, p.69–77
207 *The Cameron Highlanders At the Battles at Loos, Hill 70, Fosse 8 and the Quarries,* souvenir booklet published by the *Inverness Courier*, p.16
208 Captain Roderick McErlich, commanding A Company
209 Mackay, p.44
210 *Inverness Courier* souvenir booklet, p.17
211 Mackay, p.44
212 Actually their left
213 *Inverness Courier,* 12 November 1915, p.7
214 Mackay, p.44
215 *Inverness Courier* Souvenir Booklet, p.18
216 Lloyd, p.158
217 Rawson, p.89
218 Mackay, p.44–45
219 Atkinson, p.217
220 Mackay, p.46
221 ibid, p.45
222 ibid, p.44
223 *Inverness Courier* Souvenir Booklet, p.20–21
224 Mackay, p.45
225 Distinguished Conduct Medal Citation for Sergeant James MacBean
226 Atkinson, p.224–225
227 *Inverness Courier,* 15 October 1915, p.4
228 Mackay, p.45
229 *Inverness Courier* Souvenir Booklet, p.21
230 *Inverness Courier,* 15 October 1915, p.4
231 Atkinson, p.231
232 *The Regimental Records of the Queen's Own Cameron Highlanders,* Vol.3, p.442
233 Mackay, p.48
234 TNA Ref: WO 95/1659, War Diary of the 4th Cameron Highlanders
235 Mackay, p.47
236 ibid
237 ibid, p.47–48
238 ibid, p.48
239 ibid

240 ibid
241 ibid, p.49
242 *The Historical Records of the Cameron Highlanders,* Vol.5, p.212
243 *Inverness Courier,* 24 March 1916, p.4
244 ibid
245 ibid
246 WO95/1659, 25 February 1916
247 Papers of S Bradbury, held by the Imperial War Museum under the reference number 2528 81/35/1, p.8
248 Bradbury, p.8–9
249 ibid, p.11
250 ibid, p.14
251 *Historical Records of the Cameron Highlanders* says 1 colour sergeant and 66 men joined the 1st Camerons on the 8th May 1916 but the battalion Roll Book, kept at the Regimental Museum at Fort George only gives the names of 48 men transferring on that date.
252 *79th News*, September 1916 p.307

Bibliography

Archive Sources

Imperial War Museum, London

Private Papers of C.D. Bowdery MC (3558 85/15/1)
Private Papers of S. Bradbury (12836 PP/MCR/417)
Private Papers of M.S. Goodban (12205 P371)
Private Papers of J.B. Mackenzie (926 87/62/1)

Inverness Public Library, Reference Section

Unpublished Papers of Major Ian and Captain William Mackay

Liddle Collection, Brotherton Library, Leeds University

Interview with Hector MacDonald (M1, Tape 603)

National Archives, London

British Army WW1 Medal Index Cards (WO372)
British Army WW1 Service Records (WO/373)
British Army WW1 Pension Records (WO/374)
Bedford Regiment 2nd Battalion War Diary
Border Regiment 2nd Battalion War Diary
Cameron Highlanders 1st Battalion War Diary
Cameron Highlanders 4th Battalion War Diary
Devon Regiment 2nd Battalion War Diary

Devon Regiment 8th Battalion War Diary
Middlesex Regiment 2nd Battalion War Diary
Royal Scots Fusiliers 2nd Battalion War Diary
Royal Welch Fusiliers 1st Battalion War Diary
Royal West Surrey Regiment 2nd Battalion War Diary
Scots Guards 2nd Battalion War Diary
Staffordshire Regiment 1st Battalion War Diary
Warwickshire Regiment 2nd Battalion War Diary
Wiltshire Regiment 2nd Battalion War Diary
Yorkshire Regiment 2nd Battalion War Diary

National Archives of Scotland, Edinburgh
Soldiers Wills (SC70/8)
Will of Lieutenant Colonel Alexander Fraser (SC29/44/57)

Newspapers

Highland News
Inverness Courier
Nairnshire Telegraph
Northern Chronicle
Scotsman
Strathspey Herald

Published Sources

Anonymous, *1908 Regulations for the Territorial Force* (Portsmouth: Naval & Military Press)

______, *Historical Record of the Queen's Own Cameron Highlanders* (8 volumes, Edinburgh: Blackwood, 1928)

______, *79th News: Regimental Journal of the Queen's Own Cameron Highlanders* (Edinburgh: 1914–1918)

Asquith, H.H. *Memories & Reflections 1852–1927* (2 volumes, London: Cassell, 1928)

Atkinson, C. T. *The Seventh Division, 1914–1918* (Portsmouth: Naval & Military Press)

Bird, D. '*The Spirit of the Troops is Excellent': The 6th (Morayshire) Seaforth Highlanders in the Great War* (Garmouth, Birdbrain Publishing, 2008)

Boraston, J.H. & Bax, C. *The Eighth Division 1914–1918* (Portsmouth: Naval & Military Press, 1999)

Bridger, G. *The Battle of Neuve Chapelle: French Flanders* (Barnsley: Pen & Sword Books Ltd, 1998)
Clark, A. *The Donkeys* (London: Pimlico, 1997, first published 1961)
Farrell, S. *Ardclach & Auldearn War Memorials* (Nairn: self published, 2008)
______, *Nairn War Memorial* (Nairn: self published, 2008)
Ferguson, N. *The Pity of War* (London: Allen Lane, 1998)
French, Sir J. *1914* (London: Constable, 1919)
Gough, H. *The Fifth Army* (London: Hodder & Stoughton, 1931)
Hancock, E. *Battleground Europe: The Battle of Aubers Ridge* (Barnsley: Leo Cooper, 1998)
Holmes, R. *Tommy: The British Soldier on the Western Front* (London: Harper Perennial, 2005)
Lloyd, N. *Loos 1915* (Stroud: The History Press, 2008)
Lloyd George, D. *War Memoirs* (2 volumes, London: Nicholson & Watson, 1933)
MacEachern, Reverend D. *The Sword of the North: Highland Memories of the Great War* (Edinburgh: Robert Carruthers & Sons, 1923)
Nisbet, K. *Nairnshire Roll of Honour for the Great War* (Edinburgh: Scottish Genealogy Society, 2009)
Prior, R. & Wilson, T. *The Somme* (New Haven: Yale University Press, 2005)
Rawson, A. *Battleground Europe: Loos Hill 70* (Barnsley: Leo Cooper, 2002)
Rawson, A. *Battleground Europe: Hohenzollern* (Barnsley: Leo Cooper, 2003)
Royle, T. *Flowers of the Forest: Scotland and the Great War* (Edinburgh: Birlinn, 2007)
Strachan, H. *The First World War, Volume 1: To Arms* (Oxford: Oxford University Press, 2001)

Index

About the Author

Dr Patrick Watt holds a PhD in history from the University of Edinburgh, where his thesis examined institutional learning and organizational culture in the British army on the Western Front. He is a former curator of modern history and military collections at National Museums Scotland in Edinburgh and currently works for the Directorate of National Palaces in Istanbul. His work has been published in *Historical Research*, the *Journal of Scottish Historical Studies* and the *British Journal for Military History*, among others.